Environmental Sustainability

Techniques in Ecology and Conservation Series

Series Editor: William J. Sutherland

Bird Ecology and Conservation: A Handbook of Techniques
William J. Sutherland, Ian Newton, and Rhys E. Green

Conservation Education and Outreach Techniques
Susan K. Jacobson, Mallory D. McDuff, and Martha C. Monroe

Forest Ecology and Conservation: A Handbook of Techniques
Adrian C. Newton

Habitat Management for Conservation: A Handbook of Techniques
Malcolm Ausden

Conservation and Sustainable Use: A Handbook of Techniques
E.J. Milner-Gulland and J. Marcus Rowcliffe

Invasive Species Management: A Handbook of Principles and Techniques
Mick N. Clout and Peter A. Williams

Amphibian Ecology and Conservation: A Handbook of Techniques
C. Kenneth Dodd, Jr.

Insect Conservation: A Handbook of Approaches and Methods
Michael J. Samways, Melodie A. McGeoch, and Tim R. New

Remote Sensing for Ecology and Conservation: A Handbook of Techniques
Ned Horning, Julie A. Robinson, Eleanor J. Sterling, Woody Turner, and Sacha Spector

Marine Mammal Ecology and Conservation: A Handbook of Techniques
Ian L. Boyd, W. Don Bowen, and Sara J. Iverson

Carnivore Ecology and Conservation: A Handbook of Techniques
Luigi Boitani and Roger A. Powell

Primate Ecology and Conservation: A Handbook of Techniques
Eleanor J. Sterling, Nora Bynum, and Mary E. Blair

Conservation Education and Outreach Techniques, Second Edition
Susan K. Jacobson, Mallory D. McDuff, and Martha C. Monroe

Reptile Ecology and Conservation: A Handbook of Techniques
C. Kenneth Dodd, Jr.

Social Science Theory for Environmental Sustainability: A Practical Guide
Marc J. Stern

Social Science Theory for Environmental Sustainability

A Practical Guide

Marc J. Stern

*Department of Forest Resources
and Environmental Conservation,
College of Natural Resources and Environment,
Virginia Tech, Blacksburg, VA and The Center
for Leadership in Global Sustainability*

OXFORD
UNIVERSITY PRESS

Great Clarendon Street, Oxford, OX2 6DP,
United Kingdom

Oxford University Press is a department of the University of Oxford.
It furthers the University's objective of excellence in research, scholarship,
and education by publishing worldwide. Oxford is a registered trade mark of
Oxford University Press in the UK and in certain other countries

First Edition published in 2018
Impression: 4

Published in the United States of America by Oxford University Press
198 Madison Avenue, New York, NY 10016, United States of America

British Library Cataloguing in Publication Data
Data available

Library of Congress Control Number: 2018940565

ISBN 978–0–19–879318–2 (Hbk.)
ISBN 978–0–19–879319–9 (Pbk.)

DOI 10.1093/oso/9780198793182.001.0001

Printed and bound by
CPI Group (UK) Ltd, Croydon, CR0 4YY

For my children, Aidan and Sage, and my nieces, Eden, Dakota, and Juliana. May their generation embody the collaborative spirit this book is all about. And to my wife, Kim, who is inspiring it today.

Acknowledgments

First and foremost, I must thank my family for their patience as I worked on this project, especially my wife—she is amazing. I am also grateful to dozens of wonderful people who provided input and feedback on various parts of the book, in particular Bruce Hull, Kim Thurlow, Troy Frensley, Kristin Hurst, Michael Blackwell, Catherine Bottrill, Adam Cramer, Ashley Dayer, Daniela Franco, Elisabeth Grinspoon, Mary Jacobson, Michael Mortimer, Bob Powell, David Seesholtz, Julia Schaefers, Michael Sorice, Ken Stern, and each of the students in our graduate seminar in the human dimensions of natural resources at Virginia Tech. I'd also like to thank Bethany Kershaw and Lucy Nash at Oxford University Press for their guidance along the way, the Department of Forest Resources and Conservation at Virginia Tech for encouraging this work, and my good friends in San Miguel de Allende, Mexico, who provided great respite from the most intense periods of writing. Finally, I'd like to express my deep gratitude to Bill Burch, my academic mentor, who first taught me how to see the practical value of theory.

Contents

Part III Putting the Theories to Use

Introduction: Why would you want to read a book about social science theory?

1.1 Who should read this book?

A consultant needs to organize multiple stakeholders from different, competing organizations. An employee wants to start a company energy savings program. A small group of people wants to protect a nearby coral reef from overuse. A forest ranger wants to better engage the local public in planning for the future of a National Forest. A National Park superintendent wants to keep people out of a sensitive area. A town planner wants to devise better ways of leading people through contentious planning processes. A concerned citizen wants to bring people together to respond to threats posed by climate change. A graduate student needs theories to use in her research project. This book is for all these people.

Whether you are an environmental professional, a business person, a student, a politician, a scientist, a government employee, or simply an engaged citizen who wants to be better equipped to make sense of difficult problems and contribute to their solutions, this book is intended to serve as a reference and guide toward thoughtful action for people who want to have impact. It contains summaries of social science theories along with strategies and examples for how to apply them to solving environmental problems and promoting environmental sustainability.

1.2 What's the problem?

If you're interested in this book, I'm hopeful that you already care about environmental issues and recognize that all else depends on sustaining our planet's critical life support systems. We rely on a healthy natural environment for clean water, clean air, food, shelter, and virtually all the materials we need to have a chance to live reasonably comfortable and satisfying lives. Research tells us that healthy natural environments also provide powerful psychological and physical benefits to those who spend time in them, including enhanced short-term memory,

Social Science Theory for Environmental Sustainability: A Practical Guide. Marc J. Stern, Oxford University Press (2018). © Marc J. Stern 2018. DOI 10.1093/oso/9780198793182.001.0001

restored mental energy, stress relief, improved concentration, sharper thinking and creativity, increased motivation, boosts to the immune system, enhanced self-esteem and improved overall mental and physical health.[1] We bask in the beauty of natural scenery for restoration, inspiration, and challenge. We take pride in beautiful natural places near our home, showing them off to visitors as if they were our own. Some travel halfway around the world for the opportunity to enjoy the wonders of a coral reef, a rainforest, a flowering alpine meadow, or a roaring waterfall. Without these places of respite, our lives would be less meaningful and less enjoyable. Without the services they provide, in terms of clean air, water, and food, we'd suffer from hunger and disease and eventually cease to exist. While these benefits might seem obvious to anyone motivated enough to pick up this book, you might be asking yourself, "Why is it so hard to protect them?" Why does it seem to be a constant fight to keep our water clean, our ecosystems intact, our cherished natural spaces unpolluted, and our global climate livable into the future?

1.3 Why learn about *social* science?

Whether we are concerned with ensuring clean air to breathe, promoting sustainable use of resources, protecting endangered species, conserving special places, or protecting water sources, environmental problems are people problems, and simple straightforward fixes rarely suffice. Even the most ingenious technical solutions must be accepted and adopted by governments, corporations, and citizens to be effective. Traditional means for mandating or coercing people's behavior are rarely effective (or fair) in the long-term. Moreover, we can't simply assume that excellent rational arguments or economic inducements can convert everyone into committed environmental stewards. We should all know from personal experience that people don't always (or even typically) act in their own best interests or based on sound knowledge or advice. If they did, any number of prior environmental initiatives might have already solved many of our problems. We would have either educated people out of all of their bad habits or simply paid (or taxed) them enough to act in ways that would create a more sustainable future. In reality, problem solving in the environmental realm is inevitably entangled with social values, conflicts, and inertia. No matter what technical solutions we develop, we must navigate the complexities of human behavior to activate their utility.

This is where social science becomes helpful. Without it, we are left to our own intuitions and biases about why a particular effort should work or not. It is all too common for us to be blind to our habitual ways of seeing the world around us, especially when it comes to understanding human behavior. It is easy to assume that others should act in predictable ways that make sense to us. When this doesn't happen, we find ourselves baffled and frustrated. Relying solely on our intuitions (or what we already know) often leads us to the same dead ends. I have assembled this book to help us out of this trap—to provide access to a broader array of time-tested ways to understand human behavior.

Humans are complex creatures. Trying to understand our interactions, whether interpersonal, political, familial, communal, national, international, or otherwise, can be downright mind-boggling. Our life choices and behaviors do not result from simply weighing potential costs and benefits to choose the most beneficial path in each situation. For decades, social scientists have studied individuals, groups, and their interactions, seeking patterns in human behavior to help make sense of how people and societies function. Their work results in the development and refinement of theories, which aim to explain their observations.

> *"Your assumptions are your windows on the world. Scrub them off every once in a while, or the light won't come in." – Isaac Asimov*

1.4 What are theories good for?

Put simply, useful theories provide explanations about how or why something happens in different situations. In the social sciences, these theories explain peoples' behavior and thus illuminate strategies for influencing that behavior. The theories contained in this book comprise a small portion of those available to people working on environmental and sustainability-related challenges. They represent some of the most useful and supported that I and others have found over careers of researching and practicing the work of environmental conservation, natural resource management, and sustainability. I have intentionally simplified most of them. In some cases, I present a synthesis of multiple inter-related theories, rather than a singular pre-existing one. My goal in this book is not to trace the history of the theories provided, nor to faithfully reproduce every individual theory that might be relevant to a specific problem. I provide endnotes and references for further reading for those interested in those endeavors. Rather, my hope is that my presentation will clearly convey how the theories in this book might apply directly to contemporary problems you might be facing and how to use them to enhance environmental sustainability efforts.

1.5 How to make best use of this book

While it is every author's hope that his or her audience will read every word on every page, this book is intended to be practical for busy people. I've organized it so those who wish to read the book from cover to cover should benefit from doing so (and hopefully enjoy the experience). Meanwhile, those who prefer to use it as a general, or just-in-time, reference in times of need should also find the book easy to navigate for specific goals. To this end, I have created a table that readers can use to find what they may be looking for (Table 3.1). The table should help you to easily locate appropriate theories based on your own specific problems and contexts. The final chapter (Chapter 10) provides another means for selecting specific theories based on the degree of conflict present within the social context (see Figure 10.1). Some early readers of the book have also recommended reading any one of the vignettes in Chapter 9 as a first step to understanding how to turn theories into real world strategies.

My goal is that this book will serve as a field guide, of sorts, for busy people looking for alternative ways to tackle meaningful challenges in their work. My greatest hope is that it finds a regular place in your backpack or on the corner of your desk, and it grows worn, weary, and creased over time. Much like a birder who turns to a field guide when she sees a new bird or hears a new song, you can turn to this book whenever you hit a snag in your work, when people's behavior just isn't making sense to you, or when you need a fresh perspective on a stubborn problem.

I've divided the contents into three primary parts. Part I provides an overview of some of the most basic challenges of working with people, summarizing some of our most common cognitive biases and limitations. I intend for this chapter to serve as a baseline from which to consider a variety of approaches to understanding and influencing human behavior. Part II is creatively titled, "The Theories." This second section presents concise summaries of thirty explanatory theories (in a few cases syntheses of multiple theories) with general guidance on the types of situations in which each theory might be most (or least) useful and on how to use it. Part III, entitled, "Putting the Theories to Use," contains a series of vignettes demonstrating the theories in practice. The vignettes are designed with two purposes in mind. First, they provide examples of how one might use the theories to solve real world problems. Second, they reveal the power of considering multiple theories, rather than relying on a single favorite or any pre-conceived notions we might have about the people with whom we interact. Part III concludes with a synthesis of key principles and their potential applications to solving environmental problems.

Maintaining an adaptive mindset

I urge readers to approach this book with what I'll refer to as an "adaptive mindset." An adaptive mindset has three chief characteristics: (1) an eagerness to experiment and to learn, (2) a recognition of the value of multiple viewpoints, and

(3) a willingness to question underlying assumptions.[2] An adaptive mindset thus promotes two key qualities that I believe to be of utmost importance to modern-day problem solving. The first is a strong sense of **humility** as we grapple with questions that are not only difficult to answer, but also constantly changing. The second is a sense of ***compassion*** as we do this work together and do our best to understand different ways of seeing the world. These two elements, humility and compassion, open the door to asking the most difficult questions, considering the widest range of potential solutions, learning from failures, and being measured and thoughtful about the consequences of our actions.

With this as a jumping off point, the theories in this book should not be considered simple formulas for problem solving. The complexities and idiosyncrasies of people and contexts ensure that even the best social science theories will not apply in every circumstance. Rather, they provide multiple lenses for making sense of a situation and formulating potential courses of action. No one theory may be ideally suited for any single problem. Rather, considering multiple theories, sometimes in combination, will often illuminate new solutions that might have otherwise remained hidden.

1.6 A note to graduate students

I think you will find this book a fruitful guide to locating useful theory for any study related to the human dimensions of sustainability, conservation, or any form of environmental management. I'd be pleased if graduate students came to use this book as a short cut in this sense. However, I wish to add a word of cautionary advice. This book provides only a glimpse of each theory and its associated body of empirical research. If you plan to employ any of these theories in a research study of your own, you'll need to read far beyond the summaries I provide here. I offer some key references along with each theory only as a starting place. I wish you well on your (hopefully) long journey of discovery.

Part I

How Our Brains Work (or Don't) and Some Ideas on What to Do About It

2

Cognitive biases and limitations

2.1 An introduction to non-rational decision making

The Nobel Laureate behavioral economist Richard Thaler has long highlighted the distinction between *Humans* and what he calls *Econs*. *Econs* are the imaginary beings that populate traditional economic models. They always act rationally in a way that maximizes their own personal well-being or self-interest. Moreover, they act with full and accurate information (a sort of God-like omniscience that is rarely, if ever, the case in real world situations). *Humans*, on the other hand, are real people, like us, who exist in the real world. We rarely have full knowledge of any given problem. We often make decisions based on concerns other than self-interest, and we often lack the self-control necessary to optimize our personal well-being.

Another Nobel Laureate, psychologist Daniel Kahneman, distinguishes between two modes of operation of the brain: System 1 and System 2. System 1 represents our quick, intuitive responses to most of the daily decisions we face. System 1 is incredibly efficient and often serves us quite well, but it is prone to certain biases and systematic errors. System 2 is an effortful and slow way of thinking that requires considerable energy and concentration. When it is engaged, we are sometimes able to override the biases and systematic errors of System 1. However, because careful reasoning demands such energy, System 1 tends to dominate our decision making (unless we are specifically triggered to engage System 2—see *4.4 The Elaboration Likelihood Model*).

In short, people are prone to well-known cognitive biases and limitations. Knowing about these not only can enhance our ability to make effective arguments, but also can keep us from making common errors of judgment ourselves. This chapter provides background regarding some of the most common limitations in human thinking. My goal isn't to provide an exhaustive list of cognitive biases and limitations. For those interested, the best source I know on the matter is Daniel Kahneman's 2011 book *Thinking Fast and Slow*. Rather, I share some of the most highly relevant mistakes we commonly make every day and some ideas about how to deal with them.

Social Science Theory for Environmental Sustainability: A Practical Guide. Marc J. Stern,
Oxford University Press (2018). © Marc J. Stern 2018. DOI 10.1093/oso/9780198793182.001.0001

2.2 Common cognitive biases

The availability heuristic

The availability heuristic[1] is a mental shortcut that causes us to assess risk or the probability that something is true based on how easy it is to think of examples of it. For instance, having witnessed a flood or a car accident, we are likely to think they are more common than they actually are. Moreover, more vivid experiences typically cause us to amplify our perceptions of their effects. More recent events and events that are more personal are likely to drive decisions more than distant occurrences or reading about general trends.

This heuristic forms the basis of Winston Churchill's famous saying, "Never let a good crisis go to waste." For example, people are more likely to respond to messages about climate change after a major coastal flooding event. We are prone to overestimate or overemphasize something if we have personal experience with it. We are also prone to underestimate its significance if we lack personal experience with it.

What to do about it:

- Remember: Just because you've seen it before, doesn't mean it's common or likely. We all carry with us the baggage of our prior experiences. Recognize what your baggage might be, and do your best to check the less useful stuff at the door. Recognize also that everyone else has their own experiences that color their interpretations of you and your message. Think ahead regarding what these pre-conceived notions might be and make a plan for kindly addressing them. Creating space in which people can share some of their pre-conceived notions can be a healthy way to begin collaborative or deliberative processes (see *6.1 Trust Theory*).
- If people have witnessed something firsthand, abstract statistics alone will not easily sway their beliefs. Be sure to address personal experiences and frame communications with them in mind.
- Use vivid storytelling to create a memorable experience that will inform future thinking. Film, live storytelling, or even the sharing of personal histories across stakeholder groups can provide memorable and often emotional connections to key themes, making them salient in subsequent interactions and decision making.
- Create shared experiences that demonstrate the key elements of an issue. Experiential and environmental education research reveals that educational programs tend to achieve their greatest outcomes when they involve hands-

on, issue-based experiences, where participants can gain firsthand familiarity through direct exploration of an issue and then reflect on that experience.[2] The collaborative natural resource management literature also demonstrates the value of field trips as opportunities to build common experiences that can form the basis for common problem definition and understanding in challenging environmental planning processes.[3]

Seeing patterns where they don't exist

We are excellent at jumping to conclusions prematurely. We see patterns where they don't actually exist, and we infer causality from mere coincidence. We are evolutionarily programmed to search for causes. However, we aren't always very good at it. We are prone to believing a plausible story that aligns with our prior experiences and simple observations rather than taking the time to carefully study the complexities of an issue.

What to do about it:

- Don't make assumptions based on only a small set of observations or a few interactions with a person or group. Such assumptions are often the source of over-simplification or stereotypical beliefs that limit effective problem solving, communication, or collaboration.
- Recognize that people often make quick judgments. As a result, first impressions are particularly important. Consider how you want to be viewed before your first interaction with a new person or group and think through how you might project that image.
- Learn to tell simple, accurate, and compelling stories. People rely on stories both to inform and to justify their beliefs. People are particularly open to compelling stories that demonstrate clear and simple relationships between cause and effect.

A preference for stories over statistics

Most people find stories more memorable and easier to understand than statistics. Unfortunately, most scientists involved in environmental problem solving have been trained to construct excellent statistical arguments rather than to tell convincing stories.

What to do about it:

Tell better stories. First and foremost, be sure to connect the dots between what you know and what it means in the bigger picture. What message would you like to convey with that information? Sharing information or data alone without a well-crafted message is unlikely to have much of an impact.

A recent study of nearly 400 live interpretive programs in National Parks across the United States[4] suggests that stories exhibiting the following characteristics may have the greatest positive impacts on their audience's resulting attitudes:

- The passion and authentic emotion of the communicator.
- An introduction that captures attention and orients the audience to the key theme of the story.
- Characters and a plot (including a challenge and a resolution).
- A logical sequence with attention to smooth transitions between components.
- A clear theme that links story elements to larger universal concepts with which the audience can identify (e.g., family, love, conflict, loss).
- Provocation of the audience to imagine something or to personally reflect on the story's content and its deeper meaning.
- The conveyance of emotion, not just facts.
- Relevance of the subject to the audience's lives.
- A conclusion that connects back to the introduction in a cohesive way (coming *full circle*).

Not every good story will contain all of these elements, but each may enhance a story's impact.

Richard Maxwell and Bob Dickman provide additional advice on how to tell persuasive stories in their book *The Elements of Persuasion*,[5] stressing the importance of five key elements:

- Passion that provides the audience with a reason to listen and care.
- A hero who provides a point of view for the audience. The audience must recognize some piece of themselves somewhere within the make-up of the hero (see also *5.1 Identity Theory*).
- An obstacle the hero must overcome.
- A new awareness or realization (a learning moment) that enables the hero to overcome the obstacle.
- Transformation in the hero and the world around that results from overcoming the obstacle.

In short, the best stories are told with passion. Moreover, they help the listener to imagine themselves as a protagonist, either within the story itself or within a closely related story of even greater relevance that the original story's telling might trigger within the mind of the listener.

Anchoring

In formulating our own pictures of reality, we tend to be influenced by whatever information (especially numbers) we hear first, particularly when we are uncertain or unfamiliar with a topic. For example, let's assume I ask you to guess the amount of sea level rise predicted by scientists to take place in the next thirty years. Your response will be higher if I begin by asking if you think it will be more or less than five feet than if I ask whether you think it will be more or less than five inches (unless you are a climate modeler or someone who is well-versed in dozens of reports on the topic). This has powerful implications for negotiations (what is the starting price?) and for the power of social norms (your neighbors' electricity use will serve as an anchor by which to judge your own).

What to do about it:

- Choose examples carefully to avoid inadvertently calling attention to figures that go against the influence you hope to have. For example, don't talk about how few people recycle or how many people litter or take artifacts from a national park. These *anchors* can easily be interpreted as norms that run counter to the environmental message you wish to convey. Rather, provide accurate figures in support of the direction of the change/action you wish to see whenever they exist. Most people recycle. See *5.6 Frame Theory* and *4.1 Social Norm Theory*.
- Use default options wisely. For example, many nature centers, protected areas, or philanthropic organizations provide ideas about a "suggested donation." While too high of a request might turn people off entirely, too low of a figure might fail to capitalize on peoples' generosity. It might be wise to err on the high side of what might be considered a reasonable request given the audience, while still making it clear that any donation would be greatly appreciated. It may also be effective to provide specific information about what different levels of donation can achieve, providing a specific sense of efficacy (see *4.5 The Theory of Planned Behavior*) in addition to accommodating the effects of anchoring on message recipients.

Confirmation bias

We tend to seek out and/or overemphasize evidence that supports our pre-conceived notions. We also have a tendency to minimize, dismiss, or explain away evidence that conflicts with them. When we hear something that conforms to our pre-existing beliefs, we ask ourselves, "*Can* I believe it?" This sets a rather low threshold of evidence. When confronted with something that conflicts with our pre-existing beliefs, however, we are more likely to ask the question, "*Must* I believe it?" This latter question allows us to dismiss new information if we find even a single shred of doubt, which is usually rather easy to do.[6] In short, we have different standards for evaluating claims we like vs those we don't. This sets up high barriers to open discussion about environmental challenges and any form of persuasive messaging. For example, consider how Al Gore's *An Inconvenient Truth* was received by the majority of the conservative movement in the United States. This particular bias is treated in more detail later in the book under *5.3 Haidt's Social Intuitionist Model of Moral Judgments* and *5.4 Cultural Cognition*.

Normative bias

We tend to go with the flow. That is, we take cues from others who are important to us regarding what is right and wrong. These "others" can change from situation to situation, but they are often made up of people within our own social or cultural group that are most relevant to the question at hand—for example, our friends if we are at a party, or our political affiliation if we are evaluating an environmental policy. The norms, or accepted standards of behavior, of these groups typically define our default preferences or behaviors. Moreover, they predispose us to biased processing of new information. For more detail on this bias and what to do about it, see *4.1 Social Norm Theory* and *5.1 Identity Theory*.

2.3 Common cognitive limitations

Chunking

Working memory refers to the most easily accessible parts of short-term memory that we use every day to make sense of what is going on around us. Human working memory can only make use of a few ideas at a time. While psychologists formerly thought the number of distinct ideas we could hold in our working memory at any given time was seven plus or minus two, most have since argued that the actual amount of distinct ideas available for easy access is actually smaller for complex ideas (those beyond simple numbers or words).

Regardless of the actual number, researchers find that the human brain packages individual information fragments into bigger *chunks*. A classic example is to try to memorize a long string of letters or numbers, as shown on the left below. Once we group those characters into clusters of three or four that have some easily accessible meaning to us, even a string of 16 letters can be quite easy to remember.

RSVPPHDUSACIAFBI   RSVP PHD USA CIA FBI

Each chunk, no matter how much information it holds, occupies a single space in working memory. In other words, the working memory rule involves chunks of information, not individual numbers, digits, or words. As we grow and learn, our chunks get more complex. As our chunks develop, they become less likely to change over time. That is, we learn to classify new information quickly within pre-conceived categories of information. This quick classification pre-disposes us to sometimes ignore contrasts between new information and pre-existing knowledge. In other words, we are biased toward what we already know (see *5.3 Haidt's Social Intuitionist Model* for more on this).

This bias helps to explain our ability to jump quickly to conclusions based on very little evidence and our tendencies toward stereotyping. It also has implications for communication. If your chunks of information regarding a certain topic, such as climate change, differ largely from my chunks, it might be difficult not only to understand each other, but also to accept any new information that conflicts with what we each already think we know (see also *4.3 Cognitive Dissonance*).

What to do about it:

- Limit the number of key ideas we try to convey at any given time or group ideas in easy-to-understand ways. Storytelling can be particularly effective in this sense, as opposed to deluging a message recipient with every fact or argument that might be relevant to the issue. Aim for no more than three or four key themes.
- Consider your audience and avoid jargon and other assumptions that they have no reason to understand. Our own sets of specialized knowledge may limit our ability to communicate effectively.[7]
- Be vigilant about your own subconscious/automatic assumptions regarding new information and consider those of others. We are evolutionarily programmed to immediately search our memory for associations. As a result, we are more prone to believe someone who somehow reminds us of an old friend than someone who happens to look like our least favorite politician. While this tendency may seem illogical, it is difficult to turn off. Considering how the messenger and the message are likely to be received in different audiences can help us make better choices about each.

Choice overload

In general, we like to have choices. However, research suggests that offering people too many choices may be paralyzing, particularly in situations in which people aren't really sure exactly what they want. Researchers have shown that offering fewer options can lead to greater sales and higher levels of enrollment.[8] There is no magic number of options that will be optimal in all situations, but chunk theory suggests that five or fewer might make sense. If there are more choices, arranging them into fewer sets or categories, or offering choices in a clear sequence rather than a single overwhelming list, can also be helpful. Otherwise, people have been shown to (a) withdraw from the decision-making process altogether, (b) merely select the option that is offered first (or most conspicuously), or (c) rely on whatever default option might be offered in the absence of having to make a decision.[9]

What to do about it:

- In persuasive messaging, limit the number of suggested action items, or group them into a few lists or broad categories that will make sense to the message recipient.
- If you ever find yourself in the position of providing people with a list of potential options, place the most beneficial option, or the most desired one, in the lead position. This might be difficult to determine, however, and of course also carries the ethical burden of trying to determine what is best for both your purpose and for the message recipient. Thaler and Sunstein's (2008) bestselling book, *Nudge*, contains some great guidance on this issue.
- Provide a healthy default option in the case that the message recipient has difficulty making an active choice. For example, many employers have a default option to automatically enroll employees in retirement plans or in a good health insurance plan. Similarly, many political campaigns include an "opt out" rather than an "opt in" option. In these cases, the default is to stay engaged or informed, while it takes an active decision to remove oneself. The default option is typically perceived as a social norm in cases of multiple choice, relieving the tension of the decision maker in accepting personal responsibility for an errant decision they might make.

Hot vs cold situations

People are notoriously bad at providing accurate explanations for their own preferences or actions. This is in large part because we tend to discount the impact of emotional influences on our decision making. In other words, we are not good at predicting (or admitting) how much our emotions impact our decision making.[10] *Hot* situations involve emotions, conflict, or other forms of arousal that occur in the heat of the moment. They require quick reactions and decisions. System 1 typically takes care of these. In contrast, we are normally distanced from these stresses in *cold* situations, such as filling out a survey or reading a newspaper article. In cold situations, we may draw upon perfectly rational cost-benefit analyses, such as those conducted by Thaler's *Econs*, to predict or provide explanations for our actions. In other words, our System 2 can go to work. The problem is that we often act differently in the heat of the moment than we expect we would. System 2 stinks at predicting the actions of System 1.

This has multiple implications for addressing environmental challenges. First, we can recognize that many issues are emotionally charged and thus may crowd out our abilities to think rationally. Second, we can consider ways we might *cool off* a situation to enable more thoughtful exchanges and deliberation around a problem. Third, as marketers and advertising professionals know well, we should never ignore or discount the power of emotions in persuasive communications. Intentionally provoking specific emotions can often enhance persuasive efforts.

What to do about it:

- Create safe spaces for deliberation, in which inter-personal conflicts can be set aside, at least temporarily. For advice on how to do this, see recommendations associated with systems-based trust within *6.1 Trust Theory*, separating people from the problem within *6.2 Principled Negotiation*, and *5.2 Self-Affirmation Theory*.
- Recognize the limitations of asking people to commit to an action. While a written or verbal commitment has been shown to enhance the likelihood of performance, it does not guarantee it by any means.
- Create triggers or cues for people that might help them to *cool off* hot situations. For example, "Whenever you are faced with someone who calls into question the science behind climate change, consider the following responses . . ."[11]

2.4 Moving forward with a dose of humility

In summary, we are prone to jumping to conclusions that we already support based on limited or flawed evidence. We find it difficult to understand people who have accumulated chunking systems different from our own. We rarely activate our System 2 brains to deeply contemplate the full scope of complex problems, rather defaulting to our pre-conceived notions or those of others we trust. We're not very good at predicting how we'll act in a given situation or accurately explaining the reasons for our actions. Additionally, we are commonly blind to our own shortcomings in all of these respects. This chapter thus provides a basis for empathy and reflection on the behaviors of others as well as a list of personal checks we might use to inspect our own behaviors.

My intention in sharing these ideas is not to make us feel bad about ourselves. Our intuitions and gut feelings often serve us quite well, and we shouldn't entirely ignore them. My hope, rather, is that this introductory chapter serves as a reminder to approach the theories that follow with a strong dose of humility. We are all prone to cognitive biases and subject to the limitations of our human condition. The theories that follow do not provide infallible solutions to complex problems. Rather, they provide tested and well-reasoned approaches to operating within the common confines of the human experience. Given the constraints we all experience, I recommend a slower reading process than you might usually undertake. I am guilty of sharing far too many ideas, snippets, and suggestions in the pages that follow than anyone can be expected to digest in a quick read. I've done my best to explain any odd terms or jargon, but I'm sure my own cognitive biases have led to some shortcomings. I apologize ahead of time. My best advice is to read each theory with your own real world problems or ambitions in mind, constantly asking yourself, "How could I make use of this information in my situation?" Not all theories will apply to every situation you might have in mind (I've tried to provide guidance on that in Table 3.1), but you never know when a new set of circumstances might arise. In those cases, I hope that a small flag might wave somewhere in the recesses of your mind to remind you to have another look at something you read on your first pass through this book.

Part II

The Theories

3

Finding useful theories when and where you need them

To make navigating the book a bit easier, I've grouped the theories that follow into chapters. Each chapter contains related theories that apply most directly to certain contexts or scales. The groupings are primarily based on my own views on these matters, which of course are colored by my own experiences and biases. There are plenty of other ways the theories could have fit together that would have made just as much sense. What's most important to me is that you are able to navigate this book efficiently to find theories that will be helpful to you and your own circumstances. At the end of this short introduction, you'll find a matrix (Table 3.1) that I hope will aid you in matching the most appropriate theories in the book to your real life challenges.[1] While it might be plausible to place an "X" in nearly every box, I've tried to convey the situations in which a particular theory is *most* applicable to the task at hand. I expect that you may often find other creative uses for a particular theory that I have not envisioned. I thus urge you to read all the theories in the book at least once before relying on the table for later reference.

I chose to give cognitive biases and limitations a somewhat different treatment than the other theories in this book, even though they are also clearly theories. I intended for them to collectively provide a baseline for nearly everything that follows in subsequent chapters. In the chapters that follow, the theories (and syntheses) all adhere to a common format. Each begins with a list of potential uses for the theory and a broad question that the theory helps to answer. The question is followed by a concise summary of the components of the theory and how they fit together to provide explanations of social phenomena. The summary is followed by an "applications" section that first addresses the situations in which the theory might be most (and least) useful and second provides specific guidance on how to use the theory in those situations. Each theory section concludes with a short list of "key references." These are intended to provide important starting points for readers who wish to embark on a deeper exploration of theory.

Social Science Theory for Environmental Sustainability: A Practical Guide. Marc J. Stern, Oxford University Press (2018). © Marc J. Stern 2018. DOI 10.1093/oso/9780198793182.001.0001

Table 3.1 Matching theories to situations (descriptions of column headings are at the bottom of the table).

Theory	Persuasive communication	Political/mass communications	High conflict situations	Organizational performance	Collaboration	Negotiation	Public involvement	Governance	Cross-cultural work	Understanding systems
Cognitive Biases and Limitations	X	X	X	X	X	X	X	X	X	
Social Norm Theory	X	X		X		X			X	
Norm Activation Theory and Value–Belief–Norm Theory	X	X				X				
Cognitive Dissonance	X	X				X				
Elaboration Likelihood Model	X	X								
Theory of Planned Behavior	X	X				X				
Self-Determination Theory	X	X		X		X				
Extended Parallel Process Model of Fear Appeals	X	X	X							

	1	2	3	4	5	6	7	8	9
Motivation Crowding Theory	X				X				
Maslow's Hierarchy of Needs	X	X	X		X	X	X	X	X
Identity Theory	X	X	X		X	X	X		
Self-Affirmation Theory		X	X		X	X			
Haidt's Social Intuitionist Model of Moral Judgment	X	X	X				X		
Cultural Cognition	X	X			X	X			
Moral Foundations Theory	X	X	X		X	X	X	X	
Frame Theory	X	X	X					X	
Meyer's Culture Map	X		X		X	X	X	X	
Trust Theory	X	X	X		X	X	X		
Principled Negotiation	X	X	X		X	X	X		
The Reasonable Person Model				X		X			

(Continued)

Table 3.1 (Continued)

Theory	Persuasive communication	Political/mass communications	High conflict situations	Organizational performance	Collaboration	Negotiation	Public involvement	Governance	Cross-cultural work	Understanding systems
The Co-orientation Model			X	X	X	X	X			
Herzberg's Motivation–Hygiene Theory				X						
Team Effectiveness Theory				X	X			X		
Accountability Theory			X	X	X	X	X	X	X	X
Project Risk			X	X			X			
Nonaka's Theory of Organizational Knowledge Creation				X	X				X	X
Leadership Theory				X	X			X		
Commons Theory			X	X	X			X	X	X
Community Capitals Framework					X			X	X	X

	Persuasive communications	Political/mass communications	High conflict situations	Organizational performance	Collaboration	Negotiation	Public involvement	Governance	Cross-cultural work	Understanding systems
Collective Impact					X	X	X			
Diffusion Theory	X				X	X	X			

Descriptions of Column Headings

Persuasive communications — This category includes a wide variety of efforts to influence the attitudes and/or behavior of other people, including trying to persuade people to vote for a particular candidate, to join a volunteer effort, to enroll in a conservation program, to purchase (or not purchase) certain products, to behave in an environmentally sensitive way in a fragile environment, or to conserve resources at home. It may also include efforts to persuade groups or corporations to enroll in different efforts, change their practices, or promote specific ideas.

Political/mass communications — This category is a special case of persuasive communications involving communicating with broader stakeholder groups or the "general public." It often involves communicating through the press or social media.

High conflict situations — This category is depicted by long-standing or intense conflicts in which the people or groups involved feel meaningful threat to their values or identities. Examples include conflicts over resource use, debates about climate change, and other personally or politically charged debates.

Organizational performance — This category includes theories specifically geared to enhancing organizational performance. While many persuasive communications theories may also be highly relevant here, these theories are specific to organizational contexts.

Collaboration — Collaboration involves groups of stakeholders working together toward agreement on appropriate pathways forward and/or on a specific project. It often entails navigating diverse interests and developing procedures for joint decision making.

Negotiation — Negotiations involve discussions aimed at reaching an agreement. The theories noted here provide guidance on how to address common challenges faced in negotiations around environmental and sustainability-related issues.

Public involvement — Public involvement is typically mandated when government agencies plan and implement actions that may have meaningful impacts on the environment. Other organizations participate in public involvement in multiple roles—sometimes as stakeholders interested in a government initiative and sometimes as the leaders of a public outreach effort of their own.

Governance — The concept of governance encompasses the structures, processes, and traditions through which people in a society share power and make decisions. The theories here provide guidance on how to structure and interact within those processes.

Cross-cultural work — This category involves communicating and interacting across different cultures. The theories here are important to consider when working not only across international lines, but also across organizational, regional, political, or any other cultural divides.

Understanding systems — This final category contains theories that are focused on broader systems of interactions between social entities and their political and environmental contexts. Systems theories provide guidance for considering the bigger picture in multiple cases.

4

Theories of motivation, cognition, and reasoning

Introduction: Bounded rationality and decision making

The theories in this chapter are primarily about decision making in cases where people are primed to use their System 2 brains. That is, they explain behavior by considering people, at least partially, as *bounded rationalists*.[1] Bounded rationalists make decisions in attempts to optimize the achievement of their goals. They do so based on the information they have available (which is almost always incomplete), their own cognitive limitations, and the time they have available to make the decision. The theories in this chapter address conscious decision making, as well as the situational factors that might account for how rational or thoughtful someone might be in a situation—or whether they rely on shortcuts (also known as *heuristics*—see *2.2 Common cognitive biases*).

The theories in this chapter provide guidance on influencing and improving decision making and problem solving in situations where people can be expected to act more or less rationally. If you read Chapter 2 on cognitive biases and limitations, you know that this is not always the case. People do not always act rationally. So, when are people most likely to act as *bounded rationalists*?

Theories of motivation, cognition, and reasoning apply primarily in cases when people do not feel strong threats to their identities. These situations include, for example, everyday interactions at a place of work, consumer choices, behaviors when visiting a national park or other recreation site, a discussion with a friend or colleague, or work with known collaborators. In different situations characterized by heated or long-standing conflicts between groups, these theories will be less powerful than those presented in *Chapter 5 Morals, Intuitions, Culture, and Identity-based Theories*.

In their broadest sense, the theories in this chapter address the following general questions in everyday circumstances and others characterized by the absence of entrenched emotional conflicts:

Social Science Theory for Environmental Sustainability: A Practical Guide. Marc J. Stern, Oxford University Press (2018). © Marc J. Stern 2018. DOI 10.1093/oso/9780198793182.001.0001

1. When are people most likely to think through their actions? *And what can we do about it?*
2. How do people make decisions? *And how can we use this knowledge to be more persuasive?*
3. What circumstances provide the greatest motivation for people to act? *And how can we cultivate these conditions?*

I introduce each theory with a brief list of its uses and a simple question that it helps to answer. I then summarize the key components and claims of each theory and highlight how the theory relates to real world situations. I then provide some guidance on how to apply the theory to real world problem solving, including when it might be most and least useful and specific ideas on how to go about using it. The theories are further applied in the vignettes in Part III of the book.

4.1 Social Norm Theory

Uses: Influencing behavior, persuasive communication, organizational management

> **Can we design our approaches to go with the flow rather than against it?**

Social norms are unwritten rules[2] about how to behave within a specific setting. Understanding social norms can be particularly useful when it comes to designing a conservation project or implementing a program. For example, recognizing certain observable social norms in a community, such as maintaining an attractive garden, can provide a valuable entry point for a habitat conservation program.

While designing interactions with social norms in mind can help to catalyze a project's success, violating these unspoken rules of behavior can doom a project to failure. For example, if you are attempting to work with a community that clearly considers formal ceremonies to be important, discounting or ignoring those ceremonies can create a major barrier to working together.

Important types of social norms

Descriptive social norm: A person's perception of how people typically behave in a given situation. These types of norms can be identified through spending time and observing patterns of behavior within a group. People tend to value how other people within their own social group behave. However, which descriptive norms are most relevant might depend on the situation and who happens to be around us at the time. Descriptive norms influence behavior through our tendency to conform to the behavior of the people around us.

Injunctive (or prescriptive) social norm: Injunctive social norms are generally agreed upon standards shared by the members of a social group. In other words, injunctive norms involve our perceptions of how others think we *should* behave. These norms are believed to influence behavior primarily through social pressure, informal sanctions or rewards, or through the creation or revision of *personal norms*. **Personal norms**, in contrast to social norms, are our internalized values or beliefs about right and wrong (see *4.2 Norm Activation Theory*).

Social norms can often explain behavior that diverges from a person's narrowly defined self-interests. Social norms can influence behavior in multiple ways.

1. Through expected sanctions or rewards. These may take the form of praise, critique, agreement, disagreement, public shaming, inclusion, exclusion, or any number of interpersonal displays of acceptance or rejection.[3]
2. Through simply going with the flow. In the absence of any internalized cognitive or emotional consideration, people take cues from those around them, observing and internalizing *descriptive norms*. For example, field experiments have shown that when people are made aware of the average energy use of their neighbors, they tend to conform over time toward the group average, either up or down.[4]

Social norms and reference groups

Reference group theory can be used to trace how social norms develop. Our values, opinions, and other assessments are developed through comparison to other people we feel are important. These groups of people are called ***reference groups***.

Reference groups may consist of known individuals (e.g., friends, family members, peers, co-workers) or more distant individuals (e.g., famous movie stars, athletes). Research suggests that known individuals tend to be more influential.

Over time, we can sometimes become members of the relevant reference groups of other people, including those we hope to enroll in solving environmental problems. This can happen through active listening, positive relationship-building, sharing daily experiences, demonstrating shared values, and other trust-building activities (see *6.1 Trust Theory*). In these cases, new pathways toward environmental solutions may emerge, as the social norms of each person (or group) begin to affect the other.

Applications

When to use Social Norm Theory

- Understanding social norms and identifying relevant reference groups can be useful in designing conservation projects, in developing persuasive communication, and in facilitating collaboration.

How to use Social Norm Theory

- It usually takes some local knowledge, and sometimes research, to recognize dominant descriptive or injunctive social norms within a group. Once they are known, messages should be crafted to align with them by drawing attention to how the message fits with dominant norms.[5] For example, if it is clearly observable that people care deeply for the appearance of their home landscaping, a water savings program should focus on how to keep landscaping attractive with less water, rather than ignoring this easily observable descriptive norm.

- Call attention to the desired behavior of others who are similar to (or otherwise valued by) the message recipients. For example, "Join others in your community who have..." or, "Most people who come here care deeply about...and (act in this way as a result)."
- Do not call attention to common undesirable behaviors. In situations characterized by high levels of undesirable behavior, calling attention to the frequency of these behaviors can backfire, as they evoke a descriptive norm for the undesirable behavior. For example, messages that stress that a high number of people litter or steal fossils from a park are unlikely to be effective in halting these activities.[6]
- When possible, align the power of descriptive and injunctive norms. For example, highlight that desired activities are commonly performed *and* widely approved, or that undesired activities are relatively rare *and* unpopular. In cases where alignment is not possible, focus only on the norm that aligns with the message.
- Use negative language in normative messaging. Several researchers have found that normative messaging typically gains more attention and is more effective when negatively worded—that is, when messages focus on what people should *not* do based on descriptive or injunctive norms.[7]
- Partner with members of relevant reference groups for communicating key messages. For example, if respected local community members become spokespeople for a project, more people may join.
- Share success stories of people in similar situations. For example, bringing fishermen from a neighboring island to share lessons about conservation with local fishermen can enhance the trustworthiness of information and help local people visualize and more fully understand what is possible. Sharing success stories can influence social norms by revealing what might be otherwise invisible due to commonplace descriptive norms in a particular community.
- Consider asking people to make a public commitment to act, such as a signed pledge or other public declaration. Social norms can subsequently provide pressure to follow through.

Key references

Cialdini, R.B., Kallgren, C.A., and Reno, R.R. 1991. A focus theory of normative conduct. *Advances in Experimental Psychology* 24: 201–34.

Merton, R.K. 1968. *Social Theory and Social Structure*. New York: The Free Press.

Thøgersen, J. 2006. Norms for environmentally responsible behavior: An extended taxonomy. *Journal of Environmental Psychology* 26: 247–61.

4.2 The Norm Activation Theory and the Value-Belief-Norm Theory of Pro-Environmental Behavior

Uses: Influencing behavior, persuasive communication

At what point do people feel morally obligated to take action?

Have you ever had a nagging feeling compelling you to do something that has no obvious personal benefit to you? Perhaps it just feels like the right thing to do. Maybe it involves a favor for someone you barely know, or cleaning up after a stranger in a public space. Do you find that sometimes you act on those feelings and sometimes you don't? The *Norm Activation Theory* provides some understanding of when people are more or less likely to act in situations like these.

The *Value-Belief-Norm Theory* is an extension of the Norm Activation Theory. Both theories explain the activation of feelings of moral obligation based on personal norms. The Value-Belief-Norm Theory provides specific insights into how best to use moral arguments to influence pro-environmental behaviors.

Norm Activation Theory

Personal norms are an individual's internal standards about what is right and wrong in a given situation. The mere existence of personal norms, however, does not necessarily mean they will be considered by an individual in every situation. The *Norm Activation Theory* describes the circumstances under which personal norms are likely to be *activated*, particularly within the context of prosocial behaviors (Figure 4.1). According to the theory, an individual must (a) be aware of the consequences of a potential action (or inaction) upon something they care about and (b) accept personal responsibility for those consequences. In these cases, a personal norm becomes a moral obligation that spurs action.

For the *awareness of consequences* to evoke *acceptance of responsibility*, an individual must not only recognize a problem, but also be aware of a potential solution to the problem and feel capable to enact that solution.[8] Actions based on

Figure 4.1 Norm activation theory (based on Schwartz, 1977).

moral obligations arise when people feel unable to deny this responsibility easily. Responsibility denial is less likely when (a) people are specifically asked for help and/ or (b) other people who are watching provide social pressure to act. Responsibility denial is more likely when the individual in question is (a) not focused on the problem or in a hurry (see *4.4 The Elaboration Likelihood Model*), or (b) other people are conspicuously ignoring the problem. (If no one else is acting, why should I? Maybe it's not a big issue after all—see *4.1 Social Norm Theory*.)

Acceptance of responsibility can be weakened if the action a person might take seems like a futile effort. For example, I'm likely to be less motivated to pick up trash on a beach that is covered with it for miles than on a relatively clean beach with just one or two pieces of litter. However, if I can make the former a collective effort involving more than just myself, my motivation would likely increase. Not only might I feel more empowered that my action would be making a real difference, but also the social norms of those I involve might provide further motivation.

Value-Belief-Norm Theory of Pro-Environmental Behavior

The *Value-Belief-Norm Theory of Pro-Environmental Behavior* builds upon the *Norm Activation Theory* to explain the drivers of pro-environmental behavior specifically. According to the theory, an individual's values give rise to his or her general beliefs about an issue—in this case, the environment. General environmental beliefs influence the degree to which a person might recognize a problem and acknowledge its consequences, as well as the degree to which they might be willing to recognize their own role in either contributing to or solving the problem. As such, they influence the "activation" of personal norms and subsequent behaviors. The specific concepts included in the model are explained in more detail below (Figure 4.2).

Values represent relatively stable beliefs that individuals use as standards for evaluating attitudes and behavior. The *Value-Belief-Norm Theory* stresses three particular value orientations, or patterns of basic beliefs. A *biospheric* value orientation gives relative weight to environmental protection and non-human species in decision making. An *altruistic* value orientation places emphasis on human welfare beyond the individual. An *egoistic* value orientation focuses primarily on

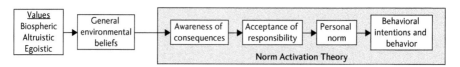

Figure 4.2 The Value-Belief-Norm Theory of Pro-Environmental Behavior (based on Stern, 2000).

self-interest in terms of costs and benefits of particular courses of action. In recent studies, biospheric and, to a lesser extent, altruistic value orientations tend to be positively related to norm activation and pro-environmental behavior. Egoistic value orientations, on the other hand, are more commonly negatively correlated with pro-environmental behavior.[9]

General environmental beliefs reflect individuals' beliefs about humans' appropriate relationships with the environment. Typical examples include beliefs about the appropriateness of human dominance over nature, the perceived fragility of the Earth's ecosystem, or faith in humans' ability to solve environmental problems. These beliefs are often reflective of the perceived social norms of an individual's reference group.

Applications

When to use these theories

- These theories are useful when trying to influence pro-social or pro-environmental behavior, such as recycling, reducing waste, carpooling, donating, volunteering, purchasing particular products, or joining a group.

How to use these theories

- Provide an unequivocal description of the problem and its consequences. Relate the consequences to something the message recipient cares about.
- Communicate what the person can do to solve the problem and provide an argument that their actions will make a difference on an outcome they care about. Without a clear, actionable solution to the problem, it is easy for an individual to deny responsibility.
- Elicit active commitments (an explicit verbal or written commitment, such as a signed pledge) to enhance the likelihood of follow-through by limiting the possibility of subsequent responsibility denial.[10]
- Use second person language "you" in communications to enhance feelings of personal responsibility and self-efficacy.
- Ask people to think about their feelings of pride and guilt associated with a desirable action. For example, "How will doing (or not doing) x make you feel?" Evoking pride has shown somewhat more consistent relationships to behavioral intentions than guilt in the literature.[11] One of my favorite anti-litter campaigns involved school children in St. Croix, U.S. Virgin Islands. They simply posted cardboard signs around the island with colorful hand-written ink that said, "Be proud. Don't litter."

- Values and general environmental beliefs are often implicit within the social norms of a particular group. For example, visitors to a National Park might commonly share a belief in the value of nature for its beauty. Sometimes, identifying these beliefs can require specific local knowledge or some basic research. Messages should be crafted to align with these beliefs by drawing attention to how the message fits with dominant norms.[12]
- Messages that highlight the pro-environmental norms or actions of other relevant people (reference groups) can cue relevant pro-environmental personal norms. For example, "Join your neighbors (or 'other visitors just like you') who are making a difference."
- In group settings, openly discussing the values of attendees with regard to a particular issue can often reveal some common ground. The recognition of a shared value or norm can help to boost feelings of moral obligation when used in concert with the principles noted above.

Key references

Schwartz, S.H. 1997. Normative influences on altruism. In L. Berkowitz (ed.), *Advances in experimental social psychology* (vol. 10), pp. 221–79. New York: Academic Press.

Stern, P.C. 2000. Toward a coherent theory of environmentally significant behavior. *Journal of Social Issues* 56(3): 407–24.

4.3 Cognitive Dissonance

Uses: Persuasive communication

> What happens when we become aware that our actions don't match our values?

Generally speaking, we aim for consistency between our values and our actions. When these things don't align, we typically feel agitated or uncomfortable and aim to reconcile the gap in one way or another. *Cognitive dissonance* describes a state of mind that coincides with the recognition of a tension or gap between two conflicting ideas or between thoughts and actions. Sometimes, pointing out this dissonance can create a re-consideration of attitudes or behaviors.

Applications

When to use it

In persuasive communication when you suspect an individual or group is acting in a way that might be inconsistent with their own interests or values.

How to use it

One technique for persuasive communication is to establish agreement about a basic value, belief, or attitude. Consequently, you can call into question another belief, value, attitude, or action held by the other person that might be in conflict with the previously agreed upon idea. If successful, this will lead the other person to question, and potentially modify, the second belief, value, attitude, or action.

However, calling attention to cognitive dissonance can result in a variety of reactions. Message recipients can:

- Ignore new information that conflicts with previously held knowledge, attitudes, or beliefs.
- Revolt or actively reject new information.
- Accept new information, but rationalize a pre-existing decision or action based on other criteria.
- Replace old knowledge, attitudes, or beliefs with new ones.
- Change their behavior to match the revealed belief, attitude, or value.

The likelihood of persuasion is enhanced by:

- The strength of agreement about the initial value, attitude, or belief.
- The strength of the connection between the initial value, attitude, or belief and the one the communicator is trying to change.
- The perceived benefits, ease, and/or cultural acceptance of the newer idea. See *4.5 The Theory of Planned Behavior.*
- Trust in and/or perceptions of credibility of the communicator. See *6.1 Trust Theory* and *8.3 Diffusion Theory.*
- The salience of the communication. Are listeners motivated to process it? See *4.4 The Elaboration Likelihood Model.*
- The overall quality of the communication/argument for change.
  - Does it address barriers to change in addition to providing motivation?
  - Is sufficient reliable evidence provided to connect beliefs, attitudes, or values to actions?

The likelihood of persuasion is diminished by:

- The strength with which the target audience holds the value, attitude, belief, or behavior the communicator is trying to change.
- The degree of personal threat to the message's recipient's identity the revelation creates (see *5.1 Identity Theory*).
  - Is the communication overly aggressive or accusatory such that defensiveness is triggered in message recipients?
  - One study found, for example, that efforts to change behavior in older people, who, on average, tend to be more resistant to change, were more successful if the communicator avoided characterizing the past behavior as wrong, rather acknowledging that the previous behavior made sense given prior circumstances.[13]

In general, we aim to act consistently with our pre-existing attitudes, statements, actions, values, and commitments. As such, an additional strategy to strengthen the likelihood of follow-through on behavior change is to ask people to make active commitments, such as signing a pledge.

Another technique associated with reducing potential cognitive dissonance is *labeling*. This involves assigning a particular trait to an individual or audience in hopes it may influence their behavior. Multiple studies have shown the power of this technique, particularly when the trait assigned is a positive one. For example, in one study, teachers were informed that a group of randomly selected students were high achievers. Sure enough, after eight months, students who were randomly assigned to this group showed greater gains in IQ. The study found that teachers treated these students differently in multiple ways.[14] In another study, randomly selected potential voters were told that they were "above-average citizens likely to vote and participate in political events," while others were told they were about average when it came to these behaviors. Those in the first group turned out to be 15 percent more likely to vote in an election held one week later.[15] In another study, students who were told they seemed like the type of students who cared about having good handwriting spent more of their free time practicing their penmanship, even when unsupervised.[16]

Key reference

Festinger, L. 1957. *A theory of cognitive dissonance*. Vol. 2. Stanford, CA: Stanford University Press.

4.4 The Elaboration Likelihood Model

Uses: Persuasive communication, influencing behavior

> Do people always need to pay careful attention to the qualities of our arguments for us to have an influence on them?

The ***Elaboration Likelihood Model*** (ELM) suggests that there are two ways to influence people's behavior—the central route and the peripheral route to persuasion (Figure 4.3). The central route involves changing a person's mind through the strength of our arguments. For example, I might be able to convince you to pick up litter based on arguments regarding its negative effects on the beauty of the place we are in and the damage to wildlife it causes. If, however, I can't get you to pay attention to my arguments, this theory suggests that you still might pick up litter anyway. The peripheral route involves the presence of "peripheral cues" that can influence behavior in the absence of an effective argument—for example, simple signs, barriers, or role modeling behavior. If everyone around you is picking up litter, you might feel compelled to do it too without giving it much thought. Knowledge of this theory can help people be persuasive, even if their central messaging efforts fail.

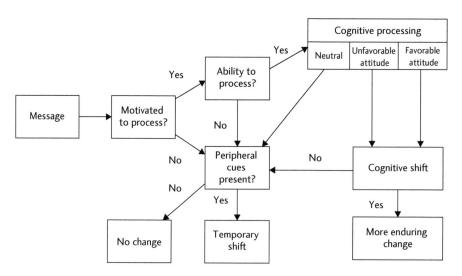

Figure 4.3 The Elaboration Likelihood Model (based on Petty and Cacciopo, 1986).

Central route to persuasion: The person receiving a persuasive message draws upon prior experience and knowledge to scrutinize and evaluate issue-relevant arguments presented in the communication. For this to occur, the person must be motivated and able to process the perceived merits of the information provided. This cognitive processing (or "elaboration") can result in the development or strengthening of an attitude that is well articulated and integrated into the person's belief structure. Attitudes developed via this route tend to be relatively accessible, persistent over time, predictive of behavior and resistant to change.

Peripheral route to persuasion: When a person's motivation or ability to process issue-relevant arguments is low, the situational context in which the information is provided may take precedence and still work to persuade the person. Examples include the use of charismatic communicators (celebrities in commercials) or the placement of environmental cues (signs) on-site. This type of attitude change tends to be less permanent than attitudes developed through the central route. If the cue is no longer present, the behavior is likely to dissipate. For example, I might pick up trash or recycle when I am with other people who do so, but not when I am on my own, unless I have developed persistent beliefs about its importance (central route).

Applications

When to use it

- Influencing immediate or on-site behaviors (both peripheral and central routes).
- Influencing longer-term behaviors (primarily central route) in combination with other persuasive communication theories, such as *4.5 The Theory of Planned Behavior* or *4.2 Norm Activation Theory*.

How to use it: to influence immediate behaviors

- Consider the use of peripheral cues, such as:
  - Role modeling desired behaviors.
  - Placing physical barriers or obstacles.
  - Simple declarative signs at the site of desired behavioral influence.
  - Placing the recycling bin (or other action trigger) in a convenient place where it can't possibly be missed.
- Remove or hide enabling cues to undesired behaviors, such as:
  - Evidence of prior undesirable behavior (e.g., litter, graffiti).
  - Informal trails to sensitive areas.

How to use it: to influence longer-term behaviors

- The following communication techniques have been shown to encourage central route processing.
  - Use multisensory media and attractive designs.
  - Design visual, verbal, or written communication to incorporate variety, novelty, and surprising elements.
  - Use questions and two-way dialogue.
  - Tell stories relevant to the lives of the audience. Demonstrate why the message should be important to them.[17]
  - Use straightforward language. Avoid jargon.
- Be responsive to questions or suggestions of message recipients.
- Call attention to cues in message recipients' personal lives that might trigger desired behaviors in the future. For example, "Whenever you see …, I'd like you to consider (what you've seen/learned here today), think, or do …"
- Consider soliciting a signed pledge or public declaration of commitment to act. Doing so can provide a memory trigger, similar to an ever-present peripheral cue that might influence decision making.[18]
- Build in regular feedback about behaviors. For example, studies have shown that thermostats that display real-time and cumulative energy usage statistics provide effective cues and motivations to homeowners to reduce their energy consumption, especially when coupled with other forms of persuasive messaging.[19] In effect, these provide ongoing cues that reinforce a persuasive message. If the monitoring efforts are then publicized to relevant others (for example, your energy usage is posted to Facebook on a daily basis), normative pressures can then further enhance the salience of the behavior.[20]
- Build personal relationships through responsiveness, active listening, demonstrations of empathy, sharing positive social experiences (see *6.1 Trust Theory*).

Key reference

Petty, R.E., and J.T. Cacioppo 1986. The elaboration likelihood model of persuasion. *Advances in Experimental Psychology* 19: 123–205.

4.5 The Theory of Planned Behavior

Uses: Persuasive communication, influencing and understanding behavior

What types of evaluations do people make when thinking through a potential course of action? Why don't people always follow through on their intentions?

The *Theory of Planned Behavior* is particularly useful in crafting arguments—for example, to get people to donate to a cause or to convince people to take a certain conservation-related action. The theory suggests that a person's intentions to perform a specific behavior are based upon three types of evaluations they make. These are labeled *attitude toward the behavior, subjective norms,* and *perceived behavioral control*. Figure 4.4 provides a schematic of the overall theory.

Attitude toward the behavior is based on an individual's evaluation of what they think will be the likely outcomes of a particular behavior. This evaluation is akin to cost–benefit analysis; if the predicted benefits outweigh the disadvantages, the person will be more likely to carry out the action.

Subjective norms refer to a person's beliefs about how other people they care about would judge them if they carried out the potential behavior. People draw their values (or judgments about right and wrong) from others who are important to them. As such, subjective norms can influence behavior regardless of expected

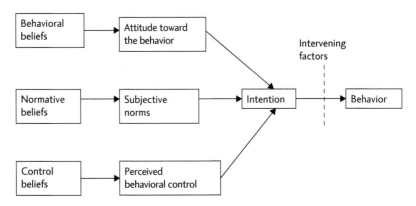

Figure 4.4 The Thoery of Planned Behavior (Ajzen, 1988; 1991). *Subjective evaluations are based on beliefs. These evaluations predict intentions. Circumstances may prevent intentions from being carried out (intervening factors).*

benefits or penalties bestowed by others. See also *4.1 Social Norm Theory*. Both descriptive and injunctive social norms can be important to this assessment.

Perceived behavioral control refers to an individual's perceptions of both the difficulty of performing the particular behavior (self-efficacy) and whether they feel they have control over decision making (autonomy). Individuals who feel empowered to carry out the behavior (the decision is theirs to make and they are confident in their abilities to do so) are more likely to carry out the action than those who lack autonomy, skills, or confidence.

Intervening factors are those that keep an individual from performing a behavior, even though they may intend to do so. For example, one might lack the skills to effectively carry out a behavior, an authority or other person might prevent them from doing so, or some physical or financial barrier may stand in the way.

The theory is only strongly predictive in cases in which the evaluations are about a specific action (for example, picking up litter or recycling), rather than general attitudes or broader beliefs (for example, about conservation more broadly). General attitudes and beliefs are rarely highly predictive of specific behaviors.[21]

Moreover, a person may have multiple evaluations about a behavior. Some, however, will be more *salient* than others. That is, not all evaluations are equally important. The more salient, or personally important, each evaluation, the more likely the intention will translate into an action. Researchers who use this theory often conduct tests to find the most salient beliefs of their subjects by asking about the importance of certain evaluations over others.

Applications

When to use it

- The *Theory of Planned Behavior* is powerful in situations where individuals are making calculations about their own behavior. In other words, they are *thinking* about it.[22] The theory is particularly useful in persuasive communications, fundraising, marketing, negotiation, and teamwork, where individuals are explicitly asked to consider an argument and make decisions about behavior. For the theory to apply in these cases, individuals must first be able and motivated to process incoming information (see *4.4 Elaboration Likelihood Model*).
- The theory can also be useful in understanding pre-existing behavioral patterns. However, not all patterns result from the conscious consideration and evaluation of likely outcomes. As such, the theory may be limited in this respect.

How to use it: persuasive communication

- Address attitudes toward the behavior:
  - Consider the benefits and disadvantages to the individual of a potential action. Can the benefits be made to outweigh the disadvantages?
- Address normative beliefs:
  - Consider relevant peer groups, potential messengers, and cultural norms in communications.
  - Perceptions that other relevant people are already engaged in the behavior, or would approve of it, enhance the likelihood of participation of the message recipient (see *4.1 Social Norm Theory*).[23] For example, try language like, "Did you know that most people we've surveyed in your community…(insert attitude or action statement here) …?" or "Join other people in your neighborhood who already…(insert action statement here)."
- Address control beliefs:
  - Enhance perceptions of self-efficacy through demonstrating the behavior, having people practice the behavior, or through other capacity-building exercises.
  - Empower people by expressing confidence in their abilities.
  - Make it feel easy to perform the desired task. For example, if you want people to recycle, provide them with a bin right outside their office door that someone else collects.
  - Emphasize personal freedom in communications about decision making. For example, "You can choose to make a difference."
  - Provide a clear course of action and provide evidence that it will actually help to achieve a desired result to empower individuals to act.
- Examine the most salient beliefs of the intended target audience to determine what concerns them most about the potential behavior. Are they most concerned with deriving direct benefits, with avoiding losses, with adhering to social norms, or about their ability (or lack thereof) to make a difference? If preliminary research is possible, this can help to determine the emphasis of communications. However, all three sets of beliefs likely matter to some extent.
- Work to find and remove intervening factors standing between an intention and a behavior. Sometimes removing a barrier to behavior can be the most effective way to encourage it. For example, some people may not vote because they have trouble getting to the polls. This is why so many campaigns provide absentee balloting or transportation on Election Day.

How to use it: understanding behavior

Consider each of the key factors of the theory to explain why or why not certain behaviors may be taking place. In particular, what is lacking? Each of the questions below can lead to the development of strategies to enhance pro-environmental or collaborative behaviors.

- Behavioral beliefs
  - What do people believe are the likely outcomes of potential behaviors?
  - Do the perceived costs outweigh the benefits of those behaviors? If so, why?
- Normative beliefs
  - What do people think others would think of them if they carried out a behavior?
    - How might prevailing norms influence this?
    - How might they be addressed?
- Control beliefs
  - Is the desired action clearly defined?
  - Do people feel like they have enough autonomy to carry out an action?
  - Do they feel like they have the necessary skills?
  - Do they feel like their action would make a difference anyway?

Key references

Ajzen, I. 1988. Attitudes, personality, and behavior. Stony Stratford, UK: Open University Press.

Ajzen, I. 1991. The theory of planned behavior. Organizational Behavior and Human Decision Processes 50: 179–91.

Armitage, C. J., and M. Conner 2001. Efficacy of the theory of planned behaviour: a meta-analytic review. British Journal of Social Psychology 40: 471–99.

Fishbein, M., and I. Ajzen 2011. Predicting and changing behavior: The reasoned action approach. New York: Psychology Press.

4.6 Self-Determination Theory

Uses: Designing collaborative processes, community engagement, workplace optimization

> **What factors can best help to strengthen people's motivation?**

According to *Self-Determination Theory*, people achieve their best when they are intrinsically motivated, and intrinsic motivation is best cultivated in situations where people are made to feel competent, autonomous, and secure in their personal relationships. The theory has powerful implications for how to design group processes, organizational or team structures, public involvement efforts, board interactions, and communications with multiple types of audiences. I first discuss the differences between intrinsic and extrinsic motivation. I then address what the theory tells us about promoting intrinsic motivation.

Motivation

Motivations for action exist on a scale from entirely intrinsic to entirely extrinsic.

Intrinsic motivation: Motivation that is self-determined, arising from personal interests or values. People are intrinsically motivated if they act for the inherent satisfaction of the activity itself.

Extrinsic motivation: Motivation driven by external pressures, accountabilities, incentives, or coercion. People are extrinsically motivated if they are acting in order to attain some separable outcome.

Intrinsic motivation generally breeds greater interest, excitement, satisfaction, and confidence. These feelings typically translate to enhanced performance, persistence, and creativity. Each of these elements then contributes to heightened self-esteem, energy, vitality, and general well-being.

Extrinsic motivators can result in a wider range of responses, including unwillingness, passive compliance, or active personal commitment. For the latter to occur, extrinsic motivators must be internalized, and ideally integrated (see Figure 4.5 below), such that they relate to a person's own sense of self, values, and interests. Extrinsic motivations can be internalized to different degrees. Figure 4.5 illustrates this spectrum. In general, the more self-determined(or internal) the cause of a behavior, the more energized a person will typically be in performing it.

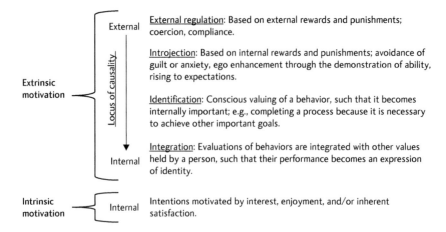

Figure 4.5 Moving from extrinsic to intrinsic motivation, based on Ryan and Deci's organismic integration theory (Ryan and Deci, 2010).

Moving toward intrinsic motivation

The work of Richard Ryan, Edward Deci, and their colleagues has identified three innate psychological needs of people that strongly influence intrinsic motivation: *competence*, *autonomy*, and *relatedness*. These elements can be considered in terms of the social environment in which behaviors may take place and the nature of the behaviors themselves.

Conditions that enhance feelings of competence:

• Providing achievable challenges, positive and constructive feedback, and freedom from demeaning evaluations.

Conditions that influence feelings of autonomy:

• Choice, acknowledgment of feelings, and opportunities for self-direction enhance feelings of autonomy.
• Extrinsic rewards that are contingent upon task performance, threats, deadlines, directives, pressured evaluations, and imposed goals undermine feelings of autonomy.

Conditions that enhance feelings of relatedness:

• Security in relationships and expressions of appreciation.
• Prompting, modeling, or overt valuing of a behavior by significant others[24] can help extrinsic behaviors to become more intrinsic.

Intrinsic motivation is typically based on individuals' interests in performing certain activities, most commonly those that have the appeal of novelty, challenge, or moral or aesthetic value. If an activity holds none of these qualities for an individual, intrinsic motivation is highly unlikely regardless of the social environment. In other words, while autonomy, competence, and relatedness can enhance the integration of extrinsic motivations, a behavior must first be of some personal interest to the individual as well for self-determined motivation to exist to any extent.

Applications

When to use it

- *Self-Determination Theory* is relevant in any situation in which you might have some control over the context in which interactions take place. For example, it can be helpful to consider if you find yourself in the position of the boss, a teacher, a negotiator, a team leader, a board liaison, or any position that can influence the terms of engagement with others.
- *Self-Determination Theory* can be particularly useful in establishing structures, conditions, or processes for organizations, boards, groups, teams, or individuals to accomplish tasks.
- It can also be useful in community engagement or public involvement. Ryan and Deci argue that all three conditions (competence, autonomy, and relatedness) are important for human well-being. As such, the design of interventions that adhere to promoting these principles in target audiences may bolster their potential for achieving goals.
- Although this is not a complete persuasive communication theory, the elements of autonomy, relatedness, and competence are highly relevant to designing and delivering effective messages.

How to use it: designing work structures, conditions, or processes for negotiation or getting work done

Enhance feelings of competence

- Enhance perceptions of the importance of tasks by clearly articulating the meaningfulness of the activities in terms of desired outcomes and broader goals.
- Empower people by expressing confidence in their abilities.
- In organizational contexts, shield team members, as much as possible, from competing tasks and provide adequate resources to get the job done. Set realistic expectations with regard to what can be accomplished given available personnel, time, and resources (*see 7.4 Project Risk*).

Enhance feelings of relatedness

- Provide spaces and opportunities for informal social interaction to build feelings of relatedness.
- Develop a shared vision for desired outcomes. Identifying shared criteria for evaluating the quality of outcomes can be particularly useful (see *6.2 Principled Negotiation*). This can take some time, but it can go a long way toward enabling people to see themselves as true collaborators.
- Develop mutually agreed upon ground rules and/or procedures for decision making, information sharing, and collaborative interactions (see also *6.1 Trust Theory*).
- Provide constructive feedback in a non-threatening way.

Enhance feelings of autonomy

- Encourage creativity and innovation in ways to get the job done.
- Share decision-making responsibility when possible and desired by team members or collaborators. This is most effective, and least risky, if desired outcomes and broader goals are clearly articulated and a shared vision is mutually agreed upon (see also *7.2 Team Effectiveness Theory* and *7.4 Project Risk*).

How to use it: community engagement

Enhance feelings of competence

- Draw on community talents for people to play meaningful roles in project planning, design, and implementation.
- Offer capacity-building opportunities that address project goals and community interests.

Enhance feelings of relatedness

- Provide spaces and opportunities for informal social interaction between external communicators and community members beyond formal meetings.
- Be transparent about goals and allow space for the exposure and discussion of underlying values, such that all parties can play a meaningful role in the design of projects that can address common interests.
- Establish clear ground rules for engagement that protect against personal attacks (see *6.1 Trust Theory*).

Enhance feelings of autonomy

- Consider means for empowering community members in decision making.
- Pay attention to and respect existing cultural patterns. Do not act without prior informed consent of, or better, partnership with, the community.

How to use it: understanding and promoting behavior, improving relationships and interactions

Consider the degree to which motivations might be externally or internally motivated. Can individuals be moved from extrinsic toward more intrinsically motivated (self-determined) behaviors?

- Do individuals feel sufficient autonomy in directing their own behaviors or do they feel micro-managed, trapped, or coerced?
- Do individuals see meaningful value in their work beyond procedural compliance or normative pressure to perform?
- Do individuals feel respected and secure in their relationships?
- Does a group have a shared sense of mission or direction?
- Do individuals feel sufficiently competent and appreciated?

Give away credit and let others shine.

- When I was a graduate student, my major professor, Bill Burch, was a master at encouraging intrinsic motivation. Whenever I would come to him with a problem, he would somehow convince me that I already had the solution. He'd say something like, "Oh, you've got. I see. You've already got this piece and that piece, and once you put them together, it makes perfect sense! Well done!" I'd always walk out feeling like *I* had solved the problem. Whether this was true or not, I *felt* that it was. I've since been able to practice this skill with my own graduate students. I find that when I provide a long-winded rationale accompanied by a proposed solution to any of their challenges,I typically see sunken shoulders and resignation in my students. When I've actually managed to guide a student to their own solution, and convince them that they did it more or less themselves, I typically see a surge of confidence and have developed better relationships as a result. Giving away credit and empowering others can provide a strong dose of autonomy, competence, and relatedness.

Key references

Ryan, R.M., and E.L. Deci 2000a. Self-determination theory and the facilitation of intrinsic motivation, social development and well-being. *American Psychologist* 55(1): 68–78.

Ryan, R.M., and E.L. Deci 2000b. Intrinsic and extrinsic motivations: classic definitions and new directions. *Contemporary Educational Psychology* 5: 54–67.

4.7 The Extended Parallel Process Model of Fear Appeals

Use: Persuasive communication

When might it be effective to use scare tactics?

Sometimes, we may try to scare someone into agreeing with us, complying with a regulation, or taking some sort of action. For example, we might reference the horrible dangers associated with a particular activity (like going off trail or burning leaves on a windy day) in an attempt to get people to refrain from doing it, or we might use fear to motivate action on climate change. The *Extended Parallel Process Model* (EPPM) explains when persuasive communications using fear (known as "fear appeals") are likely to be effective and when they are not.

The EPPM suggests that fear appeals can be effective at influencing behavior if they produce in the message recipient **both** the feeling of a salient threat and a belief that the threat can be adequately averted. If no fear is inspired, then no desired response is likely. If fear is inspired without an accompanying sense of efficacy, or belief in one's ability to avert the threat, undesirable behavioral responses, known as "fear control responses," including denial or avoidance, are likely. *Only if fear is accompanied with perceived efficacy are desired responses likely to take place* (Figure 4.6).

Threat is defined as a danger in the environment. *Perceived threat* is comprised of two components: severity and susceptibility. Severity involves beliefs about the significance and magnitude of the threat (i.e., how bad is it?). Susceptibility includes beliefs about the likelihood of experiencing the threat. If message recipients feel highly susceptible to severe threats, fear appeal messages are more likely to incite action.

Perceived efficacy is comprised of perceptions of self-efficacy and response efficacy. Perceived *self-efficacy* refers to beliefs in one's ability to carry out the recommended

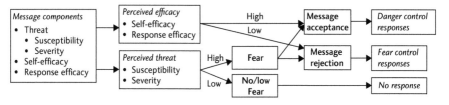

Figure 4.6 The Extended Parallel Process Model of Fear Appeals.

response to avert the threat. In other words, do I feel capable of carrying out the recommended response? Perceived ***response efficacy*** refers to beliefs about whether the recommended response will actually deter the threat. In other words, do I feel the response will actually be effective?

If perceived efficacy is high (i.e., people feel capable of averting the threat), they will reduce their fear by engaging in ***danger control responses***. These responses involve reducing the threat through the message's recommended action(s). If perceived efficacy is low, they are likely to engage in ***fear control responses***. These coping responses include avoidance, denial, and message rejection or subversion.

Applications

When to use it

- In making direct personal appeals to individuals to take (or avoid) action; in designing marketing materials or other forms of persuasive messaging; in developing instructive or persuasive signs for visitors to a sensitive site; in negotiations.
- Under the following conditions, fear appeals should be avoided:
  - If an actual threat cannot be reduced by the actions of an individual.[25]
  - If low efficacy perceptions are unlikely to be influenced through the message.

How to use it

Successful fear appeals:

- Unmistakably define a threat, making clear that the message recipient is susceptible to a meaningful negative outcome from that threat. For example, "Passing this point could be deadly. Multiple people have lost their lives by stepping past this railing."
- Clearly explain a recommended action to avert the threat (*danger control response*).
- Empower message recipients to feel that they can carry out the recommended action (promote *self-efficacy*).
- Demonstrate that the recommended action can reduce or deter the threat (promote perceived *response efficacy*).

Unsuccessful fear appeals:

- Fail to make the severity of the threat or its relevance to the message recipient clear.

- Fail to empower message recipients to feel capable of averting the threat. Messages that include threat without a powerful efficacy component may scare audiences to fall deeper into fear control responses. This is one reason why climate adaptation strategies, which involve local responses to the effects of climate change, can often feel more empowering than climate mitigation strategies, which involve trying to lessen climate change through global atmospheric carbon reduction. Local strategies often feel more doable, and the effects of the work are more visible. For fear-based messaging about climate change mitigation to be effective, they may need to either be linked to another issue or focus on collective efficacy. In the first case, people might drive less to mitigate local air pollution which threatens their health. In the latter case, an argument should focus on how the message recipient's actions can work together with the actions of others to make a real difference. See *5.6 Frame Theory* for a more detailed discussion on this idea.

Fear appeals may work differently for different people and different cultures:

- Strong individualists or people from individualist cultures tend to perceive greater threat when exposed to messages about severity and susceptibility of a threat to themselves. Meanwhile, collectivistic people perceive greater threat when exposed to messages about severity and susceptibility of a threat to a larger group to which they belong.[26]
- People with prior knowledge or direct experience with the threat may be more strongly influenced by powerful efficacy messages than those who are made aware of the threat for the first time.[27]
- High sensation-seekers may be less affected by fear appeals than low sensation-seekers.[28] High sensation-seekers are people who commonly take risks in search of varied, novel, complex, and intense experiences.

Key reference

Maloney, E.K., Lapinski, M.K., and Witte, K. 2011. Fear appeals and persuasion: a review and update of the extended parallel process model. *Social and Personality Compass* 5(4): 206–19.

4.8 Motivation Crowding Theory

Uses: Persuasive communication, enrolling people in projects, sustaining participation

> **When and why might providing incentives backfire?**

Traditional economic theory suggests that increasing incentives, particularly monetary incentives, should enhance performance. *Motivation Crowding Theory* suggests that under certain circumstances the opposite may be true. That is, providing or increasing incentives can actually decrease motivation and subsequent performance. This is due to what is known as a *crowding out* effect, in which intrinsic motivations, or those that arise from personal interests or values, are replaced (or "crowded out") by extrinsic motivations, which are those driven by external pressures, incentives, or sanctions.

Intrinsic motivations are typically intertwined with the values of those who hold them. People who are intrinsically motivated act based on what they feel is right or just, or for the inherent satisfaction of the activity itself. Intrinsic motivation is typically associated with greater interest, excitement, satisfaction, and confidence. These feelings typically translate to greater commitment, enhanced performance, persistence, and creativity.

Extrinsic motivations may or may not align with the values of those influenced by them. Extrinsic motivators, such as incentive payments or penalties (carrots or sticks), can have more variable effects on recipients, ranging from passionate commitment through passive compliance to active resistance. The responses may rely on the size of the incentives, social norms, and whether the extrinsic incentive aligns with intrinsic motivations.

Figure 4.7 demonstrates the effects of a shift from intrinsic to extrinsic motivation on overall motivation and resulting effort. The line to the right represents a case in which intrinsic motivation exists, while the line to the left indicates its absence. In both cases, theoretically, as reward increases, effort increases as well. However, when intrinsic motivation is crowded out by external rewards, the line shifts to the left, such that greater rewards are necessary to generate a similar amount of effort. For example, in the absence of intrinsic motivation, the same external reward might only result in the amount of effort indicated by point B instead of point A. To achieve the same amount of effort, the external reward would need to increase significantly (to point C). Note that effort goes to zero in the absence

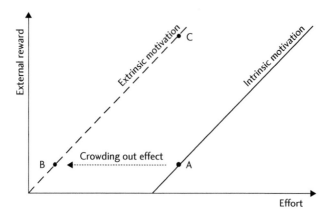

Figure 4.7 The motivation crowding effect. *Adapted from Frey and Jegen (2001).*

of intrinsic motivation with no external reward. However, effort is not zero when intrinsic motivation is present in the absence of an external reward.

The motivation crowding effect raises three important questions to consider when attempting to motivate people to participate in environmental problem solving, conservation or other sustainability-related efforts:

1. Under what conditions might monetary (or other external) incentives support or enhance intrinsic motivation? In other words, how can we stay on the intrinsic motivation line (the one to the right) in Figure 4.7?
2. Under what conditions might these same incentives *crowd out* intrinsic motivation?
3. What happens if external incentives cannot be maintained in the long run?

I provide some answers to each question below.

External incentives can work *with* intrinsic motivation in cases where:

- The incentive works primarily as the removal of a barrier to doing something the recipient would like to do anyway, rather than as the primary motivation for undertaking the task. For example, a rural farmer would like to protect bird species on his property but can't afford to monitor nests and purchase nest markers. An appropriate external incentive would be to provide the capacity, labor, and/or start-up costs to perform these tasks. However, providing additional incentive payments would increase the likelihood of crowding out intrinsic motivation for bird protection. In another example, a private landowner in the United States might wish to protect a large forest on their property, but can't afford to continue paying property taxes. They feel pressure to sell the land, even though they would prefer to maintain their forest. A conservation easement, which provides tax relief in exchange for preservation, removes a barrier to satisfying the landowner's pre-existing intrinsic motivation toward nature protection. Similarly, subsidies or tax breaks for installing solar panels on private homes or businesses might do the same, without displacing intrinsic motivations.

- Within an organization, when payment is already part of the equation, increasing incentives can increase effort. However, crowding out is sometimes observed in these cases as well. Research has found that increasing payments is less likely to crowd out intrinsic motivation when payments are given unexpectedly or are not designated as contingent upon the performance of a specific task. For example, an unexpected reward (or bonus) payment for a job well done is less likely to crowd out intrinsic motivation than the promise of a salary increase contingent on performing a specific task or solving a particular problem. While each might increase effort in the short run, future expectations in the contingent scenario may be more oriented toward extrinsic motivation (the promise of increased payments) rather than intrinsic motivation (the satisfaction of a job well done, and potentially the social recognition that comes with it).

- See *7.1 Herzberg's Motivation–Hygiene Theory* to further explore motivation crowding within an organizational context.

External incentives crowd out intrinsic motivation in these situations:

- When extrinsic motivations don't align with intrinsic motivations or with social norms, they can crowd out intrinsic motivation if they are large enough. For example, if I want to convince small farmers in Indonesia to maintain their rice fields to contribute to water protection, and I pay them to do so, I might crowd out the powerful religious, communal, and aesthetic beliefs that serve as intrinsic motivations. If, as noted above, the payment merely removes a barrier to continued rice cultivation, these motivations may not be crowded out. If, however, the payments (and associated communications monetizing the act) are great enough, water conservation may become contingent upon the payment, effectively crowding out intrinsic motivations.

- When external rewards (or penalties) are seen as so large that recipients feel they have no choice but to accept them, they can be seen as controlling (limiting the autonomy of the recipients). This is sometimes the case in developing countries where local people are encouraged to enter the formal economy through ecotourism or other forms of exchange aimed at providing incentives for nature protection. As some people join, they quickly gain tremendous wealth relative to those who don't. That inequality compels others to join the formal economy. Whatever intrinsic motivations there might have been for nature protection have now been replaced by market forces or other incentives. Without strong linkages to nature protection, these programs are now subject to the whims of the free market and have to compete with other incentives that might conflict with conservation goals or promoting sustainable development. For example, if I can make twice as much money by selling my land to a developer than I could participating in an ecotourism or agroforestry program, I'm likely to sell unless I have intrinsic reasons for continuing in the conservation venture.

• In any case in which behaviors are effectively monetized, people may feel absolved of moral obligations. For example, if people in a community have jointly maintained a community forest based on collective agreement about its social or other intrinsic value, introducing monetary compensation for doing so could potentially crowd out intrinsic motivations as people begin to expect payment for their services.

What happens if external incentives cannot be maintained in the long run?

• Crowding out shifts the motivational focus toward external rewards (e.g., monetary payments) or penalties (e.g., avoiding getting caught). When the external reward ceases, whatever intrinsic motivation may have been present has now been replaced and may be quite difficult to recover. If an external contingent reward is guaranteed in perpetuity, efforts might continue. However, other external rewards are likely to have an easier time competing with extrinsically motivated activities.

  – For example, one conservation program in Africa provided a health clinic in exchange for local promises to limit illegal resource extraction. It worked for a few years, but then illegal activities increased again. When the project team met with villagers, they demanded a school.[29]

  – To provide another example, consider whether you would expect the rural farmer in the United States introduced above to continue to protect birds on his property when additional incentive payments run out. If intrinsic motivation has been replaced with the expectation for compensation, the likely answer is *no*.

Applications

When to use it

Motivation Crowding Theory is highly relevant when trying to enroll people in a conservation program or attempting to influence the behaviors of individuals or groups. Providing incentives can have multiple potential effects, depending on the pre-existing dispositions of target audiences and the conditions in which they live:

- In cases where any degree of intrinsic motivation for conservation behavior exists, *Motivation Crowding Theory* suggests first focusing on this form of motivation prior to considering the implementation of an extrinsic reward or penalty system.
- Intrinsic and extrinsic motivations can work together, provided that the external reward or sanction is not so large that it replaces all intrinsic motivation. In ideal cases, the external incentive is provided to remove a barrier to action, rather than be the primary motivation of that action.

Motivation Crowding Theory is irrelevant when intrinsic motivation doesn't exist—for example, in simple task environments, such as assembly line work, where pay-for-performance has been shown to enhance efforts. In the absence of pre-existing intrinsic motivations, many other theories in this book (in particular, persuasive communication theories—see Table 3.1) can be useful for building interest in conservation.

How to use it

Before making a decision to use rewards or sanctions to encourage or discourage any particular activity, first consider whether intrinsic motivations already exist or might be activated. In other words, are people already oriented toward the activity or the program?

- If so, focus most effort on activating intrinsic motivations for action. Theories such as *4.6 Self-Determination Theory*, *4.3 Cognitive Dissonance*, and *4.2 Norm Activation Theory* can be particularly helpful. In cases where distrust or identity threats may be perceived, also consult *5.1 Identity Theory*, *5.2 Self-Affirmation Theory*, *5.5 Moral Foundations Theory*, and *6.1 Trust Theory*. Each provides direct links to intrinsic motivation.
- Does the activity encourage the continuation of a cherished lifestyle? Does it avert threats to health, identity, beauty, or social order? Does it promise enjoyment or inherent satisfaction? Does it feel good? Again, if so, intrinsic motivation can be activated.
- If your goal *only* involves trying to influence a one-time behavior or commitment, such as the transfer of a property or a sale, this theory may not apply. However, in any case involving long-term engagement or relationships, it should always be considered.

In some cases, small monetary payments or monitoring systems can remove barriers, such that intrinsic motivations can be fulfilled.

- Monetary payments make sense in cases where people cannot afford a preliminary investment to shift their activities toward more environmentally friendly practices.
- Ideally, external rewards remove barriers rather than provide incentives. In cases where intrinsic motivations can be activated, preliminary investments and capacity-building efforts are typically preferable to periodic payments, which may be subject to uncertain future funding.
- Monitoring systems, or those that involve penalties for non-compliance, can help to level the playing field and enable people to feel safer that they won't be outcompeted by others who neglect to do their part. These are particularly helpful in cases that are highly susceptible to such "free riders" (see *8.1 Commons Theory*).

In cases where intrinsic motivations do not exist, external incentives, monitoring, and sanctions may be more worthwhile investments.

Key references

Deci, E.L., R. Koestner, and R.M. Ryan 1999. A meta-analytic review of experiments examining the effects of extrinsic rewards on intrinsic motivation. *Psychological Bulletin* 125(3): 627–68.

Frey, B.S., and R. Jegen 2001. Motivation crowding theory. *Journal of Economic Surveys* 15(5): 589–611.

4.9 Maslow's Hierarchy of Needs

Uses: Any form of communication, enrolling people in projects, managing work teams, monitoring organizational climate

How can we help people reach their maximum potential?

Maslow's Hierarchy of Needs suggests that people can rarely (if ever) achieve their full potential ("self-actualization") without first having their basic physiological and psychological needs met. Figure 4.8 depicts a sequential hierarchy in which lower needs must be met before higher levels of needs become achievable. For example, if I don't feel safe, it may be difficult for me to focus on building my self-esteem. Similarly, if I feel ostracized (lack of belonging) or have particularly low self-esteem, it will be difficult for me to reach my full potential (self-actualization). While some researchers have found flaws in the linear sequential proposal of the hierarchy, the basic premise driving the hierarchy has stood the test of time—that without meeting lower needs first, it is difficult to achieve higher levels of the hierarchy.

Self-actualization refers to the state in which a person maximizes their motivation (and achievement) in service of both the self and others. While self-actualization will look different for different people, the hierarchy asserts that maximizing motivation for service to environmental (or other) causes likely requires that lower-level needs first be met.

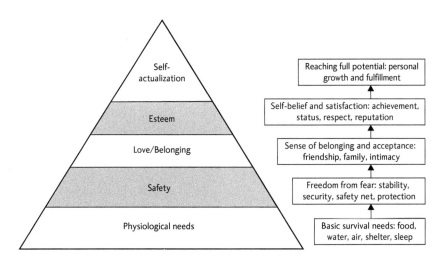

Figure 4.8 Maslow's Hierarchy of Needs.

Applications

When to use it

In an organizational sense, the theory illuminates the importance of building an organization or team environment in which all needs are met to maximize the potential of each employee or team member.

In a conservation project or environmental communications context, the theory is useful both for understanding what might be expected of a target audience and for designing projects that fit the context of potential participants. For example, if basic needs are not met, any intervention that doesn't address them is unlikely to be successful. Conversely, efforts that consider each level of the hierarchy prior to calling for action are more likely to be successful.

How to use it

Begin designing any effort with the lowest level of the hierarchy that needs attention. I provide suggestions in Table 4.1 for two different contexts: (1) teams and organizations; (2) conservation projects with external audiences/participants.

Table 4.1 *Applying* Maslow's Hierarchy of Needs *to organizations and conservation projects.*

Need	Teams/organizations	Conservation projects
Physiological needs	The health and well-being of team members should be considered. Are people appropriately compensated for their time? Is their time respected? Are there accommodations for personal family or health issues? Are working conditions reasonable?	Projects involving marginalized or poverty-stricken populations must address livelihoods in project design. People cannot be expected to comply with conservation regulations or participate in a project if it threatens their livelihood. Projects that aim to change behaviors of the poor typically require much longer time periods to deliver the capacity-building necessary to provide reasonable alternative livelihoods to resource extraction.[30] Any project or event should address physical conditions, in terms of the need for food, drink, shelter, shade, rest, childcare, transportation, compensation, and gear.

(Continued)

Need	Teams/organizations	Conservation projects
Safety	Can the work environment minimize risk associated with physical and psychological harm? Do employees or team members feel secure in their jobs? Are they free from demeaning evaluations or any form of unfair treatment? Is there recourse for addressing perceptions of unfair treatment? Transparency in procedures and a priori team agreement on processes can enhance feelings of security. See also the discussion of systems-based trust in *6.1 Trust Theory*.	Personal risk is often involved in conservation projects— especially projects that go beyond fundraising or simple volunteer work. Consider what is at stake, materially, socially, and psychologically for project participants. What are the sources of risk? These might emanate from distrust of project staff (the fear of getting taken advantage of), material risks associated with behavior change (such as changing livelihood means), or social risks associated with potential ridicule or ostracization by peers, among other sources. What are people risking to participate? Take steps to avoid or directly minimize these risks.
Belonging	Team-building exercises and the encouragement of social interaction outside the work environment can help to build a sense of belonging, as can the development and public broadcasting of organizational principles that encourage mutual respect as well as commitment and pride to the team/organizational mission. Agreement on, and shared commitment to, clearly defined goals can also enhance a sense of belonging. See also *7.2 Team Effectiveness Theory*.	In addition to considering social risks, as noted above, particularly in projects that may not coincide with dominant social norms, consider strategies for building a sense of camaraderie or belonging between participants and with program staff. Strategies may include events that clearly demonstrate commonalities between all parties, field trips, and other social interactions. See also *6.1 Trust Theory*.
Esteem	Provide the necessary resources, training, and support for accomplishing tasks. Provide positive feedback to individuals and teams that acknowledges their role in achieving meaningful impacts. Regularly reinforce the importance of the mission and progress toward it. Provide opportunities for work or service that makes employees feel good.	Provide positive feedback to participants, particularly feedback that demonstrates the positive impacts of the project and people's role in creating that impact. Celebrate successes and share credit where culturally appropriate.

(Continued)

Table 4.1 (Continued)

Need	Teams/organizations	Conservation projects
Self-actualization	As other levels of the hierarchy are met, self-actualization can be promoted through increasing the autonomy of individuals (or teams) to pursue the mission in their own ways.	As other levels of the hierarchy are met, self-actualization can be promoted through supporting community-formulated projects that align with conservation goals—providing capacity-building, material support, networking, and positive feedback that strengthen these efforts.

Key references

Maslow, A. 1943. A theory of human motivation. *Psychological Review* 50(4): 370–96.
Maslow, A. 1954. *Motivation and personality.* New York: Harper.

5

Morals, intuitions, culture, and identity-based theories

Introduction: Beyond bounded rationality

The theories within this chapter move beyond bounded rationality to incorporate a wider array of situations common to our daily lives. Most of the decisions we make on a daily basis don't involve deep cognitive thought in which we carefully weigh options, consider multiple viewpoints, and maybe even question our own assumptions. We rather rely on our intuitions, or *gut feelings*, to guide us. Intuitive decision making generally happens in two common circumstances: (1) any time we aren't specifically provoked to think deeply, and (2) when we feel threatened. Our intuitions serve us well in many circumstances. After all, they are built on the accumulation of our prior experiences and deeply engrained preferences for particular activities or outcomes. However, an over-reliance on intuitionist decision making can preclude learning, innovation, and problem solving, as we fail to consider possible alternatives. Moreover, our intuitions are often colored by our own implicit biases, making it hard to open our minds to people we disagree with or feel threatened by.

This chapter examines intuitive decision making as well as what happens when our intuitive predispositions are challenged. When we feel threatened, it typically proves difficult to calmly evaluate information and make rational decisions. A great deal of environmental work lies clearly within this realm. Debates about environmental regulation, climate change, wilderness preservation, resource extraction, and the appropriate balance between economic and environmental concerns, among many others, often trigger deep-seated emotions and defensive reactions that create seemingly intractable conflicts, precluding productive deliberation and problem solving. The theories within this chapter help to explain why and how this happens and provide some ideas for what to do about it.

Social Science Theory for Environmental Sustainability: A Practical Guide. Marc J. Stern, Oxford University Press (2018). © Marc J. Stern 2018. DOI 10.1093/oso/9780198793182.001.0001

5.1 Identity Theory

Uses: Collaboration, persuasive communication, public involvement, team processes, conflict resolution

> **Why do people seem to take things so personally, and what can we do about it?**

Identity Theory helps us understand how our perceptions of ourselves interact with the perceptions and behaviors of those around us to produce different outcomes. Put simply, people generally don't like to be misunderstood or mislabeled. Conversely, we typically feel good when we believe we are well understood and that others see us the way we want to be seen.

Identity theorists distinguish between three major types of identities, or self-definitions:

Person identity: How people define themselves as unique individuals across contexts. "I am this type of person." Person identities are relatively stable and primarily reflect our own personal or moral norms (see *4.2 Norm Activation Theory*).

Role identity: How people define themselves when occupying a particular role in a social situation or structure (e.g., a teacher, a parent, a boss). Role identities reflect the interactions between personal norms and shared expectations attached to social positions in society. In short, we may act (and judge ourselves) differently when we occupy different roles within a group.

Social identity: We sometimes use our membership in a group or category of people (e.g., Republicans, Liberals, Catholics) to define ourselves. In these cases, we identify the prototypical attributes of the category and see ourselves as having these attributes. Social identification with a particular group leads us to act in accordance with the relevant group's goals, values, beliefs, and behaviors (see also the discussion of *reference groups* within *4.1 Social Norm Theory*).

The famous sociologist Erving Goffman argued that we spend much of our waking time managing how people perceive us. Any social encounter involves a balance between who we want to be and whether the situation enables or disables the realization of that identity. In other words, to Goffman, social actions are motivated by people's desire to control the impression they create in the eyes of others. Identity theorists similarly stress the importance of ***identity verification***, which describes the degree to which individuals perceive that others see them in the same way they see themselves.

When an identity is activated in a situation, people compare their perception of their own identity (known as the ***identity standard***) to the feedback they receive from others. When these perceived meanings correspond, the resulting *identity verification* arouses positive emotions. Meanwhile, non-correspondence, or "role confusion" as Goffman calls it, results in negative emotions, such as embarrassment, anger, or shame. These negative emotions can drive various behaviors. When the non-correspondence is small, individuals typically adjust their behaviors in an attempt to change the perception of others. When the non-correspondence is large, people may engage defensive behaviors, such as withholding information, refusing to collaborate, withdrawing from the situation, or diminishing or devaluing others or the entire undertaking.

Key definitions

Identity verification: the degree to which people are able to confirm what they believe about themselves through observing the actions of others (how much we think others perceive us in the way we perceive ourselves).

Identity non-verification: the state in which people's perceptions of themselves appear to conflict with how other people perceive them.

Identity prominence: how important a specific identity (or self-concept) is to someone.

Identity commitment: how devoted someone is to maintaining a specific identity—typically based on the strength of relationships with other people who are connected to that identity.

The more prominent the identity is for a person, the more powerful their reaction is likely to be. ***Identity prominence*** represents an internal ranking of how important a particular identity is to a person. Identity prominence is driven by ***identity commitment*** and prior instances of identity verification. In general, the more a particular identity has experienced identity verification, the more prominent the identity. *Identity commitment* reflects the degree to which a specific identity is tied to particular social networks, both in terms of the number of such connections and the amount of discomfort a person would feel if they were to no longer engage with others associated with that identity.

The expectation that a situation might include identity non-verification can have both positive and negative consequences.[1] In some cases, the expectation of being misunderstood or mislabeled can cause us to adjust our expectations and think through how we might respond adaptively to identity threats we could face in an upcoming interaction. In other cases, we can put up defensive mechanisms that shut down positive interactions. These negative responses can include denial, diminishing or de-valuing the source of the threat, hiding information in anticipation of negative feedback, dishonesty, discounting the importance of the undertaking, justifying our own inflexibility through comparison to people who are "even worse," or withdrawal from the situation entirely.

Applications

When to use it

Our self-concepts (i.e., the ways in which we view ourselves) are always in play in any social interaction. Therefore, *Identity Theory* is nearly always relevant, but in different ways in different situations.

- In most situations, enhancing opportunities for identity verification and minimizing likelihood of non-verification can catalyze more productive exchanges. This doesn't mean avoiding disagreement, but rather separating disagreement on issues from identity-threatening rhetoric.
- In long-term or highly politicized conflicts, identity threats are common, as different groups label each other in ways that often conflict with self-definitions. In these cases, threat alleviation is paramount to breaking long-standing patterns of unproductive communication. Moreover, understanding the moral foundations of different groups can enhance cross-constituency communications (see *5.5 Moral Foundations Theory*). In some cases, *Identity Theory* can be used to activate people against a common enemy. However, this tends to exacerbate conflict rather than diminish it.
- In persuasive communications on less-polarizing issues, appealing to personal identities (and associated moral norms) and social identities (and associated social norms) can enhance messaging (see *4.1 Social Norm Theory* and *4.2 Norm Activation Theory*).

How to use it: Across all contexts

- The strongest antidote to identity threats, real or perceived, is the development of trusting interpersonal relationships. While these relationships can develop in innumerable ways, *6.1 Trust Theory* provides insights on how to reach out to those with whom we have less natural affinity.

- References to both personal and social norms can be powerful, particularly when relevant reference groups can be identified (see *4.1 Social Norm Theory* and *4.2 Norm Activation Theory*).

- Pay attention to the identities others are trying to project. First and foremost, this means listening and observing attentively. Allow space for these identities and try to avoid non-verification. This may be difficult in adversarial circumstances. When people take on role identities that are harmful to collaboration, such as the role of an enemy or harsh critic, validation of their intended identity doesn't necessarily mean condoning their behavior. Rather, it means recognizing and allowing their expression. Oftentimes, this can lead to de-escalation of inflammatory rhetoric. Specific strategies include repeating someone's arguments, asking if you have heard their concerns correctly, and asking for more detail about the bases of their interests before responding.

- Some studies have found that simple language shifts can make an issue more personal and activate identity concerns. For example, talking about the importance of being a "voter" as opposed to the importance of voting was shown to increase voter turnout by eleven percentage points in one study.[2] Invoking the consideration of the self through the use of positive identifying nouns or labels can be more powerfully persuasive than merely asking people to undertake a specific activity.

How to use it: In direct social interactions, deliberations, team settings, negotiations, or collaborative groups

- Reduce the potential for identity threat by delineating clear rules of engagement that create a safe space for disagreement and building rational, affinitive, and procedural trust between the parties. See *6.1 Trust Theory* for additional advice on how to do this. A few key suggestions include:
  - Stressing the importance of reasoned debate and compromise with clearly defined and agreed upon goals can help to lessen the salience of identity threats—if participants are able to agree upon clear rules of engagement. In particular, rules regarding appropriate ways to express disagreement (e.g., focusing on the content of the argument rather than the person or their group; providing evidence both in favor and against) can be particularly helpful.
  - Promising confidentiality, when appropriate, beyond the meeting space can also lessen concerns of social identity threat.

- Give people the opportunity to explain the origins of their point of view. Listen for identity-relevant language (e.g., "I am…," "I have…," "I consider myself…") or other clues about how people view themselves. Validate and/or demonstrate understanding of people's professed values or identities whenever possible and appropriate. Repeating back key elements and checking to see if you heard right can ensure a clearer understanding. When the threat of being misunderstood is removed, deeper communication is possible (see also *5.2 Self-Affirmation Theory*).
- Try to focus on the content of the argument, rather than the person's credibility or identity in your interactions. This means avoiding negative labeling. Attacking a person's identity may galvanize one side of the argument, but it likely only further antagonizes those who identify with the person being attacked. While such attacks might help to win a short-term argument, the longer-term divisions created may preclude opportunities for working together in the future.
- Breaking larger groups into smaller ones can often enable some of these strategies to work better, as identity threat can be diminished through building more personal understandings, which may not be feasible in larger groups.

How to use it: In long-term or highly politicized conflicts

- Listen (or read) carefully and ask questions to try to reveal the values underlying the messages of others. If we can understand the moral foundations of antagonistic arguments that have rallied others against our cause, we can often begin to empathize and craft more appropriate messages that may align with a wider array of identities (see *5.5 Moral Foundations Theory*).
- Consider using some form of self-affirmation to buffer participants in a dialogue against identity threats (see *5.2 Self-Affirmation Theory*).
- Consider conducting some baseline research to understand the most likely sources of identity threats (see *6.3 The Co-orientation Model*).
- In some cases, purposefully highlighting identity threats can activate groups against a common adversary. For example, the 2017 March for Science and Women's March in protest of the Trump administration gained momentum through organizers highlighting identity threats to scientists and to women. Threats can be made particularly salient if framed in terms of moral foundations (see *5.5 Moral Foundations Theory*), and they can motivate action if coupled with communications about clear actions that can be taken to avoid potential losses (see *4.7 The Extended Parallel Process Model of Fear Appeals* and *5.6 Frame Theory*). These actions of course carry high potential to further polarize issues and inhibit collaboration across partisan lines.

How to use it: In persuasive communications on less-polarizing issues or situations with low conflict

- We generally aim for internal consistency in our self-concept. As such, we aim to act consistently with our pre-existing attitudes, statements, actions, values, and commitments.
  - Soliciting active commitments (an explicit verbal or written commitment, such as a signed pledge) enhances the likelihood of follow-through, particularly if the pledge is made publicly.
  - Efforts to promote a particular change in behavior are likely to be more successful if people aren't made to feel shame about their prior experiences. Acknowledging that a previous behavior was understandable given prior circumstances or knowledge can circumvent perceived direct threats to one's identity (see also *4.3 Cognitive Dissonance*).
- Storytelling/narrative framing.
  - Consider using stories to demonstrate key elements of an argument. One of the reasons people are predisposed to stories, as opposed to facts and figures, is that stories allow for the clear articulation of identity in their characters. Crafting stories that relate to the moral foundations or social or personal norms of an audience allows audiences to see themselves within the narrative (see *4.1 Social Norm Theory* and *5.5 Moral Foundations Theory*). This creates opportunities for identity verification.
  - See *2.2 Common cognitive biases* for more guidance on constructing effective stories.
- A cognitive dissonance approach aligns somewhat with *Identity Theory* as well. Consider beginning an interaction by establishing some level of agreement on important principles. Subsequently, demonstrate how the other person's attitudes or actions seem to be opposed to those principles. Although the cognitive dissonance generated is likely to produce negative emotions, it also sets up an explicit opportunity for someone to directly address identity non-verification (see *4.3 Cognitive Dissonance*).
  - Perhaps the most important element of protecting against harmful effects of identity threat in this scenario involves providing the opportunity to save face. Creating cognitive dissonance should thus be accompanied with recognition of identity-affirming alternative courses of action. For example, instead of a threatening, "what are you going to do about it?" or "how can you live with that?," one could provide easy ways out of the dissonance—for instance, "We've thought about this too and have decided that this makes sense to us (for resolving the dissonance). What do you think?" or

"Some people have resolved this issue by doing x." If accompanied with normative pressure from others, trust development, and/or clear ground rules for debate (see *6.1 Trust Theory*), this could trigger an honest reconsideration of the dissonant information.

Key references

Goffman, E. 1956. Embarrassment and social organization. *American Journal of Sociology* 62(3):264–71.

Sedikides, C. 2012. Chapter 16. Self-protection. In Leary, M.R., and J.P. Tangney (eds), *Handbook of self and identity*, pp. 327–53. New York: The Guilford Press.

Stets, J.E. and R.T. Serpe 2013. Chapter 2. Identity theory. In DeLamater, J., and A. Ward (eds), *Handbook of social psychology*, pp. 31–60. Netherlands: Springer.

5.2 Self-Affirmation Theory

Uses: Collaboration, public involvement, team processes, conflict resolution

> How can we help people feel less threatened when trying to resolve heated issues?

Bringing together people who have a history of conflict, or even just different opinions, can be downright uncomfortable. People tend to get defensive when their beliefs are challenged, especially when those beliefs are tied to their personal or social identities. They either close themselves off to new information or filter it in a way to confirm their pre-conceived notions (see *5.1 Identity Theory*). This ***identity-protective reasoning*** can lead to seemingly intractable conflicts that preclude the possibility for productive conversations, learning, deliberation, or collaboration.

Self-Affirmation Theory is built on the premise that people get defensive first and foremost in an effort to protect their sense of self-worth. While traditional theories of bounded rationality suggest that better arguments (factual, normative, or otherwise) should help to change minds, *Self-Affirmation Theory* suggests that this is unlikely in situations where people feel their personal or social identity is threatened. In these cases, their focus is rarely on the merits of an argument, but rather on dissonance in how they perceive themselves and how new information calls those self-definitions into question.

Self-Affirmation Theory suggests that if people can be reminded that their self-worth derives from sources other than their attitudes about the issue at hand, feelings of identity threat can be diminished. Research supports that self-affirmed people are less prone to biased processing (see Chapter 2) of new information or defensiveness (see Figure 5.1).

In their most basic sense, ***self-affirmations*** are any acts that demonstrate to oneself one's adequacy. Self-affirmations can take many forms, ranging from participating in simple activities that reinforce a sense of self-worth, such as volunteering at a local animal shelter or posting a self-validating comment on Facebook, to writing about core personal values. In some experiments, participants have been asked to identify and write about a particular value (unrelated to the debate at hand) that they feel is important to them prior to receiving counter-attitudinal information (information that contrasts directly with their pre-existing attitudes). In these cases, self-affirmation is self-generated and thus individually tailored to

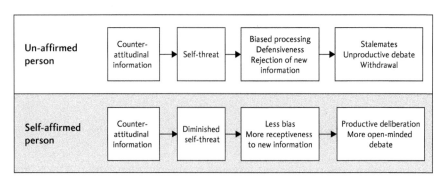

Figure 5.1 Differential processing of un-affirmed vs. self-affirmed people when presented with counter-attitudinal information.

activate a personally valued self-concept. For these types of self-affirmations to be effective, they should not be directly related to the subsequent challenging information or debate that will ensue. If they are, they can work to make people more certain of their pre-conceived notions rather than more open. The idea is that self-affirmation buffers a person against a threat to her identity by reinforcing her belief about herself as an adequate, or "good enough" person. Self-affirmations are not intended to make people feel superior or "correct," especially within the specific domain of debate.

> *"Without the self on trial, people are better able to evaluate evidence on its merits." –Cohen and Sherman 2014, p. 348.*

Self-affirmations can also be based on positive feedback from others. In some cases, research participants have been given positive feedback on a task related to identity validation but still unrelated to the subject matter of the counter-attitudinal information they were about to receive. For example, in one experiment, participants took a phony quiz and were then congratulated on their far-above-average scores in their degree of "social perceptiveness" (Cohen et al. 2000). Interventions such as these have influenced participants to subsequently focus more on evidence than on the norms of their groups or other pre-conceived notions when confronted with information that conflicts with their pre-existing attitudes. For self-affirmations based on positive feedback to be effective, people must feel praiseworthy, rather than merely praised. In other words, empty or disingenuous forms of praise not associated with a specific action or trait of an individual are likely to backfire.

Applications

When to use it

The theory is most directly applicable to face-to-face communicative environments, such as public involvement processes, teamwork or conflict resolution situations, or collaborative group processes with diverse stakeholders.

Research suggests that self-affirmations are only effective at decreasing bias and increasing open-mindedness and pragmatic compromise when identity threats are present. Self-affirmations are thus likely to be unnecessary in homogeneous groups with high levels of moral agreement on the issues under discussion. Rather, self-affirmations are more likely to have a positive effect in long-standing conflicts, partisan policy arguments, or other situations in which people are triggered to focus on their personal or social identities or group allegiances.

How to use it

First, assess whether the situation constitutes a clear identity threat. Situations in which identity threats are likely have the following characteristics:

- When someone feels unfairly or inaccurately categorized by another person or group.
- When one group has been harshly criticized or negatively evaluated publicly by another.
- When issues and positions have been highly politicized and participants are well aware of that politicization.
- In any case involving long-standing conflict between two or more people or groups.
- In any case when one's self-esteem or self-concept is doubted, diminished, or de-valued.
- In any case involving obvious cultural differences between groups, especially when stereotypes can or have been evoked.
- In any case with large power differentials (real or perceived) between stakeholders or groups.

These characteristics apply to a wide array of environmental issues and debates, including those associated with climate change, environmental regulations, public lands management, environmental justice, international conservation and development projects, land use planning or permitting, access disputes, or resource extraction.

In cases when threats to identity are clearly not present (when all of the conditions listed above are absent), self-affirmation can actually make people more certain of their own pre-conceived ideas. Thus, it is not only unnecessary, but can also have a detrimental impact on open-mindedness and innovation.

In cases where identity threat is apparent (any of the conditions above are present):

- Consider using self-affirmation in a domain outside the one under debate.[3] Preliminary activities known commonly as "icebreakers" provide great opportunities. Here are some potential techniques that could be used or adapted:
  - Precede an interaction by having participants rank a list of values and qualities in terms of their personal importance (these values should be general and outside the domain of debate)—for example, "sense of humor, relations with friends/family, spontaneity, compassion, creativity."[4] Ask participants to spend five minutes to write about a few personal experiences in which they felt good about exemplifying their most highly rated characteristic. If possible, participants could then be asked to pick one of those experiences to write a short story describing the event and their feelings at the time. This exercise mimics those found to make a difference in experimental research. While this exact activity might be a bit cumbersome or feel overly contrived for some settings, its private nature serves to remind people of their value as human beings outside the conflict setting.

  Begin an interaction with a short task that enables participants to demonstrate a positive value that they hold. In some groups, participants report on something they feel personally proud of over the past few weeks in their personal lives. This enables a public acknowledgment of one's self-identity, ideally buffering potential threats to come. It can also influence affinitive trust (see *6.1 Trust Theory*).
- Reduce the potential for identity threat by delineating clear rules of engagement that create a safe space for disagreement. See *5.1 Identity Theory* and *6.1 Trust Theory* for some advice on how to do this.
- While other opportunities may emerge to validate stakeholders' identities within an interaction, self-affirmations typically take place prior to engagement in debate. They are intended to remove initial threats participants might feel prior to a deliberation.

Key references

Cohen, G.L., J. Aronson, and C.M. Steele 2000. When beliefs yield to evidence: Reducing biased evaluation by affirming the self. *Personality and Social Psychology Bulletin* 26(9): 1151–62.

Cohen, G.L., and D.K. Sherman 2014. The psychology of change: Self-affirmation and social psychological intervention. *The Annual Review of Psychology* 65: 333–71.

Cohen, G.L., D.K. Sherman, A. Bastardi, L. Hsu, M. McGoey, and L. Ross 2007. Bridging the partisan divide: Self-affirmation reduces ideological close-mindedness and inflexibility in negotiation. *Journal of Personality and Social Psychology* 93(3): 415–30.

McQueen, A., and W.M.P. Klein 2006. Experimental manipulations of self-affirmation: A systematic review. *Self and Identity* 5(4): 289–354.

5.3 Haidt's Social Intuitionist Model of Moral Judgment

Uses: Collaborative problem solving, persuasive communication, avoiding grid-lock in joint or interdisciplinary decision making, understanding and addressing common biases

Why is it so hard to change people's minds?

Moral judgments are decisions about what is right or wrong (for example, the degree to which we should focus on environmental protection). People typically base these judgments on intuition (or "gut feelings") rather than rational analyses of new information or alternative points of view. ***People primarily use reasoning to justify their pre-conceived notions rather than to carefully weigh new information and make decisions based on that information*** (Figure 5.2). This is known as *motivated reasoning*, and reflects our propensity to focus our attention only on information that confirms our intuition. This tendency is known as *confirmation bias* (see Chapter 2).

The implications for environmental problem solving are tremendous. To demonstrate, Philip Tetlock and Jennifer Lerner distinguish between **exploratory thought** and **confirmatory thought**.[5] Exploratory thought describes reasoning that even-handedly considers multiple points of view in search for truth or an optimal decision or solution. Confirmatory thought describes reasoning focused on justifying a specific point of view. Decades of research clearly demonstrate that we are all prone to confirmatory thought. This is due not only to our inclinations toward intuitionist thinking, but also our natural concern for defending our reputations (see *5.1 Identity Theory*). Confirmatory thought is a major hurdle to finding collaborative and socially acceptable solutions to environmental challenges, as it limits the consideration of new evidence or multiple viewpoints and promotes *post hoc* reasoning rather than open-minded deliberation.

Intuitions are typically quick, automatic evaluations that require little to no conscious thought.[6] Our intuitions tend to be relatively stable, but they can change through experience. As we interact with other people who hold different beliefs,

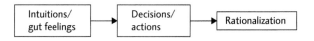

Figure 5.2 Haidt's Social Intuitionist Model of Moral Judgments.

our ideas can shift if we experience reasoned exchange or build new relationships, altering our intuitions about moral judgments going forward.

Although we certainly shouldn't ignore our intuitions (after all, they often serve us well in signaling an issue that needs attention), relying entirely upon our gut feelings in complex situations limits our ability to find innovative solutions and to broaden our networks to people who don't typically see things in the same way as we do.

While we are all pre-disposed to confirmation bias and motivated reasoning, certain conditions can promote exploratory thought and more rational deliberation. These include cases in which (1) we feel high degrees of external accountability or (2) we are explicitly encouraged and feel safe enough to explore our own underlying values.

Applications

When to use it

The *Social Intuitionist Model* is useful to consider in any situation in which differences of opinion seem intractable (or create hurdles that seem insurmountable). This might include publicly contentious issues such as climate change, planning processes for public lands, regulatory processes that involve deeply held beliefs about the appropriate role of the government, or conservation efforts that don't align clearly with pre-existing social norms (trying to change people's habits or behaviors).

The model is relevant to both decision makers interested in improving their decisions as well as external stakeholders who would like to hold decision makers accountable in a more constructive way than partisan posturing.

How to use it: Interactions or communications with others in any context

Recognize the intuitionist within ourselves and others, and that intuitions, which are often deeply intertwined with emotions, drive us toward certain conclusions, which may not align with the facts. This recognition can have two positive consequences. First, we can limit our own confirmation biases and search for information that might challenge our intuition and improve our decision making. Second, this recognition can help us to develop empathy for others, as we acknowledge that it is normal for people to have gut reactions and immediately feel driven to defend them. Empathy in this sense can enable more reasoned conversations if we aim to understand rather than to demonize.

Resist the urge to react quickly to rapid judgments and first impressions. Rather than attacking a claim that seems irrational as stupid, uninformed, or disingenuous, recognize that our intuitions are driven by deeply held values associated with our personal histories and the social norms of our peer groups. *Ad hominem* attacks or others that threaten the values or identity of an individual are likely to generate defensiveness, rather than exploratory thought. Consult other theories in this book, such as *4.1 Social Norm Theory*, *5.1 Identity Theory*, and *5.5 Moral Foundations Theory*, to try to understand the underlying values driving the claim. Begin conversations based on an acknowledgment of the validity of those values, rather than with an attack of what appears to be a false claim. For example, in the 2016 Clinton–Trump presidential election in the United States, most Americans were pre-disposed to believe "fake news" that aligned with their pre-conceived notions of each candidate. Yet, most were utterly dismayed when fake news about their candidate seemed to hold sway with the other side. These judgments were based almost entirely upon confirmatory thinking.

Look for common values. Conversations that begin with a focus on who or what is right or wrong are likely to only further entrench each participant within their pre-existing stances. Rather, turning a conversation toward the values that undergird people's pre-existing stances may reveal less tumultuous waters on which to promote rational discussion. See the discussion of separating interests from positions in *6.2 Principled Negotiation* for more detail on how to do this and *5.5 Moral Foundations Theory* as a starting point for identifying potential commonly held values and for crafting messages that address them.

How to use it: In public meetings, debates, negotiations, team processes, or collaborative efforts

Recognize the limitations of individuals' abilities to reason without motivation and confirmation bias, especially when self-interest and reputations are involved. This speaks to the importance of creating safe spaces where people with different ideas can question the claims of both themselves and others and work toward collective reasoning. Creating fair, transparent, and agreed-upon rules for negotiation can reduce perceived identity threats. Many of the other theories within Chapter 5 and some elsewhere in this book are focused on creating these conditions. See *5.2 Self-Affirmation Theory*, *6.1 Trust Theory*, and *6.2 Principled Negotiation*, in particular. See also *9.3 Moving from traditional public involvement toward more collaborative engagement.*

Create opportunities for participants to recognize common values. These values do not necessarily need to be directly associated with the particular debate at hand, but rather any values that display similarities between participants (see *5.5 Moral Foundations Theory* and *6.1 Trust Theory*). Strategies may include:

- facilitated dialogue, in which people share what is important to them personally;
- field trips, retreats, or social events, designed so that people come to know each other outside the realm of intense debate or conflict;
- discussion of desired futures prior to debating means for achieving a shared (or mutually acceptable) vision.

Stress the importance of exploratory thought directly by explaining the *Social Intuitionist Model* and our common tendencies toward confirmatory thought. Challenge audiences (and/or create specific ground rules) to check their assumptions and consider other viewpoints in light of this model.

Create a team atmosphere, in which the debate is framed as a specific challenge to work together as a team toward a collective goal. Humans are evolutionarily programmed to operate in teams (consider our tendencies to form sports teams, social cliques, or other groups that defend against external threats). If a contentious group can come to see themselves as a team working together to achieve something specific, individual compromise becomes more likely. When we experience common struggle together, we often build mutual respect and can enter each other's relevant reference groups (see *4.1 Social Norm Theory*). In doing so, we can begin to place greater value on each other's opinions and insights.[7]

How to use it: To influence decision makers

To enhance the likelihood of exploratory thought in decision makers, politicians, or other officials, overlay accountability into the situation. Accountability in this sense emerges from a person's expectation that they might have to justify their beliefs, decisions, or actions to others. In general, accountability increases exploratory thought (as opposed to confirmatory thought) when (1) a person learns *prior to making a decision* that they will be held accountable to an audience; (2) the audience's views are unknown; (3) they believe the audience is well-informed and interested in accuracy, and (4) they believe the audience has a legitimate reason for inquiring into the decision-making process.[8] Therefore, we can:

- Generate public interest in decision-making processes, not only outcomes. This involves demanding information about how decisions are being made, as well as their potential consequences, and publicizing this information. Demanding transparency on the criteria through which alternative courses of action will be evaluated (rather than the desirability of the outcome alone) can shift attention from pre-conceived solutions or political alignments toward more thoughtful evaluation.

- Educate diverse stakeholders on the relevance of decisions to their lives and on the background information necessary to understand decision-making processes. See *6.4 The Reasonable Person Model.*
- Stress to decision-makers that relevant audiences are interested, educated, and diverse, and that they have a legitimate stake in the process.[9]
- Inform and involve the press.

Key references

Haidt, J. 2001. The emotional dog and its rational tail: a social intuitionist approach to moral judgment. *Psychological Review* 108(4): 814–34.

Haidt, J. 2012. *The righteous mind: Why good people are divided by politics and religion.* New York, NY: Vintage Books.

5.4 Cultural Cognition

Uses: Science communication, persuasive communication, understanding and addressing common biases, conflict resolution

Why can't people be convinced by the facts?

The concept of *Cultural Cognition* rests on the premise of motivated reasoning, similar to *Haidt's Social Intuitionist Model*, that reasoning may often come after the fact, if at all, to justify our pre-conceived notions. In other words, our evaluations of new information are not often based on a careful unbiased consideration of the facts. Rather, they are more commonly based on our pre-existing beliefs or prior cultural commitments.

The principle foundation of *Cultural Cognition* is that people endorse "whichever position reinforces their connection to other people with whom they share important commitments,"[10] regardless of the facts or other persuasive arguments. For example, we are more likely to think a penalty called against our favorite sports team is unfair than would someone who favors the other team, regardless of the evidence.[11]

Despite what many people think, scientific facts don't change people's minds when cultural commitments are in play. In multiple studies, researchers have found that increasing scientific knowledge is not consistently linked to the acceptance of the existence of environmental risks, such as anthropogenic climate change. Rather, prior cultural commitments, such as party allegiance (e.g., Republican vs Democrat), political orientation (e.g., conservative vs liberal), or the dominant cultural beliefs of one's self-identified peers, family, or community, are far better predictors of their acceptance. The more powerfully a person identifies with a particular cultural group that denies climate change, the more likely they are to use whatever knowledge they have to justify their pre-conceived notions, rather than to consider new information that might adjust those pre-existing beliefs. For example, a common strategy is to stress the inherent uncertainty in the scientific process (or the biases of scientists) to justify nearly any claim that seems contrary to the majority of the evidence.

Dan Kahan and colleagues call out the importance of specific group identities, which exist along two spectra: from egalitarian to hierarchical and from communitarian to individualist.[12] The sets of meanings associated with these identities tend to be relatively stable for people, reflecting their views about ideal societies. Conflicting information thus threatens both individual and collective identities.

When a message or a messenger's identity or delivery style does not align with the values held by the message recipient (or their group), the message is likely to have little to no effect. When either directly conflicts with the values of the recipient (or their group), the message may result in an even deeper commitment to pre-existing beliefs or opinions. The following dichotomies represent the ends of these spectra.

Egalitarian vs hierarchical:	People with egalitarian values are concerned with equality for all people, regardless of their race, religion, socioeconomic status, or other cultural identities. Hierarchical individuals are more concerned with fairness than equality, typically believing that concerns about equality are either overblown and/or that they represent attempts to unfairly redistribute wealth or weaken traditional values.
Communitarian vs individualist:	Communitarians stress that it is society's responsibility to make sure everyone's basic needs and rights are protected. They typically see this as a primary responsibility of governing bodies. Individualists are more concerned about government overreach and think people should be responsible for themselves.

Cultural Cognition research has shown that those who subscribe to a hierarchical or individualistic worldview tend to be skeptical of environmental risks, as they are more averse to restrictions on industry. Meanwhile, egalitarians and communitarians tend to be skeptical of industry to which they often attribute social inequality. They are thus typically more concerned about environmental risks. Similar distinctions are likely amongst other classifications or categorizations of cultures as well.[13]

Cultural Cognition can happen intuitively, without much thought, or through conscious efforts to align oneself with (or justify) the attitudes, beliefs, or actions of important reference groups (see *4.1 Social Norm Theory*). Research associated with this field powerfully undermines the hypothesis that simply providing people with factual evidence is likely to change minds—especially in the case where opinions are broadly shared within a particular social group.

Applications

When to use it

Understanding *Cultural Cognition* is useful in public communications and in any effort that involves bringing together diverse stakeholders around a contentious or debated issue.

How to use it

Cultural Cognition suggests a number of potential actions for communicating across value sets.

1. Present information in a way that affirms, rather than threatens, people's cultural identities. This involves creating narratives (stories with settings, characters, plots, and a moral) that address the underlying values of different audiences. See *5.1 Identity Theory, 5.5 Moral Foundations Theory*, and *5.6 Frame Theory* for more specific advice. Also, see *5.2 Self-Affirmation Theory* for advice on reducing identity-related threats.

2. Consider the identity of the communicator(s). These could be people who are clearly members of message recipients' cultural communities or people who demonstrate particular qualities in their communication style (e.g., egalitarian or hierarchical) that match target audiences. If audiences are diverse, consider diverse communicators who demonstrate agreement with each other, though perhaps based on different moral foundations.[14]

3. Recognize that traditional persuasive communication efforts, such as those described in Chapter 4, are less likely to be effective on people with deeply entrenched political identities or pre-determined stances. Rather, identity-based theories are likely more appropriate for understanding these groups.

Key references

Kahan, D.M. 2012. Cultural cognition as a conception of the cultural theory of risk. In S. Roeser, R. Hillerbrand, P. Sandin, and M. Peterson (eds), *Handbook of Risk Theory: Epistemology, Decision Theory, Ethics, and Social Implications of Risk*, pp. 725–9. Netherlands: Springer.

Kahan, D.M., H. Jenkins-Smith, and D. Braman. 2011. Cultural cognition of scientific consensus. *Journal of Risk Research* 14(2); 147–74.

Kahan, D.M., E. Peters, M. Wittlin, P. Slovic, L.L. Ouellette, D. Braman, and G. Mandel 2012. The polarizing impact of science literacy and numeracy on perceived climate change risks. *Nature Climate Change* 2: 732–5.

5.5 Moral Foundations Theory

Uses: Collaborative problem solving, persuasive communication, understanding and addressing common biases, conflict resolution

> **Why is it so easy to think the people on the other side of an argument are crazy? How can we bridge the divide?**

How is it that so many people reject climate science? Why are there such intense and divisive debates about the rights of endangered species, environmental regulations, and issues like universal healthcare, gay marriage, and taxes? One explanation is that different people have different sets of morals, developed over the course of their unique life histories. These moral systems "bind and blind" us, according to Jonathan Haidt, binding us to people who share our moral system and blinding us to the validity of any moral system other than our own.

Moral systems are sets of values, norms, and practices that keep our self interest in check and make cooperative societies possible. They are based on at least six moral foundations, identified by Haidt and colleagues through extensive worldwide research. Each foundation is comprised of two opposing concepts—one that is generally morally desired, or "good," and the other which is not. Haidt and colleagues argue that all humans share this common set of fundamental moral judgments, though different people place varying emphasis on each. In the United States and other wealthy Western countries, for example, liberals place greatest moral emphasis on the care/harm and fairness/cheating foundations, while conservatives place relatively stronger emphasis on the loyalty/betrayal, sanctity/degradation, and authority/subversion foundations (though they still care about the others to some degree). Libertarians place greatest emphasis on the liberty/oppression foundation.

Moral judgments are typically intuitive judgments. That is, they don't require conscious thought. Rather, they typically emerge as gut feelings and urge us to judge a person or action by what *feels* right to us. In other words, the foundations that underlie our judgments are often invisible to us. Learning to recognize which moral foundations are important to different audiences can improve our communications with prior adversaries. Recognizing shared moral foundations can also help us find common ground between conflicting parties. Specific actions that exemplify or mark violations of each foundation will vary for different people, communities, and cultures. However, the underlying foundations that drive judgments may be universal.

The six moral foundations

1. *Care/Harm*: This foundation is concerned primarily with easing suffering and avoiding harm to others. An action is good if it demonstrates care. An action is bad when it harms others.
2. *Fairness/Cheating*: This foundation is concerned with rewarding good work or good deeds appropriately (or proportionately) and punishing cheating.
3. *Loyalty/Betrayal*: This foundation drives us to trust and reward those who display commitment to their group and want to punish those who betray or ignore larger group values or causes.
4. *Authority/Subversion*: This foundation enables us to recognize and respect legitimate authority and hierarchy that brings order to groups or societies. It also makes us sensitive to signs that people are not behaving properly based on their position (abusing power as a leader or subverting legitimate authority as a follower, thus threatening societal order).
5. *Sanctity/Degradation*: This foundation drives appreciation of intrinsic purity and disgust. We feel some things are inherently good because they represent purity, God's will, or perhaps beauty. We feel others are bad because they are disgusting, regardless of whether they have any tangible consequence that involves our self-interest or any other moral foundation.
6. *Liberty/Oppression*: This foundation is concerned with maintaining personal freedoms or rights and avoiding being dominated. It triggers our urge to band together against bullies, tyrants, or repression. It also drives feelings about the appropriate role of government in society.

Applications

When to use it

Moral Foundations Theory can be particularly useful in any situation where one party is in conflict with another (or multiple parties are in conflict). The theory can apply to persuasive communications, planning processes, public involvement efforts, negotiations, conflict resolution, or political communications.

Moreover, activating and/or revealing common moral foundations can help to build teams, enhance commitment to organizations, or grow social movements. We empathize with those who conform to our moral system. The belongingness that comes from sharing moral foundations typically engenders service and generosity. Groups that can elicit commitment to shared moral foundations tend to thrive and grow.

How to use it: In public or political communications

We tend to try to convince other people what is right and wrong based on our own moral systems, rather than considering the moral systems of the people we are trying to convince. When we advocate for environmental issues in our own moral terms, we speak convincingly only to others who likely already feel similarly about those issues. *Moral Foundations Theory* suggests two pathways for enhancing our persuasive powers, depending on what we know about the moral systems of others.

When we don't know much about the moral systems of our target audiences, we might consider crafting messages that touch upon as many of the moral foundations as possible. Because these foundations are broadly applicable across multiple cultures,[15] making an argument that appeals to each improves our chances of aligning with the moral values of a greater proportion of message recipients. For example, in crafting a message about the importance of curtailing water pollution, we might not only address the typical liberal moral foundations prominent in most contemporary environmental messaging, like care/harm (pollution hurts people; our children are especially vulnerable) or fairness (polluters get rich while we all pay the price in terms of clean-up costs, ugly rivers, and illnesses), but also other moral foundations, including loyalty (pollution makes our country weaker; let's be proud of our community and protect it from these threats; it's our civic duty; together we can do it), sanctity (polluted water is disgusting, an abomination; its impurity makes us sick), authority (let's follow the advice of important leaders and do what's asked of us to keep our waterways clean), and liberty (pollution is a form of oppression; it is our inherent right to be free of contaminants unjustly thrust upon us by polluters). In different communities or cultures, the arguments may be different, but evoking each moral foundation may enhance the likelihood of activating a positive evaluation of the message.

When we do have information about the moral systems of our target audiences, for example in the case of conservatives or liberals in the United States, aligning messages with the moral foundations emphasized by each group can shift attitudes. Matthew Feinberg and Robb Willer[16] have demonstrated the effects of alternative framing using *Moral Foundations Theory* in a series of experiments with conservatives and liberals in the United States. They found that reframing pro-environmental messages in terms of the sanctity/degradation moral foundation largely eliminated the pre-existing difference between liberals' and conservatives' environmental attitudes—that is, conservatives cared as much about taking environmental action as liberals after reading about degradation and the importance of purification of the environment (and viewing pictures of degradation). Meanwhile, exposure to messages framed within the care/harm foundation, which emphasized the harm humans cause to the environment and the need to care for it (along with similar images), made no difference. They also tested the framing power of moral foundations in other arenas, including same-sex marriage, military spending, and adopting English as the nation's official language. In each case, they found framing messages within the dominant moral foundations of the group known to oppose the given policy (fairness for liberals; and loyalty, authority, and sanctity for conservatives) increased their support for it. Fairness messages used words like "unfair," "unjust," "equality," and "discrimination." Sanctity messages used words like "unclean" and "disgusting." A combined authority and loyalty message used words like "nation," "loyal," "leader," and "oppose." A separate loyalty message used words like "patriotic" and "community."[17]

Because moral judgments are typically driven by intuition and gut feelings, factual arguments that lie outside the dominant relevant moral frame of the message recipient are likely to be rejected. They just *feel* wrong. For example, those who continue to deny the science of climate change in the United States may do so because they see it as a threat to their way of life (liberty/oppression frame) or as a ploy by foreign governments to damage U.S. interests (loyalty/betrayal). For these people, arguments that are morally framed by the fairness/cheating or care/harm foundations are unlikely to be effective, as they don't address their intuitive moral concerns. Moreover, factual scientific arguments will be subject to motivated reasoning, limiting their effectiveness (see *5.3 Haidt's Social Intuitionist Model of Moral Judgment* and *5.4 Cultural Cognition*). Rather, reframing climate change as a form of oppression that threatens our way of life, or the act of ignoring it as betrayal of our national interests, might provide an entryway to more open discussion.

Does this sound strange? If so, you probably emphasize the care/harm or fairness/cheating foundations yourself. It is not an easy jump to communicate using an unfamiliar moral foundation. Can addressing climate change be an act of patriotism (loyalty)? Probably, if we frame our national interests as winning the race to reaping the greatest profits from alternative energy innovations vs stagnating our economic interests on finite resources and being left behind by other countries. Can it be about fighting oppression? Again, it probably can be, if ignoring climate change is framed as limiting our freedom to compete in the global economy or as maintaining the dominance of corporate power over others.

No specific framing strategy is guaranteed to work, and poor framing can always backfire. However, considering *Moral Foundations Theory* can expand our thinking about how to communicate more effectively with others who don't share our beliefs.

How to use it: In conflict resolution or negotiation situations

As a facilitator, mediator, or participant, consider drawing attention to shared moral values of antagonistic parties.[18] This can happen in one of two ways. The first way involves reframing the argument. For example, perhaps environmentalists and timber industry representatives can't agree on whether (or where) a road should be built in a public natural area. Environmentalists put forth arguments focused on the care/harm foundation (concern for species or habitats); industry folks argue about feeling oppressed by environmental regulations that infringe upon their right to make a living (liberty/oppression). These arguments fall on deaf ears, as each side feels it has the moral high ground. Might it be possible to find common ground by reframing the argument in terms of a different moral foundation, such as the sanctity/degradation frame? Possibly. Both sides might appreciate the value of a pristine nature experience and be amenable to preserving that as much as possible. However, it would be difficult to predict such a reaction without considerable knowledge of both parties. Facilitated visioning processes of desired futures[19] can sometimes reveal shared values in this sense. Alternatively, if the industry argument could be reframed in terms of care for employees who might lose their jobs, and the environmentalist argument could be reframed to consider the liberty of recreationists in the area who have long-standing connections to this place and feel some ownership over it, both sides might become more amenable to working out a compromise, as they can better empathize with the opposing group.

The second way involves demonstrating shared moral foundations outside the context of the debate. Through interpersonal communications and informal interactions, we can begin to see ourselves in our adversaries, as we come to know them as parents or grandparents, members of common community groups, or as people who like to spend their free time in ways similar to us. These types of interactions can reveal stories that demonstrate values like commitment to one's family or one's employees (loyalty) or common respect for an important social/institution (authority). A shared sense of morality enhances feelings of empathy. Oftentimes, revelations such as these between adversaries can soften deeply entrenched positions, enabling and encouraging people to look for win–win solutions (see also *6.1 Trust Theory* and *6.2 Principled Negotiation*).

How to use it: In collaborative group or team processes

In addition to considering each of the above strategies, call attention to similarities shared by group members. Take the time for group members to build a shared understanding of the mission of the group. Facilitated conversations about goals and appropriate processes to achieve them early on in group formation can create an agreed upon moral system in which the group will operate (see also *6.1 Trust Theory*). Shared moral foundations can enhance commitment to the team, motivation to work, and innovative thinking toward common goals in the absence of moral conflict (see *7.2 Team Effectiveness Theory*).

Key reference

Haidt, J. 2012. *The righteous mind: Why good people are divided by politics and religion.* New York, NY: Vintage Books.

5.6 Frame Theory

Uses: Persuasive communication, negotiation

Are some ways of presenting the same information more persuasive than others?

Frame Theory, as I describe it here, doesn't constitute a single standalone theory. This section rather summarizes a body of knowledge based on multiple theories and empirical research on the ways in which people tend to interpret information. In the broadest sense, people use *frames* to understand and respond to particular events and situations.

There are two different types of frames that fall under the general umbrella of *Frame Theory*. Each type of frame is relevant to understanding different people's points of view and for effective communication across diverse audiences. The first, which I will call *interpretive frames*, refers to collections of beliefs that people use to define a situation, understand their role within it, organize and evaluate information, and make decisions within a particular context. We can think of these frames as similar to those around a painting in a museum. They constrain what is visible to us, drawing our attention to certain aspects of a situation rather than others. This first type of framing is implicit within many of the other theories summarized in this book. For example, *Moral Foundations Theory* and *Cultural Cognition* each suggest that different people see the world in different ways and focus on different aspects of a problem. In a practical sense, making use of interpretive frames involves being a great listener and/or conducting some preliminary research on your audience. It then involves aligning communications with pre-existing knowledge, norms, moral foundations, or intuitions to minimize unproductive conflict or defensiveness.

The second type, which I'll refer to as *communicative frames*,[20] denotes ways in which information can be conveyed (or "framed") to influence the evaluations and responses of message recipients. These frames are crafted by communicators and aim to prime participants to place emphasis on certain types of information over others, based on what is known about human psychology.

Interpretive frames

Most commonly, researchers use interpretive framing to understand the worldviews or mental maps of their research subjects. In a practical sense, interpretive frames can be influenced by (1) directing the focus of interactions toward certain topics or subjects or (2) changing the relationships of those involved in a debate or other interaction.

In the first sense, climate change action arguments could be framed as an issue of economic opportunity (improving economic competitiveness in alternative energies), national security (decreasing dependence on foreign oil; reducing environmental pressures that trigger foreign conflicts), religious stewardship (caring for the Earth; compassion toward those most vulnerable), or public health (improving air quality; limiting the spread of infectious disease; reducing the likelihood of extreme weather events). Research has revealed little consistency in which types of topical or thematic frames might be preferable in different situations.[21] Rather, the underlying moral foundations of the arguments, social norms, and relationships between the parties seem more powerful drivers of outcomes in various contexts.

In the second sense, people and groups label (or *frame*) each other in ways that are sometimes not conducive to productive interchange. These frames, known as **characterization frames** or **identity frames**, set up significant barriers to meaningful communication through escalating feelings of risk and threat. Strategies that reveal common values, create positive shared experiences between parties, or set up procedures to minimize risk and enhance feelings of safety can help to shift these frames over time. See *5.1 Identity Theory, 5.2 Self-Affirmation Theory*, and *6.1 Trust Theory* for more on these strategies.

Communicative frames

Communicative frames research has shown that the ways in which identical information is framed (communicated) can influence responses drastically. Four types of framing, in particular, have been well studied: risk frames, goal frames, attribute frames, and moral frames.

Risk framing is largely based on *Prospect Theory*,[22] which explains that people are more sensitive to losses than to gains. Specifically, people will be more likely to take a risk if they are told their action will avoid a loss than if they are told it will achieve a gain, even if the odds of success are exactly the same in each scenario.

Goal framing is an extension of risk framing, except that it does not necessarily involve a risky behavior. In goal framing, a positively framed message stresses the positive consequences of performing a behavior. A negatively framed message emphasizes avoiding the negative consequences of performing (or not performing) a behavior. Messages that focus on avoiding a loss (negative goal framing) tend to have stronger impacts on responses than those focused on gains (positive goal framing). For example, messages about the dangers of not performing a breast exam have been more compelling than those that focus on the benefits of the exam.[23] Similarly, if I could convince you that you had a 50 percent chance to avoid a huge loss of income by joining the local ecotourism co-op, you'd likely feel more compelled to act than if I instead convinced you that you had a 50 percent chance to achieve the same amount of new income from the same action.

Both risk and goal framing are subject to ***the certainty effect***, or the tendency for individuals to prefer a certain outcome to an uncertain one. When a suggested behavior leads to a relatively certain outcome, gain-framed messaging can work. However, as uncertainty increases, loss-framed messages, those focused on ***avoiding a loss***, are more persuasive. This is primarily because losses are more emotionally salient to us than gains. Their emotional power can counteract uncertainty better than thinking about potential gains. Uncertainty has also been found to interact with self-efficacy (the feeling that one can take an action and that the action will actually make a difference). Situations with high degrees of uncertainty that are not accompanied with a strong sense of self-efficacy can promote the convenient justification of self-interested actions or denial.[24]

Attribute framing involves foregrounding a particular attribute of an argument. Examples of attribute framing relevant to the environmental arena include positive vs negative framing; individual vs collective framing; local vs distant framing; and future vs past framing.

- ***Positive framing***: In attribute framing, positive and negative mean something slightly different than in goal framing. In this case, positive framing means highlighting the positive side of an issue. For example, I could communicate to you the same information by telling you that you have a 20 percent chance of success or an 80 percent chance of failure. Your response is likely to be more favorable when I communicate with the positive frame (in this case, the 20 percent chance of success) instead of the negative frame (80 percent chance of failure). For example, one study showed people felt that ground beef was tastier and less greasy when they were told it was 75 percent lean versus being told it was 25 percent fat.[25] An important caveat to this type of attribute framing is that it is less effective when topics involve pre-existing strongly held attitudes or high personal involvement.
- ***Collective efficacy framing***: Focusing on collective efficacy (actions "we" can take together to avoid a loss) has been found to be more effective than messages about individual sacrifice ("I'll have to forego this").[26]
- ***Local framing***: Research shows that focusing on local impacts and actions produces greater motivation than communication focused on more distant or global events or processes.[27] This goes for social distance as well. That is, communicating about impacts on people who are more similar or known to

the audience are likely to resonate more than discussing more distant or different populations.

- **Diagnostic and prognostic framing:** Research on social movements reveals the importance of both diagnostic and prognostic framing to motivate enrollment.[28] Diagnostic framing involves clearly describing a problem and attributing to it a specific cause or set of causes. Prognostic framing involves pairing diagnostic frames with an articulation of promising solutions. Similar to the *Extended Parallel Process Model of Fear Appeals*, articulation of a problem and its causes is not likely to motivate action without a parallel articulation of realistic solutions.

- **Future vs past framing:** Baldwin and Lammers (2016) found environmental messages with a temporal focus on the past were significantly more effective at promoting pro-environmental attitudes and actions for conservatives in the United States than those focused on the future. Meanwhile, the particular temporal framing used had no consistent effect on these outcomes for liberals. Their research was based on common philosophical differences between conservatives and liberals in the United States—that conservatives more strongly endorse tradition and tend to view progressive policies as movements away from a cherished past. Meanwhile, liberals tend to view change as progress. Examples of the specific messages used in the study are shared in Figure 5.3. This serves as a strong example of how knowing your audience can make a huge difference on the effectiveness of different message framing.

Past-focused framing	Future-focused framing
"Looking back to our nation's past, I think that our society has gone too far in its desire for material wealth (among other things). It seems like life in the past was simpler and people were happy with the little that they had. There was less traffic on the road, the air was clean, and there was plenty of land. I sort of feel like we have changed the world that our forefathers lived in . . . would they be happy with what we've done to it? I want to make our founding fathers proud, and if we do not make changes to the way we treat the environment now, it will continue to get worse. I think we need to undo what we've done so that the world can go back to how it was supposed to be back then."	"Looking forward to our nation's future, I think that our society has gone too far in its desire for material wealth (among other things). It seems like life in the future is getting too complex and people will never be happy with all they have. There is increasing traffic on the road, the air is becoming polluted, and land is disappearing. I sort of feel like we are changing the world that future generations will live in . . . will they be happy with what we are doing to it? I want to make future generations proud, and if we do not make changes to the way we treat the environment now, it will continue to get worse. I think we need to stop what we are doing so that the world can be what it's supposed to be in the future."

Figure 5.3 Past and future framing passages from the Baldwin and Lammers study (2016, p. S1). *Study participants were asked to read one of these messages (they were told it was a passage from a prior study participant). They then evaluated the message and answered questions about their environmental attitudes. Similarly, they read past-focused and future-focused messages from environmental charities. Conservatives were more likely to donate to past-focused charities than liberals.*

Moral framing is based on the premise that different people (or groups of people) may place varying degrees of importance on different moral values. Framing arguments within the context of the moral values of an audience, when they are known, or a wider array of moral values, when they are unknown, can enhance an argument's persuasiveness. See *5.5 Moral Foundations Theory* for more detail on this form of communicative framing.[29]

Applications

When to use it

Interpretive frames are relevant in any communications. Their consideration can help to understand diverging rationales, produce empathy, and expand the range of deliberation between parties.

For ongoing or deeply entrenched conflicts, most forms of **communicative framing** are unlikely to prove successful, as most people may have already aligned strongly with a social group and will defend that group's norms in light of new information. *Moral framing* currently shows the most promise in this respect, if the message can link with the opposing group's underlying moral foundations.

Furthermore, using **communicative frames** for persuasive purposes is unlikely to be successful in situations in which the communicator is distrusted or lacks legitimacy or when a suggested action or behavior seems unrealistic (self-efficacy is low).

How to use interpretive frames

Using interpretive frames involves understanding the underlying assumptions and beliefs of the stories people tell. This typically entails intensive listening and/or considerable analysis. Understanding these frames, however, can help to bridge gaps in communication in many ways—in particular by looking for common elements across the narratives of different people or groups and using the common elements as bases for setting goals or coming to agreement. I can offer no simple guidance for doing this other than paying careful attention and respecting differences.[30] See also *6.1 Trust Theory* and *6.2 Principled Negotiation*.

How to use communicative frames

Using communicative frames is a bit more straightforward. Here are some guidelines for more successful communications based on communicative framing:

- Stress loss avoidance rather than the opportunity to create something new or generate a new gain. The only exception to this would be in cases where an outcome is perceived as relatively certain by the message recipient. This is rarely the case in environmental communications.

- Explain suggested actions in terms of their likelihood of success (to avoid a loss) rather than their likelihood of failure.
- Stress collective efficacy ("we can do it") rather than individual sacrifice ("I'll have to forego this"). Messages of individual sacrifice, especially for environmental issues, which are inherently collective, do not enhance (and can lower) feelings of self-efficacy.
- Discuss local impacts as much as possible. Also, avoid framing messages in terms of the distant future or impacts on faraway people or people with whom the message recipient has no connection.
- If we know we are dealing with conservative audiences, consider past-focused messages, rather than future-focused messages. Liberal audiences tend to prefer future-focused messages. See also *5.5 Moral Foundations Theory* for more tips on communicating environmental themes to conservatives vs liberals. Words also matter in this sense. Can we use words like "protection," which can invoke the sanctity foundation and stress loss avoidance in place of words like "regulation" or "restriction," which can invoke feelings of oppression and threats to liberty?

Key references

Kahneman, D., and A. Tversky 1979. Prospect theory: an analysis of decision under risk. *Econometrica* 47(2): 263–71.

Levin, I.P., S.L. Schneider, and G.J. Gaeth 1998. All frames are not created equal: A typology and critical analysis of framing effects. *Organizational Behavior and Human Decision Processes* 76(2): 149–88.

Lewicki, R.J., B. Gray, and M. Elliott (eds.) 2003. *Making sense of intractable environmental conflicts*. Washington, DC: Island Press.

5.7 Meyer's Culture Map

Uses: Identifying norms, working in foreign contexts

> When working in different cultures, how can we recognize norms and avoid accidentally offending people so that we have a better chance to accomplish our goals?

Erin Meyer identified eight dimensions that differentiate the ways in which people in different countries tend to perform common business practices (Table 5.1). Her work identifies categories of descriptive norms that vary across cultures in ways that matter to carrying out environmental work. The categories alert us to practices we should pay attention to as we attempt to work in cultures different from our own. Violations of these norms can lead to undesirable outcomes, including not being taken seriously or initiating identity-defensive mechanisms in the people

Table 5.1 *The eight dimensions of Erin Meyer's Culture Map.*

Scale	Cultural normative preferences (ends of spectra)	
Communicating	**Low context**	**High context**
	Preference for direct, precise, and straightforward language intended to be understood at face value.	Preference for less direct, nuanced, or layered communication with intention for the listener to read between the lines.
Evaluating	**Direct feedback**	**Indirect feedback**
	Preference for direct (often blunt) feedback.	Preference for softened or indirect feedback, in which criticism is implied rather than directly spoken.
Persuading	**Principles-first**	**Applications-first**
	Develop theory before presenting conclusions. Conceptual principles underlying arguments are highly valued.	Begin with key conclusions first, then add concepts or principles later to explain the conclusion as necessary. Desire to get to the point quickly.
Leading	**Egalitarian**	**Hierarchical**
	Small distance between boss and subordinates; boss is facilitator among equals; communication can skip hierarchical channels.	High distance between boss and subordinates; boss is out-front leader; status and hierarchy are important; communications follow hierarchical structures.

(Continued)

Scale	Cultural normative preferences (ends of spectra)	
Deciding	**Consensual**	**Top-down**
	Favoring group deliberation and agreement.	Relying on the boss (or other expert in specific role) to make decisions.
Trusting[31]	**Task-based**	**Relationship-based**
	Trust is built on consistent adequate performance.	Trust is based on personal relationships developed through positive social experiences.
Disagreeing	**Confrontational**	**Confrontation-avoiding**
	Open debate and disagreement is considered positive and appropriate.	Open debate and disagreement is considered negative and damaging.
Scheduling	**Linear time**	**Flexible time**
	Emphasis on sticking to well-defined deadlines and sequential schedules, promptness, and predictability.	Work is approached fluidly, changing as opportunities or challenges arise with an emphasis on adaptability and flexibility.

with whom we hope to work. Each dimension is measured on a scale, with two opposing practices on each end of a spectrum. Most cultures exist somewhere between the two polar ends.

While Meyer created these scales through years of observations of business interactions across the globe and in consultation with prior literature attempting to categorize cultures at the national level,[32] the dimensions represent cultural elements that also likely vary at much smaller scales. While national trends and norms undeniably exist, subgroup variation does as well. For example, working with an indigenous tribe in Peru will involve drastically different norms of interaction than working with Peruvian government officials or a multi-national firm based in Lima. Moreover, certain individuals may not conform to the overall norms of their local communities, organizations, or groups. The value of the dimensions lies in their ability to direct our attention to different categories of norms that may enhance our interactions if we spend the time and energy necessary to understand them.

Other frameworks that provide similar types of insights, but at the individual level rather than the group or national level, include the Myers–Briggs Type Indicator (MBTI) personality inventory,[33] the Five-Factor Model of Personality (also known as the Big Five),[34] and the Riso-Hudson Enneagram Types.[35] Each of these models examines the traits or general preferences of individuals and provides guidance for self-improvement, team building, leadership, and enhancing interactions between those with similar and different types. These models high-light that general trends at the national, regional, or even local level inevitably interact with personal histories, traits, and preferences to produce actual behaviors. They thus raise a flag of caution for those who might be quick to label a group or a culture as one way or another or assume they understand individuals' preferences based on cultural norms. They also provide some guidance on selecting the right person for a particular task or upcoming interaction—considering who might have the natural dispositions to be effective bridge-builders or communicators to certain audiences (see *8.3 Diffusion Theory*).

Applications

When to use it

Whenever working in a culture different from our own, the dimensions identified within the *Culture Map* are worth consideration.

While Meyer offers explicit information about national cultures in her book,[36] be careful about assuming these general trends will apply to smaller scales, such as organizations, groups, or individuals. Rather, they may provide a starting point for understanding how best to interact with the dominant cultures in the area. Deeper understanding requires direct observation or other forms of investigation (see below).

How to use it

Talk with key informants about the dominant cultural norms of the communities and people with whom you intend to work. Key informants are typically people from within the targeted group we hope to understand with whom we've developed some level of trust or understanding. The eight scales of the *Culture Map* provide worthwhile dimensions for discussion. They also may direct our observations in our early interactions with different groups. Meyer has identified behavioral categories known to make or break cross-cultural business transactions. Thus, understanding where different groups (or key individuals) lie on the spectrum of each scale enables us to adjust our own behavior to better align with respected norms and expectations and to avoid (or lessen the likelihood of) identity threats or other gaffs we might otherwise make. We might also consider having explicit conversations about expectations along each of these spectra with potential cross-cultural partners to come to agreements about appropriate modes of interaction that work for each party involved.

Meyer's website[37] provides a way to map national trends for each scale. Meyer notes that it is critical to consider one's own relative position to another culture on each scale, rather than to consider any absolute score (or notion) of a particular culture on any scale.

Each scale implies simple adjustments in our own behaviors as we work in cultures different from our own. For example, we may need to resist our temptation to openly debate a leader in front of their subordinates in a hierarchical and confrontation-avoiding culture. We may need to soften our feedback to others in a culture that prefers indirect feedback. We may consider switching the order of our arguments or presentations depending on whether our audience prefers principles-first or applications-first communication. And so on.

For prolonged interactions with collaborators or other types of partners, individual level personality tests, such as the MBTI, the Big Five, or the Enneagram of Personality Types, may provide some valuable insights for improving interactions *if facilitated by a trained professional*. These tests can sometimes result in self-labeling and the labeling of others. As a result, their casual use or misuse can lead to identity threats and associated challenges (see *5.1 Identity Theory*).

Key reference

Meyer, E. 2014. *The culture map: Breaking through the invisible boundaries of global business.* New York: PublicAffairs.

6
Trust, negotiation, and public involvement

Introduction: Navigating a diverse social landscape

People in just about every profession or pastime must navigate the diverse ideas and values of others to accomplish their goals. For environmental professionals, public involvement processes are often mandated by law. Environmental impacts and other details of potential actions must be disclosed, and the public is encouraged to comment. These types of interactions are typically referred to as *public involvement*. In other cases, people involved in environmental or sustainability-related initiatives must interact with diverse stakeholders to plan and implement their work. These interactions represent efforts at *collaboration*.

Public involvement efforts can serve various purposes, which can be labeled *procedural*, *substantive*, *instrumental*, or *normative*.

Procedural: Some may see their obligations to interact with the public as no more than a procedural or legal requirement. In these cases, public officials or others may simply go through the motions and meet minimum obligations for informing or educating public audiences about their actions.

Substantive: Public knowledge is solicited in an effort to improve the basis of facts that inform management actions. The premise for substantive public involvement is that external audiences might have useful information otherwise unavailable to decision makers.[1]

Instrumental: Public involvement processes can provide a means to head off conflict and manage external relationships to avoid legal or other challenges to planned efforts. This primarily entails strategic and persuasive communications or making programmatic adjustments to circumvent or avoid potential resistance.

Social Science Theory for Environmental Sustainability: A Practical Guide. Marc J. Stern, Oxford University Press (2018). © Marc J. Stern 2018. DOI 10.1093/oso/9780198793182.001.0001

Normative: Public involvement can also been seen as opportunity to more fully incorporate the values or desires of stakeholders in decision making. This view typically entails greater efforts at dialogue rather than one-way communications.

Research suggests that public involvement can serve all of these functions, and those that combine substantive, instrumental, and normative goals, aiming to incorporate diverse knowledge and values and resolve points of conflict along the way, tend to achieve the best outcomes.[2]

In multi-stakeholder settings, collaborative approaches can result in the consideration of a broader array of ideas and strategies, the resolution or diminishing of unproductive conflict, and the leveraging of diverse talents and social networks to achieve goals. While adversarial approaches can also be effective in certain situations to achieve gains or avoid catastrophic losses, they rarely represent a sustainable long-term strategy. Moreover, they forego the opportunities and benefits of bringing more people and ideas into our efforts.

Of course, collaborative approaches present challenges of their own. They often require extensive negotiation and compromise. They are not easy, and they can feel overly time-consuming and inefficient. Recent research, however, suggests that greater efforts at collaborative deliberation in planning processes can actually enhance efficiency in the long term by averting subsequent deficiencies in project design and stakeholder conflict.[3]

The theories in this chapter explicitly deal with managing relationships within these interactions. They provide strategies for structuring interactions between stakeholders, for enhancing trust and understanding between diverse parties, and for addressing conflict.

6.1 Trust Theory

Uses: Engaging potential participants, communities or stakeholders, negotiation, understanding behavior, structuring teams or processes, persuasive communication, public involvement

> **What is trust, how does it come about, why is it so frequently lacking, and what can we do about it?**

Years ago, I conducted a study in communities surrounding protected areas in South America, the Caribbean, and the mainland United States.[4] I was trying to understand conflicts between national parks and the people that live around them. I examined economic concerns, environmental values, pathways of information exchange, land disputes, political contexts, and just about everything you might imagine could influence conflict in these areas. One factor alone, however, could predict with nearly 80 percent accuracy (within a sample of over 400 people) who was actively opposing their nearby park (through illegal resource extraction or other acts of protest) and who was not. That factor was whether people trusted park managers to be fair and honest with them or not.

Across diverse contexts, trust has been associated with better cooperation, collaboration, conflict resolution, compliance with rules, teamwork, and project outcomes. Meanwhile, distrust is commonly associated with multiple forms of unproductive conflict.

This section provides a synthesis of numerous trust theories, beginning with definitions of key components of each.

Trust is typically defined as the willingness of a person to accept vulnerability to another party in the face of uncertainty. Components of *Trust Theory* include a *trustor*, a *trustee*, an action in question, and the context in which an evaluation about trust is made. While a *trustor* is most commonly an individual, a *trustee* can take multiple forms, such as a person, a group of people, an organization, or even an object, such as a map.[5]

Distrust is theoretically distinct from a lack of trust. A lack of trust happens when there is not enough information for someone to formulate a positive or negative expectation of another entity. Distrust, on the other hand, indicates an explicit expectation of harm or other undesirable outcome. Distrust can emerge from similar sources as trust, just their opposites (see *Trust ecology* below). It is also commonly associated with identity threat, as discussed in *5.1 Identity Theory* and *5.2 Self-Affirmation Theory*. Though distrust can often be damaging, small degrees of it can

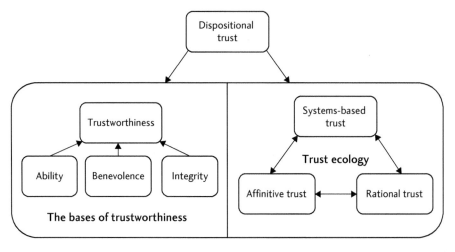

Figure 6.1 The bases of trustworthiness and trust ecology. *Predispositions (dispositional trust) will influence both.*

promote active deliberation and engagement. People who have some level of distrust are often those most likely to show up to a public meeting, for example.[6]

Trustworthiness is a perceived set of characteristics of a person, group, or thing. Theories of trustworthiness primarily provide lessons on how to be a trustworthy person or organization. Theories of trust, on the other hand, provide broader insights that go beyond how we should comport ourselves toward how we might structure a negotiation, collaboration, or other interaction to achieve positive outcomes. Two theories shared below (*The bases of trustworthiness* and *Trust ecology*) provide the broadest views of each, summarizing a tremendous body of literature that spans multiple disciplines (Figure 6.1). A third theory about *trust repair* specifically addresses how to go about restoring trust after it has been lost.

The bases of trustworthiness

Trustworthiness is most commonly theorized in consideration of an individual person, a group of people, or an organization as the "trustee." It is based on trustors' perceptions of the ability, benevolence, and integrity of the trustee.

Ability: The trustors' perceptions about the competence of the trustee to carry out expected actions that result in expected outcomes.

Benevolence: The trustors' perceptions that the trustee holds good will toward them.

Integrity: The consistency with which the trustee adheres to an acceptable set of principles or values.

Trustees appear most trustworthy when they consistently perform in a way that is seen as beneficial to the trustor, follow through on their promises, demonstrate competence in their work, treat people well and with respect, and act in a way that reflects a clear and consistent code of ethics or values.

Trust ecology

Trust ecology applies to group situations and accounts more directly for contextual influences as well as interpersonal interactions and pre-existing tendencies of trustors. Peoples' reasons for trusting (and potentially acting on that trust) in these situations can be classified into four categories: dispositional, rational, affinitive, and systems-based.

Dispositional trust: A general pre-disposition to trust or not to trust in a given situation. Dispositional trust is based on the past experiences and culture of the trustor, which result in a tendency to be trusting or distrusting of other entities in general. Dispositional trust sets the baseline from which other forms of trust emerge or are eroded.

Rational trust: Rational trust is based upon trustors' evaluations about what they believe will be the likely outcomes of potential trustees' likely actions. As such, it is grounded in perceptions of competence, predictability, past performance, and perceived alignment of goals between the trustor and trustee. If I can confidently predict that your behavior will benefit me, I can develop rational trust in you.

Affinitive trust: Affinitive trust emerges from an affinity for the trustee, rather than any specific prediction of a behavior and associated outcome. It may come about through feelings of social connectedness, positive shared experiences, demonstrations of genuine caring or active listening, perceptions of shared identities, or assumptions of similar values. The more I like you personally, the more likely I am to trust you.

Systems-based, or procedural, trust: Trust in a system or set of procedures or rules, rather than trust in an individual or organization. Where procedures are jointly agreed upon as fair, participants can place greater faith in the compliance of others, thus reducing their own risk. This can allow for other types of trust to develop more easily.

Dispositional trust is relatively stable, changing slowly, if at all, over long periods of time. The other three forms of trust are fluid and can change more quickly through the individual and joint actions of both trustors and trustees.

Any management system or collaborative effort can be successful in the short term based on any one of these forms of trust. However, long-term collaboration likely requires adequate stores of each of the "actionable" forms of trust above: rational, affinitive, *and* systems-based. As challenges arise that may threaten or eliminate one form of trust, other forms may buffer the system while the lost form of trust is rebuilt. For example, if we have high levels of affinitive trust, I am more likely to forgive a performance failure. If our system (policies, laws, or other broader contextual factors) changes, we can rely on interpersonal forms of trust to maintain our working relationships while we adjust or rebuild the system.

Trust diversity may enhance both the efficacy and resilience of any sustainability initiative, collaborative effort, or natural resource management institution up to a certain point. However, an overabundance of trust can breed complacency and/or disengagement. For example, if I completely trust the management authority on all fronts, why would I even show up to the meeting? Small degrees of skepticism can be beneficial to maintain active participation and deliberation.[7]

Trust repair

Following any trust violation, people tend to pay more heed to negative evidence that reinforces their distrust rather than positive evidence that might rebuild trust. Trust repair efforts must thus overcome salient negative expectations while simultaneously aiming to restore (or create) positive expectations about future trustworthiness. Gillespie and Dietz (2009) refer to these efforts as *distrust regulation* and *trustworthiness demonstration*, respectively.

Distrust regulation involves efforts aimed to prevent future trust failure, such as instituting new regulations, rules, contracts, monitoring processes, or other controls. If these controls are implemented voluntarily or are self-induced, they typically function better for restoring trust than if they are externally imposed.

Trustworthiness demonstration incorporates both affinitive and rational elements. Suggested efforts at rebuilding affinitive trust include acknowledgment of responsibility, expressions of regret, voluntary penance, and offers of reparations. Efforts at rebuilding rational trust involve setting up opportunities for rapid displays of competence.

Research suggests that failures in performance (rational trust failures) may be best addressed through trustworthiness demonstration—apology and rapid displays of competence. Affinitive trust failures, such as integrity breaches (inconsistency between professed values and actions) or relationship breaches, call for greater efforts at distrust regulation. Individuals tend to weigh positive information more heavily when evaluating performance (rational assessments) and negative information more heavily when evaluating the repair of affinitive (or integrity-related) violations.

Cross-cultural dimensions

Different people may rely more on different types of trust assessments (rational vs affinitive, for example) than others. Similarly, different situations (for example, a business transaction vs a friendly conversation at a party) might pre-dispose certain people toward elevating different bases for trust over others. Research on these situational effects is still in its infancy. However, some general trends across cultures have been observed. For example, trust may commonly emerge from different bases in collectivist vs individualistic societies. Collectivist societies, particularly common in Asia, value group goals and achievement above individual needs and desires, whereas individualistic societies, such as the United States of America and other highly developed Western nations, place high value on individual freedom and independence, emphasize personal achievement, and are accustomed to competition. In individualist societies, individual performance, prestige, and personal relationships are typically highly important to generating trust. In collectivist societies, trust is often related to fulfilling expected roles, identities, duties, and obligations associated with specific situations.

In each case, differing cultural norms dictate that different specific practices might be key to building or eroding trust. Moreover, different sets of procedures or systems will likely influence feelings of risk differently for people from different cultures. In short, while the four forms of trust summarized by *trust ecology* are likely relevant to interactions in all societies, they will be influenced by different specific practices in each. See *5.7 Meyer's Culture Map* for additional guidance.

Applications

When to use it

- In virtually any communication effort, trust in the communicator can be critically important.
- In understanding observed behaviors.
- In designing work teams, work processes, collaborative structures, negotiations, and public involvement processes.
- In communications following any form of crisis or mistake (trust repair).

How to use it: general communications

- Trustworthiness is difficult to fake. As such, consistent demonstrations of ability (competence), integrity (adhering to specific values or principles), and benevolence (caring and responsiveness) are helpful.
- Be honest.
- Don't make promises that you are unsure you can keep.
- Affinitive trust is often the most elusive in new or stressful situations. A few key strategies include:[8]
  - Expressing appreciation for someone else's ideas, even when you disagree— for example, finding merit in and expressing understanding and appreciation of someone else's reasoning, concerns, or efforts.
  - Establishing commonalities with another person—for example, calling attention to shared roles, experiences, or memberships based on common age, rank in an organization, family status, personal history, or pastime through informal conversation.
  - Working to understand the other person's core interests by asking for clarification and resisting the urge to express quick judgment. See *6.2 Principled Negotiation.*
- In formal settings, shifting blame or responsibility can weaken trust. Communicators who try to hide behind their organizations, or absolve themselves of responsibility by claiming ignorance about actual decision-making processes, may be opening the way for dubious speculation and conspiracy theory. Transparent processes, on the other hand, in which decision-making procedures are made clear, tend to engender higher levels of trust in both individuals and organizations.[9]
- More specific techniques that may build trust in one culture may not be helpful in others (see *5.7 Meyer's Culture Map).* Rather, the broader themes of *trust ecology* likely transcend most cultural barriers. Considering context-specific ways to build each should always be helpful.

How to use it: understanding behavior

- Consider each of the key trust forms (dispositional, rational, affinitive, and systems-based) to understand why or why not certain behaviors may be taking place. In particular, is there any form that is missing? Is there any type in which *distrust* exists? If so, what might be some contextually appropriate ways for building those trust forms?

How to use it: designing constructive interactions

Collaborative environments need healthy stocks of each form of actionable trust to persist:

- Rational trust is typically built by demonstrations of competence in mutually beneficial actions. Creating opportunities for quick demonstrations of competence by all parties can foment rational trust. This involves developing quick, achievable tasks aligned with the capabilities of each entity that enable early successes to be celebrated.

- Affinitive trust is typically developed through positive social interactions, active listening, and responsiveness to the concerns of others. Setting up respectful ground rules for communication and creating opportunities for participants to recognize common ground through shared experiences can help engender affinitive trust. This common ground need not be directly related to the issue(s) at hand within the collaborative effort (though this is certainly helpful). Catalyzing informal social interactions through field trips or other activities can often enable the development of affinitive relationships, as can sharing personal stories.

- Systems-based trust commonly relies on perceptions of fair, transparent, and consistent application of procedures and rules, particularly regarding group membership and decision making. Joint development and/or revision of such procedures can further enhance their legitimacy. Jointly establishing shared criteria that can be used by the group to evaluate the appropriateness of potential decisions can also enhance systems-based trust (see also *6.2 Principled Negotiation*). "Joint" procedures refer to those that are co-created by all parties involved, such that clear collective ownership of the rules is established.

- In cases where dispositional trust is low at the outset, establishing systems-based trust through joint procedural development and other means can pave the way for other forms of trust to develop.

- Overall, trust relies on reducing perceptions of risk. Different situations may call for different means for reducing these perceptions and creating safe spaces for deliberation. Perceptions of risk can also often be associated with identity threats. See *5.1 Identity Theory* and *5.2 Self-Affirmation Theory*.

- Developing specific procedures for addressing common challenges to trust, such as turnover of key personnel or values conflicts, can further enhance systems-based trust.

- Often, the use of a third-party facilitator can enhance and maintain levels of trust necessary for networks to collaborate.[10]

- Sometimes, representatives of government agencies or other organizations choose to shift responsibility for unpopular stances to their superiors or their organization's policies or to claim their own ignorance of how decisions will actually get made above their station. In effect, this sacrifices systems-based and organizational trust in the hopes of maintaining interpersonal trust or simply just avoiding uncomfortable conversations. Being transparent about upward accountabilities can be helpful for generating trust. Hiding behind them, however, can frustrate other parties and foment distrust and dissatisfaction in the collaborative process.[11] The participation of empowered decision makers can thus be critical to successful collaboration, as can making decision-making criteria and processes known.

How to use it: trust repair

- Acknowledge, take responsibility, and apologize for mistakes early.
- Voluntarily develop new regulations, rules, contracts, monitoring processes, and/or controls to prevent a recurrence of the mistake. This is particularly important in the case of affinitive or integrity-based failures (e.g., being caught lying, betraying a partner).
- Create opportunities to demonstrate competence, particularly regarding reparations relevant to the mistake. This is particularly important in the case of performance-based failures (e.g., failing to achieve expected goals, unexpected outcomes, or mistakes in production or delivery).
- For example, when Volkswagen was caught cheating on emissions tests in 2015, its best course of action was to publicly accept responsibility for the violation, apologize, self-impose stringent ongoing external monitoring of its plants to avoid future violations, quickly and effectively recall its vehicles, fix the problem, and compensate its clients.

Key references

Gillespie, N., and G. Dietz 2009. Trust repair after an organization-level failure. *Academy of Management Review* 34(1): 127–45.

Mayer, R.C., J.H. Davis, and F.D. Schoorman 1995. An integrative model of organizational trust. *Academy of Management Review* 20(3): 709–34.

Stern, M.J., and T.D. Baird 2015. Trust ecology and the resilience of natural resource management institutions. *Ecology & Society* 20(2): 14.

Stern, M. J., and K. J. Coleman 2015. The multi-dimensionality of trust: applications in collaborative natural resource management. *Society and Natural Resources* 28(2): 117–32.

6.2 Principled Negotiation

Uses: Negotiation, persuasive communication, collaborative processes

How can we better facilitate agreement between parties who want different things?

When opposing parties seem to have already made up their minds regarding how a problem should be resolved, we may often wonder why we showed up to the conversation in the first place. How we can break stalemates and use our interactions with others to improve decision making, rather than arriving at suboptimal compromises or clear winner–loser situations?

Principled Negotiation was developed by the Harvard Negotiation Project and introduced to the world in the book, *Getting to Yes: Negotiating Agreement without Giving In*. The book was developed as a reaction to the shortcomings of positional bargaining, which involves each party making a specific demand followed by subsequent arguments and concessions. This type of bargaining is typically inefficient, ignores the underlying concerns, or "interests," of each party, and may damage the relationships of the people involved.

Principled Negotiation, an alternative to positional bargaining, is based on four primary principles:

1. *Separate people from the problem.* Every negotiation involves both the substance of the problem and the relationship of the negotiators. Each needs attention.

2. *Focus on interests rather than positions.* Put simply, your position is a specific solution or action you've decided upon. Your interests are what caused you to decide. Positional bargaining typically leads to suboptimal compromises, as it focuses on pre-determined courses of action. As a result, negotiations create winners and losers and curtail creativity that might emerge if the focus were on the underlying interests of each side rather than their stated positions.

3. *Generate options for mutual gain.* By focusing on underlying interests, rather than positions, common ground is typically easier to find. Each side's interests may be addressed through multiple potential pathways. This makes win–win solutions possible.

4. *Develop shared criteria to evaluate outcomes.* In simple negotiations, this might mean examining external reference points for a fair price or market value. In environmental negotiations, developing shared criteria typically involves

identifying the underlying interests of each side. If parties can share their most important concerns, discussion about appropriate criteria for evaluating potential courses of action becomes possible. If these criteria can be agreed upon, making decisions about the best paths forward for all involved becomes easier, as the likely outcomes of each path can be judged against a common set of standards.

Applications

When to use it

In any effort that involves multiple parties with different beliefs about what should be done.

Principled Negotiation assumes that the parties can agree on what the problem actually is and are willing consider the interests of the other side(s) involved in the debate or negotiation. Thus, to make the theory useful, it needs to be preceded (or accompanied) by clear problem definition in which parties agree on the content and scope of the problem at hand. It also requires all parties to agree to its general principles.

How to use it: separating people from the problem

Positional bargaining often trades substance for relationships, and vice versa, as people sometimes agree to a suboptimal outcome to maintain a relationship or choose to damage a relationship in order to "win" an argument. Separating people from the problem involves disentangling the substance of the negotiation from the relationship, such that both can be treated appropriately. If negotiators can see themselves as partners rather than adversaries, their chances of achieving mutually beneficial solutions increase. Guidance for doing so includes:

- *Try to see the situation from your counterparts' perspective*. Many of the theories in this book can help us to envision the world from someone else's point of view. Who are their most important reference groups? To whom do they feel most accountable? What components of their identities do they hold most dear? What triggers threats to these? How might their frames differ from mine? What moral foundations are most salient to them? What are the costs and benefits to them of different potential outcomes? Consideration of these questions can help us to better understand our counterparts' points of view and provide us with meaningful conversation starters to understand underlying interests. Open and honest discussion of each side's perceptions can uncover opportunities for producing feasible concessions and goodwill.

- ***Don't assume others' intentions based on your fears.*** Overly defensive or suspicious attitudes tend to preclude gaining an accurate perception of your counterparts' real intentions.
- ***Don't blame others for your problem.*** Even if blame is justified, it is usually counterproductive, as it tends to provoke defensiveness and/or counterattacks rather than productive dialogue.
- ***Seek opportunities to act inconsistently with others' misperceptions.*** This might involve acknowledging the merits of their arguments, displaying empathy, or sharing an unexpected area of agreement.
- ***Don't discount the importance of saving face.*** All parties need to be able to reconcile an agreement with their principles and self-image. This is often related to their accountability to their home organizations or the people they represent. Plan carefully to avoid compromising the integrity of your counterparts.
- ***Acknowledge emotions as legitimate and make them explicit if possible.*** Sometimes, laying emotions on the table can clear the way for productive discussions. The *Getting to Yes* authors (Fisher et al. 1991, p. 30) suggest that it might be helpful and proactive to say something like, "You know, the people on our side feel we have been mistreated and are very upset. We're afraid an agreement will not be kept even if one is reached. Rational or not, that is our concern. Personally, I think we may be wrong in fearing this, but that's a feeling others have. Do the people on your side feel the same way?"
- ***Allow the other side to vent.*** Airing grievances might be necessary for some. Allowing space for this can be helpful, as long as you don't respond defensively. Sometimes, including a specific space within a discussion explicitly for letting off steam with no response allowed from the other side can allow for the release of tensions prior to continuing conversation. A simple acknowledgment, and even better, an apology where appropriate or a gesture of empathy can go a long way.
- ***Practice active listening.*** Give the speaker your full attention. Occasionally summarize their points to confirm your understanding. Doing so in the form of a question is typically less confrontational and can ensure more accurate understanding.
- ***Orient discussions to feel shoulder-to-shoulder, rather than face-to-face.*** Talk about your concerns and the substance of the problem. Use "I" or "we" rather than "you" whenever possible. Talk as if you are partners trying to solve a problem, rather than adversaries trying to defeat each other.
- ***Build a relationship before the negotiation.*** See *6.1 Trust Theory*.

- *Make sure all relevant parties are involved in the negotiation.* Even in the case of a favorable agreement, excluded parties may look upon it skeptically if they haven't been involved in the negotiations.

How to use it: focusing on interests rather than positions

Positions are what we assert we want as outcomes. Interests, on the other hand, are the reasons that lie underneath our desires associated with a particular position. For example, environmental advocates may be opposed to the construction of a new paved road in a National Park. Meanwhile, local people may be in favor of its construction. These are their positions. The environmental advocates may argue that the road will cause irreparable environmental damage and impair backcountry recreation. Local people may argue that the road will provide greater recreational access as well as economic benefits to the local area from tourism. They may also argue that their side of the park lacks the tourism benefits of the other side, as there is no direct access into the park from here, and that the sacrifices their ancestors made for the park to be created have gone unrecognized. Underlying interests in a case such as this might include environmental protection and the preservation of backcountry experiences for environmental advocates, and economic benefits, cultural recognition, and increased access to recreation for local people. If they hope to benefit from the National Park, environmental protection is also likely of high interest to local people. Here, we can see that moving away from entrenched positions (road vs no road) toward underlying interests can reveal various solutions that would not otherwise come to light. For example, a cultural heritage-focused visitor center near the local community might be agreeable to all parties. Other forms of access, such as a boat launch across the local lake or expanded, but regulated, access on pre-existing unpaved National Park roads, might also be a reasonable option.[12]

In cases that don't move beyond positional bargaining, people often take extreme positions that are designed to counter their opponents' positions. This can often create stalemates and ill will, as each side tries every strategy imaginable to "win." In some cases, this can cause such antipathy between parties that new unproductive interests emerge, such as beating the other side. Even then, it may be possible to reframe interests like revenge and anger more productively, often as desires for acknowledgment and respect. In this way, the search for mutually gainful solutions can potentially resume if relationships can be repaired over time.

A more complete understanding of each other's interests can enable a search for win–win solutions and can help to define potential criteria that can be used jointly to evaluate potential pathways forward. To uncover interests, ask why your counterparts hold the positions they do. Why don't they hold some other alternative position? Ask yourself the same question. What do you really care about and why do you care about it? This can help each side to identify and describe their interests more clearly. Each should explain their interests completely and acknowledge the interests of the other side as legitimate, focusing on possible solutions rather than on assigning blame.

How to use it: generating options for mutual gains

We are often prone to premature judgment, searching for a single best answer, assuming that a win for one party means a loss for another (zero sum game), or focusing too intently on our own concerns rather than the concerns of another—leaving it up to them to modify a solution to fit their own interests. Each of these tendencies lessens the likelihood of finding a win–win solution. Some key principles for enhancing that likelihood follow.

1. Separate the act of identifying options from deciding upon which is the best. Tips for brainstorming potential options include:
   - Defining a clear purpose for the brainstorming session.
   - Breaking into smaller groups if your initial group is large—between five and eight people seems to be near ideal.
   - Consider brainstorming with the other side—while risk may be higher, the benefits to relationships and the resulting broadening of possible ideas may be worth it.
   - Change the environment—distinguish brainstorming sessions as much as possible from regular discussions. Go outside. Take a walk. Design an informal atmosphere where people can relax. See also *6.4 The Reasonable Person Model*.
   - Choose a facilitator who keeps the meeting on track, enforces agreed upon ground rules, stimulates conversation by asking questions, ensures everyone gets a chance to speak, and manages the overall flow of the session.
   - Consider seating people side-by-side facing the problem (flip chart or screen), instead of facing each other. This can focus participants more on the substance rather than interpersonal conflicts.
   - Jointly develop ground rules; include a no-criticism rule. That is, in the idea-generating phase, no ideas should be criticized yet.
   - Record ideas in full view of participants.
   - After brainstorming, mark the ideas the group feels have greatest promise.
   - Discuss potential improvements for the most promising ideas.
   - Set up a time to evaluate the ideas and decide on a path forward.

2. Broaden the options on the table rather than looking for a single solution:
   - Consider and discuss different ways of defining the problem.
   - Consider how people in different roles would view the problem and potential options.
   - Consider changes in the pacing or scope of different options as well.
3. Search for mutual gains:
   - Identify shared interests, such as a healthy environment in the road example above.
   - Dovetail differing interests when possible. If one thing is of interest to one party but of little consequence to another, it provides grounds for satisfying both. For example, consider the cultural heritage center in the example above.
4. Make the decision as easy to agree to as possible:
   - Consider the individual(s) who is(are) negotiating for the other side(s). What are their accountabilities? How can you help them save face? See *7.3 Accountability Theory.*

How to use it: developing shared criteria for evaluating outcomes

In sustainability-related negotiations, developing shared objective criteria for evaluating potential options can be tricky, as most pathways involve challenging trade-offs with unknown or vague desired future conditions. For example, imagine that a group can agree that "forest health" is important in an area. Developing shared criteria for assessing impacts on forest health requires agreement on what each party believes makes a healthy forest. This could include ideas as diverse as: maximizing plant and animal diversity, mimicking a desired past condition, maximizing resilience to fire regimes or forest pests or disease, maximizing recreational opportunities of one sort or another, maintaining aesthetic beauty, guaranteeing sustained access and use to the widest array of local users, maximizing carbon sequestration or other ecosystem services like flood control, water capture, or oxygen production, or even ensuring the sustainable yield of timber into the future. Each of these ideas reflects a viable interpretive frame (see *5.6 Frame Theory*) and would be accompanied by a distinct set of judgments about the quality and appropriateness of a potential agreement about forest management. Without first identifying the key interests of stakeholders about the forest in question, developing shared criteria for evaluating options is nearly impossible.

Shared criteria can range widely in terms of metrics and values. For example, natural resource economists have developed complex methods for placing dollar values on nearly everything. Meanwhile, others may focus on environmental measures, such as acres of riparian zone or wildlife habitat restored. The most critical aspect is that all relevant parties agree prior to making a decision on met-rics they can live with.

In the forest health example above, relevant criteria may be rather diverse to reflect all stakeholders' interests, including, for example, sustaining enough habi-tat in perpetuity for critical species, enabling enough economic activity to sustain industry stakeholders and/or local communities, reducing risks of catastrophic wildfire, and protecting enough space for desired recreational activities. If the par-ties can agree on these general principles, all possible pathways forward can be judged appropriately with regard to how they will affect each desired criteria. The more specific the criteria, the easier it is to develop and select mutually agreeable outcomes. Third party facilitation can be particularly valuable in the development of these standards, structuring conversations to reveal the underlying interests of all parties and insisting on agreement of criteria for evaluation before moving forward.

Shared criteria can also be used to assess the perceived fairness of procedures. Similar facilitated discussions can move groups toward agreement on the charac-teristics of fair procedures for debate and decision making. This can foster systems-based, or procedural, trust that can diminish feelings of risk within the negotiation or debate (see *6.1 Trust Theory*).[13]

How to use it: developing a "BATNA"

Not all negotiations result in an agreed upon solution, especially if one party abuses their power and/or refuses to use *Principled Negotiation*. When unequal power dynamics are at play, the weaker party should develop what is known as a "best alternative to a negotiated agreement" (BATNA). This enables the weaker party to establish a bottom line that marks a clear standard by which to turn down proposed solutions that would be worse than their BATNA.

Key reference

Fisher, R., W. Ury, and B. Patton 1991. *Getting to Yes: Negotiating agreement without giving in.* Second Edition. New York: Penguin Books.

6.3 The Co-orientation Model

Uses: Public outreach, communicating across organizations, interest groups, or stakeholders.

> **How can we better understand others' viewpoints such that we can improve our chances of working toward common understandings of problems and collaboration?**

Oftentimes, we may feel misunderstood or unfairly labeled. Similarly, we may often hold assumptions about other entities that are incorrect and preclude our ability to find common ground or work together toward problem solving. If we can correct these misconceptions, we might find more agreement than we expect. Alternatively, we might find that groups we thought shared common values with us actually don't. In each case, there are important implications for what we might do about it.

Co-orientation research is concerned with identifying similarities and differences in the viewpoints of two or more parties and the assumptions each party holds about the other. It can provide powerful insights into conflict resolution, public relations, collaboration, or negotiation.

The Co-orientation Model highlights three different relationships between entities: agreement, congruency, and accuracy (Figure 6.2).

Agreement: The extent to which different groups hold similar values, attitudes, or opinions (and sometimes practices) about an issue relevant to each.

Accuracy: How accurate each group's perceptions are about the values, attitudes, or opinions of the other.

Congruency: A measure of perceived similarity—the extent to which each party's estimate of the other's values, attitudes, or opinions is similar to their own.

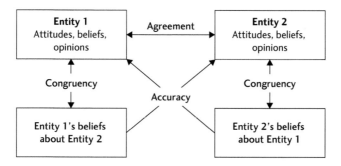

Figure 6.2 Co-orientation analysis. *Adapted from McLeod and Chaffee (1973).*

		Accuracy	
		Low	High
Agreement	Low	False consensus	Dissensus
	High	False conflict	True consensus

Figure 6.3 Potential outcomes of co-orientation analysis.

Four situations may result from co-orientation analyses: ***true consensus, dissensus, false conflict***, and ***false consensus*** (Figure 6.3). True consensus occurs when both agreement and accuracy are high. In other words, the two groups share similar values and are aware of their agreement. Dissensus occurs when there is low agreement and high accuracy; the two parties disagree and recognize that this disagreement exists. There are two false states in which the groups hold inaccurate views of the other's positions on the issue. When agreement is high and accuracy is low, false conflict occurs. In false conflict, the groups actually agree on an issue, but incorrectly believe that they disagree. False consensus occurs when both agreement and accuracy are low; the groups do not agree, but mistakenly believe that they do.

The identification of any of these states can suggest avenues for subsequent communications and actions. These actions often entail efforts to create, enhance, or maintain congruency.

In ***dissensus*** states, stakeholders should engage in understanding the bases for the different evaluations of the situation held by each group. This necessarily involves self-reflection as well as dialogue with the other party (or parties) to discover underlying interests. From here, communications may be reframed to better reflect the underlying interests or moral foundations of the other party, and *6.2 Principled Negotiation* may ensue.

In ***false conflict*** states, strategies for enhancing relationships need to focus on improving congruency. This may involve communication in multiple forms about shared values, including interpersonal exchanges, facilitated dialogue, formal communications through various media, and demonstrations of values in action (making commitments to actions that demonstrate a shared value and following through).

False consensus states can lead to unwanted surprises when disagreement eventually surfaces. If we assume there is agreement, we are likely to move forward with actions based on our own self-interest. This can lead to subsequent conflict that might have been avoided if the false state was identified earlier. Moreover, *false consensus* can obscure opportunities for healthy deliberation of different viewpoints. If we assume we agree, we may be less motivated to deconstruct our strategies and the theories that underlie them, missing opportunities for improving our approaches.

Avoiding *false consensus* requires regular reflection and exchanges between stakeholders. Reflection involves exploring our own assumptions, or *mental models*, associated with a particular problem. Mental models are our personal theories of how something works. They are comprised of our assumptions about the key components of an issue and how those components interact to produce different outcomes. When combined with our perceptions of which outcomes are most desirable, they provide a holistic picture of how we view a particular issue. An explicit consideration of our mental models can unearth underlying assumptions of why we expect x to lead to y and why we feel one potential outcome might be better than another. This can enable us to question our assumptions and to compare our mental models to those of others. The latter requires dialogue and exchanges between stakeholders.

In *true consensus* states, effective deliberation and collaboration are possible. The danger in *true consensus* lies in complacency, in which groups fail to effectively critique their shared assumptions, missing opportunities for improving their efforts.

Applications

When to use it

The Co-orientation Model can be useful whenever two or more parties can be defined as stakeholders in a particular issue. Stakeholders are groups or individuals who can have an effect or be affected meaningfully by the actions under consideration.

How to use it

Oftentimes, *The Co-orientation Model* is used by researchers to investigate relationships between two parties, commonly an organization and its constituents or two organizations or groups. This involves measuring the values or evaluations held by each entity and their perceptions of the other's values in survey research. While such research is often highly revealing of important relationship dynamics, co-orientation analyses need not involve survey research. Rather, co-orientation states can be identified through regular processes of reflection and dialogue between stakeholders.

Reflection should be focused first on examining our own assumptions and mental models regarding the issue at hand. This often involves internal conversations within a group or organization. Concept mapping or logic modeling can often be quite useful. These exercises entail the diagramming of cause and effect relationships between key components of the system involved. They require us to be explicit about our assumptions about why we would expect any particular cause to lead to any specific effect. They can often reveal weaknesses in our own logic as well as opportunities we may not have previously considered. Explicitly listing the assumptions revealed in these exercises can provide a basis for healthy internal reflection as well as dialogue with other stakeholders.[14]

Dialogue, in this sense, can be defined as "a sustained collective inquiry into the processes, assumptions and certainties that comprise everyday activities."[15] In other words, dialogue is not comprised of a series of one-way communications, such as press releases, written comments, or public comment periods. Rather, it involves active interchanges in which stakeholders learn reflectively about the assumptions of other stakeholders. This is often not an easy process, especially when strategic actors perceive high degrees of risk in revealing their motives or desires. See *5.2 Self-Affirmation Theory*, *6.1 Trust Theory*, *6.2 Principled Negotiation*, and *6.4 The Reasonable Person Model* for some advice. The key to identifying and improving co-orientation states involves a focus on revealing and sharing mental models and their underlying assumptions.

Each co-orientation state benefits from reflection (i.e., mental modeling and the surfacing of assumptions) and dialogue, though the process of accomplishing these activities may be somewhat different in each case.

In states of ***dissensus***, mental modeling exercises may be followed by *6.2 Principled Negotiation* techniques to move toward mutually acceptable pathways forward.

In ***false conflict*** states, congruency can be improved by increased dialogue about shared mental models and underlying values, as well as explicit displays of actions that clearly demonstrate shared values. In areas of high perceived conflict, third party facilitators can help to enhance trust in information. See *5.1 Identity Theory*, *5.2 Self-Affirmation Theory*, and *6.1 Trust Theory* for additional advice.

While ***false consensus*** may enable one entity to move forward more rapidly, it can lead to future conflicts that could have been avoided. These states are thus often best treated by identifying the areas of ***dissensus*** and moving through the steps of *6.2 Principled Negotiation* to determine pathways forward.

True consensus states are also benefitted by reflection and dialogue. However, in these states, stakeholders use their mental models primarily to identify areas for improvement in strategies to achieve mutually agreed upon goals.

Key references

Brønn, P.S., and C. Brønn 2003. A reflective stakeholder approach: co-orientation as a basis for communication and learning. *Journal of Communication Management* 7(4): 291–303.

McLeod, J.M., and S.H. Chaffee 1973. Interpersonal approaches to communication research. *American Behavioral Scientist* 16: 469–99.

6.4 The Reasonable Person Model

Uses: Designing public participation, creating optimal environments for volunteers, employees, or other participants in projects

How can we design interactions to suit the needs of participants?

The Reasonable Person Model stresses the importance of people's basic informational needs, positing that people are more likely to be reasonable (and possibly collaborative) in environments that support these needs. These needs are thought to fall within three domains.

Model-building: People use mental models, or "cognitive maps" to make sense of information and to learn. See *6.3 The Co-orientation Model*.[16] Environments that provide (1) enough information for people to build upon pre-existing cognitive maps and (2) opportunities for exploration of new knowledge at their own pace best support people's need for model-building to make sense of new situations (see also *7.5 Nonaka's Theory of Organizational Knowledge Creation*). In practice, this means relating information to what people already know, providing common experiences to which to relate more structured information, and providing sufficient amounts of relevant information such that people can build hypothesized causal linkages in their minds.

Becoming effective: People can best accomplish their goals when they (1) are clear-minded and (2) feel competent. The concept of clear-mindedness draws from *attention restoration theory*.[17] Information can sometimes feel overwhelming. Directed attention, such as that required when listening to a challenging lecture or actively multi-tasking, creates mental fatigue. Restorative experiences replenish that mental fatigue and are relatively effortless. These experiences typically emerge in settings that are fascinating or compelling, such as beautiful or unique nature settings, and that represent a departure from the setting of directed attention. Restorative experiences are thought to renew one's ability to resume directed attention. *Feeling competent* involves knowing how to do things, knowing how things work in the specific domain in which one wants to make an influence, and understanding what is possible within that domain. When people are clear-minded and feel competent, they are empowered to be at their most effective.

Meaningful action: People want to know they can make a real difference. This generally involves both having an opportunity to create consequential positive change and feeling heard and respected. These feelings can create a sense of empowerment and reduce feelings of helplessness.

Applications

When to use it

- *The Reasonable Person Model* can be particularly useful in establishing structures, conditions, or processes for groups, teams, or individuals to accomplish tasks.
- It can also be useful in public involvement processes or other forms of community engagement. However, this theory alone is insufficient to address situations of long-standing or heated conflict. In those situations, *6.1 Trust Theory*, *6.2 Principled Negotiation*, and identity-based theories are likely to provide more complete guidance.
- *The Reasonable Person Model* is not particularly useful for persuasive communication. Information provision and well-structured processes alone will rarely effect changes in attitudes. Rather, see Table 3.1 for persuasive communication theories.

How to use it

- Structure activities such that participants (or team members) have freedom to learn and explore at their own pace.
- Consider developing specific experiences that provide necessary background knowledge to participants. The experiences should supplement other forms of knowledge provision and may come with the additional potential benefit of creating common understanding and shared knowledge amongst participants.
- Build in time and opportunities for restorative experiences. These may take many different forms, depending upon the interests of participants, ranging from quiet time in nature settings to fun group activities that provide a break in the need for directed attention. Don't always just push through when attention or patience is clearly waning.
- Provide both subject-related knowledge and procedural knowledge to enhance both model-building and perceptions of competence. If participants understand how decisions are made and the processes through which those decisions can be implemented, they not only can build a more coherent model of what is possible, but also feel more competent in their ability to effect change. See also the concept of procedural, or systems-based trust, within *6.1 Trust Theory*.

• Ensure that participants (or team members) understand what will happen with their input and provide evidence that their voices have been heard through specific responses to suggestions.

Key reference

Kaplan, S., and R. Kaplan 2009. Creating a larger role for environmental psychology: The reasonable person model as an integrative framework. *Journal of Environmental Psychology* 29: 329–39.

Organizational theories

Introduction: Considering organizational learning and effectiveness from multiple angles

Addressing organizational theory in a book like this is complicated by multiple factors. First, readers will find themselves in different positions relevant to organizations, ranging from the boss to middle managers to employees further down organizational hierarchies. Some readers may work outside of organizations entirely. Organizational theories can look quite different from different points of view. Second, the variety of types of organizations is truly staggering. Some of the simplest distinctions include those between for profit companies, non profit organizations, and government agencies; between large, medium-sized, and small organizations; and between those with formal hierarchical structures and those with less formal and horizontal structures. The theories in this chapter apply broadly to these various structures and can be useful from many vantage points.

Given the challenging nature of addressing issues associated with environmental sustainability, my selection and treatment of organizational theories in this book take collaboration and innovation as implicit goals of performance. In other words, this chapter is heavily geared toward organizational learning, innovation, and adaptation. The theories here directly address questions of accountability, leadership, appropriate levels of worker discretion, monitoring and evaluation, and performance. They thus provide insights into organizational effectiveness and the well-known principal/agent problem, which spans multiple disciplines.[1] In organizational theory, this problem arises from the common circumstance in which workers, or "agents," don't always act in accordance with the best interest of their organizations, or "principals."

I urge you to read these theories first and foremost based on the position you currently occupy within your organizational structure (or outside of one), regularly asking how each theory applies to your own set of challenges, responsibilities,

Social Science Theory for Environmental Sustainability: A Practical Guide. Marc J. Stern, Oxford University Press (2018). © Marc J. Stern 2018. DOI 10.1093/oso/9780198793182.001.0001

and relationships. Also, consider each theory from the perspective of your supervisors, other co-workers, and people in other organizations with whom you interact. What are the accountabilities and pressures they face? A better understanding of the multiple perspectives of people occupying different roles can often reveal pathways for improving relationships and performance.

7.1 Herzberg's Motivation–Hygiene Theory

Uses: Developing organizational structures, motivating employees

Which factors best motivate people at work?

In an ideal world, workers would show up every day motivated to perform at their highest level. In the real world, however, motivation ebbs and flows based on numerous factors, including the nature of the tasks we face, how we feel about our place of work and our colleagues, and whatever might be happening in our personal lives. *Herzberg's Motivation–Hygiene Theory* provides insights into which factors, within the control of the organization, are most likely to influence motivation at work.

Herzberg makes a few critical distinctions in how to conceptualize motivation, the factors that influence it, and what to do about them. First, Herzberg distinguishes between ***motivation*** and ***movement***. ***Motivation*** entails intrinsic motivation. Motivated workers work because they want to. ***Movement*** entails extrinsic motivation. Moved workers accomplish tasks because they feel compelled by external rewards or threats. Intrinsically motivated workers tend to outperform moved workers (see also *4.6 Self-Determination Theory*). Moreover, they typically don't need as much *movement*, which Herzberg gracefully defines as "KITAs," or "kicks in the ass." KITAs can include increasing wages, providing additional fringe benefits, fines, admonishments, or more frequent standardized reviews.

Herzberg's research suggests that the factors that motivate people at work are different from the factors that tend to de-motivate them. He termed the de-motivating factors ***hygiene factors***. Hygiene factors are necessary for the basic maintenance (or movement) of an organization, but they are not sufficient for motivating employees in the long term. Rather, if hygiene factors fall below a certain level, they may cause dissatisfaction. ***Motivation factors***, on the other hand, tend to produce greater job satisfaction and motivation. Managers need to pay attention to both hygiene and motivation factors to maximize employee satisfaction and motivation.

Hygiene factors: If these factors fall below a certain level, dissatisfaction settles in. They may also provide short-term motivation (KITAs).

- Company policies, relationships with supervisors, working conditions, pay, relationships with peers, relationships with subordinates, status, and security.

Motivation factors: These factors generate satisfaction. They are associated with longer-term motivation.

- Achievement, recognition, the nature of the work itself (meaningfulness and challenge), responsibility, advancement, personal growth.

These factors are well-aligned with both *Self-Determination Theory* and *Maslow's Hierarchy of Needs*. Hygiene factors are primarily concerned with the work environment and lower levels of Maslow's Hierarchy. Meanwhile, motivation factors are concerned primarily with the nature of the work itself and higher levels of Maslow's Hierarchy (esteem, self-actualization). As Herzberg's theory has been tested, studies suggest that social elements, in particular relationships to co-workers,[2] might play either role (hygiene or motivator) depending on the individual and the situation. These factors occupy the middle levels of *Maslow's Hierarchy of Needs* (love/belonging) and reflect *Self-Determination Theory*'s emphasis on relatedness.

The third important distinction that Herzberg makes involves what to do with this knowledge. Herzberg distinguishes job enrichment from job enlargement. *Job enrichment* involves vertical job restructuring, in which employees are provided with opportunities for greater responsibility, achievement, recognition, and personal growth. *Job enlargement* simply increases the number of tasks, providing variety without achieving these outcomes (Table 7.1). Job enrichment has high potential to enhance motivation; job enlargement typically does not have long-term impacts on intrinsic motivation.

Table 7.1 *Examples of job enrichment vs job enlargement.*

Examples of job enrichment	Examples of job enlargement
• Removing some oversight (while still retaining accountability for outcomes).	• Providing variety in mundane tasks—for example, rotating assignments.
• Giving people responsibility for more complete projects, rather than assigning them only small pieces of a larger job.	• Challenging an employee by increasing expectations about the amount of work they should be able to do or outputs they should be expected to create.
• Granting additional autonomy to employees.	• Adding additional meaningless tasks.
• Encouraging creative problem solving and providing avenues for upward communication and broader dissemination of these ideas.	
• Demonstrating employees' impacts on larger projects through increased communication about their contributions.	
• Encouraging employees to take on new tasks and to become experts in specific tasks they enjoy.	

Table 7.2 *Ideas for addressing hygiene and motivation factors for motivating employees.*

Addressing hygiene factors	Addressing motivation factors
• Limit over-burdensome reporting requirements to the extent possible. • Ensure that wages are competitive. • Provide opportunities for positive social interaction among staff. • Create a culture of respect for all team members by establishing core values for interactions. • Ensure safety and security. • Consider work–life balance issues, providing adequate flexibility whenever possible for addressing personal, family, or health issues. • Create a pleasant physical environment for work interactions whenever possible. • Establish processes for constructive evaluations and feedback in both directions (upward from employee to supervisors and downward from supervisors to employees).	• Be realistic in balancing commitments with available, energy, time, and resources within an organization. This typically entails thoughtful prioritization processes, such that tasks are achievable and staff are not spread too thin. • Ensure the necessary training, time and resources to accomplish meaningful goals. • Redistribute commonplace tasks, such that each employee has an acceptable (ideally high) ratio of interesting work to mundane work. • Build consensus around the importance of the organizational mission, critical tasks, and goals of teams. • Set challenging but realistic goals to build a sense of accomplishment. • Provide positive feedback that demonstrates how employee performance has contributed toward larger goals. • Match employees to tasks they enjoy and that match their skills. • Provide opportunities for personal growth through professional development. • Encourage adaptation and innovation geared toward achieving agreed upon goals. • Enhance autonomy by encouraging creativity and experimentation in improving ways to get work done. • Encourage employees to document and share their learning in performing their work. Provide venues for celebrating such learning and disseminating it within the organization. • Share decision-making responsibility whenever possible. • Provide opportunities for promotion. • Maintain good communications between levels within an organization. Adopt good ideas from wherever they arise and acknowledge their source. • Celebrate successes and share credit. • See also the examples of "job enrichment" above.

Applications

When to use it

Attending to both hygiene and motivation factors is generally beneficial in nearly any organizational context. These factors may be especially important to work on when organizations face employee burnout, high turnover rates, or declines in morale.

How to use it

While hygiene factors rarely draw people into the field of environmental problem solving, they should never be ignored. Most people are not, however, motivated solely by pay and working conditions—particularly with regard to environmental and sustainability issues. Regularly consider both hygiene and motivation factors in the design of all work processes. Also, recognize that different people will be motivated by different approaches. Table 7.2 provides some ideas for specific actions. However, other approaches might accomplish similar goals in different contexts.

Key reference

Herzberg, F. 1968. One more time: how do you motivate employees? *Harvard Business Review* 46: 53–62.

7.2 Team Effectiveness Theory

Uses: Structuring, motivating, and maintaining teams to enhance effectiveness, learning, innovation, personal satisfaction, and commitment

> What factors most commonly enhance the effectiveness of working teams?

Most work gets done in teams, especially when it comes to dealing with complicated problems that require diverse sets of knowledge and skills. These types of problems can benefit tremendously from the creative products of collaboration and the collective thinking of talented people. However, we've all likely been on teams that don't work for one reason or another. Sometimes teamwork feels painful and seems to lead nowhere. Other times, magic seems to happen. Why? In this section, I synthesize the findings from decades of research on teams to identify the factors that most consistently distinguish successful from unsuccessful teams.

What are teams and how can we understand them?

A team refers to two or more individuals who socially interact to achieve a common goal or goals. Teams may be virtual, in-person, or a mixture of the two. Although no single, concise, and consistent overarching theory has emerged to explain team effectiveness, the field is rich with hundreds of empirical studies spanning decades of research. These studies have been based on dozens of theories and have yielded numerous key principles for enhancing teamwork. I provide a simple overview and share some of the most consistently validated principles here.

The most common framework for evaluating teams examines the qualities and interactions of inputs, processes, emergent states, and outcomes (Figure 7.1).

Inputs: Antecedent factors which influence a team's operations, such as the organizational context, initial goals and task design, and the characteristics of the resources and people assigned to a team at its outset.

Processes: The operations and activities of the team throughout its existence.

Emergent states: Characteristics that develop over time as teams undertake their work, such as intra-team trust, shared mental models, or conflict between teammates.

Outcomes: The observable results of the team's work, usually evaluated in terms of their quality and the extent to which the team's efforts have achieved meaningful goals. These goals typically relate to high quality products, but they may also include less tangible outcomes, such as innovation, team member satisfaction, efficiency, and enhanced relationships with clients or other stakeholders.

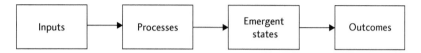

Figure 7.1 A simple model of the drivers of team effectiveness.

These characteristics of teams interact throughout different stages in teams' life cycles, and lessons have emerged that relate to each. I start by summarizing the emergent states that most consistently and directly relate to team outcomes. I then divide teams' life cycles into two main stages to discuss the impacts of specific inputs and processes on key emergent states and outcomes:[3]

1. **Team establishment**, in which teams are created and charged with pursuing specific goals.
2. **Team action processes**, in which team members engage in planning, accomplishing tasks, coordinating actions, managing relationships, and monitoring progress.

Emergent states that influence team effectiveness

Certain emergent states have been identified as particularly important drivers of team outcomes across contexts (Table 7.3). They reflect individual and shared feelings, perceptions, and practices that over time come to constitute team norms.

Team establishment

Teams are strongly influenced by the contexts in which they are created and decisions made about membership and resource allocation. Key questions that have been explored through prior research involve the appropriate degree and types of diversity represented by team members, team size, role clarity for team leaders and team members, and desired team member capacities. Table 7.4 identifies key inputs and processes that affect team performance in the team establishment phase.

Table 7.3 *Key emergent states that consistently influence team outcomes.*

Emergent state	Key lessons
Goal clarity	• Team consensus on clearly defined goals is consistently among the strongest predictors of team effectiveness across multiple contexts.
Commitment	• Stronger commitment to shared goals leads to better outcomes. This commitment is commonly related to perceptions of team cohesion, task meaningfulness, and team identity.
Team identity	• Stronger identification with the team (team members' feelings of investment and membership in the team) promotes more effective cooperation, greater commitment to team goals, and stronger motivation for team performance (see *5.1 Identity Theory*).
Cohesion	• Cohesion refers to feelings of team spirit, belongingness and attachment to the team. It is thus strongly related to team identity and is a consistently strong driver of team effectiveness.
	• Cohesion is typically strongest in teams with a clear purpose shared by all team members, where team members feel supported by each other, and where communication is focused on improvement rather than critique.[4]
	• Cohesion is also typically stronger in teams whose members embody the following personality traits: agreeableness, extraversion, and emotional stability.[5]
Task meaningfulness	• Team members' perceptions that their work is worthwhile and important are consistently linked with enhanced performance. See also *4.6 Self-Determination Theory.*
Intra-team conflict[6]	• ***Task conflict*** involves disagreement among team members about team-related analyses or decision making. It can include debates about how to best get the work done or about the meaning or significance of specific information.
	– When allowed to surface through active and courteous dialogue among team members, task conflict often shows positive relationships with outcomes. When it is openly debated and resolved, task conflict ensures greater attention to detail. Its resolution can also increase satisfaction of team members who feel like they have had a voice in decision making. This, in turn, can enhance their commitment to the work.
	– Task conflict is most beneficial in cases where decisions are made relatively quickly and not drawn out over long periods of time.
	• ***Relationship conflict*** is a perception of personal incompatibility resulting in negative emotions and interactions between team members.
	– Relationship conflict is consistently related to less positive team outcomes. It can distract team members from team tasks, increase anxiety, and inhibit constructive deliberation.

(Continued)

Emergent state	Key lessons
	• Task conflict tends to turn into relationship conflict in contexts of low trust between team members. In low trust conditions, people tend to interpret the actions and arguments of others skeptically, assuming hidden agendas, dubious intentions, or just incompetence. This can create a negative feedback loop. If I feel distrusted by you, I will commonly begin to distrust you in return. Collaborative teamwork can unravel in this way.
Intra-team trust	• Trust between team members can drive collaborative culture on the team, enabling enough psychological safety to facilitate productive deliberation, risk-taking, creativity, and workload sharing. • Trust may emerge from dispositional, rational, affinitive, or procedural sources. See *6.1 Trust Theory* and "How to use it: Managing team relationships and performance" below for more.
Interdependence	• ***Task interdependence***: the extent to which team members are dependent on each other to carry out their tasks. • ***Goal interdependence***: the extent to which team members' goals or rewards are intertwined, such that individual team members can only achieve their goals if other team members achieve theirs. • Goal interdependence has shown more consistently positive relationships with outcomes than task interdependence.[7] • Teams with greater interdependence generally require a greater proportion of team members' time to produce positive outcomes.[8]
Shared mental models	• Mental models are perceptions about how something works (see *6.3 The Co-orientation Model*). Shared mental models among team members about how to approach the team's work are consistently related to more positive team outcomes. • Shared mental models emerge from collaborative goal setting, group deliberation about how to best accomplish shared goals, and knowledge sharing. These processes build shared expectations and understandings.
Transactive memory systems	• Transactive memory systems (TMS) reflect knowledge of who on the team knows what. In other words, how well do all team members understand the talents and knowledge of each other? Teams with better TMS perform better. • TMS can be informal (through the tacit knowledge of team members) or formal (through shared documentation or information management systems—see *7.5 Nonaka's Theory of Organizational Knowledge Creation*). • In teams using either formal or informal systems, higher degrees of face-to-face interaction, familiarity, and shared experience enhance TMS.
Accountability	• Feelings of accountability to teammates and to professional standards have been shown to enhance team effectiveness. Too much pressure from superiors to meet pre-defined targets has been shown to negatively affect team outcomes.[9] See *7.3 Accountability Theory* for more detail.

(Continued)

Table 7.3 (Continued)

Emergent state	Key lessons

Autonomy	• Teams with more autonomy have greater freedom to make decisions, plan work activities, and adapt to changing conditions.
	
	   – For tasks with moderate to high degrees of uncertainty, or when creative problem solving or innovation may be a goal, greater team autonomy is strongly related to improved team performance, given sufficient capacity within the team.
	
	   – For routine tasks, team autonomy is not always ideal, as it makes coordination more difficult and can decrease efficiency.

Reflexivity	• Reflexivity refers to the degree to which a team monitors its progress and adapts. It can emerge formally, through specific procedures, or informally, through a team's norms of communications and interactions. Reflexivity is particularly important to team performance in challenging, uncertain, or changing working conditions.

Table 7.4 *Key inputs and processes during team establishment and their impacts on team outcomes.*

Inputs/ processes	Key lessons
Team member traits	• Socio-demographic diversity (gender, ethnicity, race, etc.) has not shown consistent relationships to the quality of outcomes. • Functional diversity, which refers to variety in the specific skills and technical training of team members, is believed to enhance teamwork for creative tasks, but not always for clearly defined, routine, or repetitive tasks. Increased functional diversity increases the need to focus on team coordination and cohesion. • Key traits of team members on successful teams include: emotional intelligence (the capacity to be aware of, control, and express one's emotions tactfully and judiciously, and the capacity for empathetic communication); functional competence (being good at one's job); willingness to work collaboratively; reliability; and flexibility. These individual traits, when included in studies, often are the most powerful drivers of team outcomes.
Team size	• There is no clear consensus in the literature regarding optimal team size, regardless of the context. In general, smaller teams tend to have greater cohesiveness, greater commitment, and coordination. Larger teams, however, can draw from a wider array of expertise and networks. Most scholars suggest five to nine members as an optimal core team size, and that larger teams should be divided into smaller working sub-units.
Resource allocation	• Sufficient material resources and time allocations are critical for successful team outcomes. This often requires explicit efforts to balance the loads of team members by supervisors, especially on projects with high interdependence or uncertainty. See also *7.4 Project Risk*.

(Continued)

Inputs/ processes	Key lessons
Setting team boundaries	• Clearly defining who is on the team and who is not can aid in the development of stronger team identity and cohesion.
Goal setting	• Setting challenging goals with clear performance expectations leads to better performance than establishing easier goals or being unclear about performance expectations.
	• Team participation in goal-setting can help to enhance team identity and commitment.
Team structures	• **Functional team structures**: Team members are assigned different specializations and focus on their own specific tasks.
	• **Divisional team structures**: Each team member is trained to be able to accomplish all of the team's subtasks.
	• In predictable task environments, functional team structures are generally more efficient.
	• In unpredictable task environments, divisional team structures can perform better. Though few teams in the environmental context are entirely divisional, common understanding of each other's roles and some functional redundancy can contribute to better outcomes.
	• The fit between the team's context and its appropriate structure may need to be monitored and updated over time.
	• Shifting from a functional structure to a divisional structure is easier than shifting from a divisional structure to a functional structure.[10] This is because divisional structures typically fail to prompt the development of advanced coordination skills. As a result, if moving from a divisional to a functional structure is foreseen (as task environments become more predictable), additional training on coordination skills can ease the transition.
Team member roles	• Role clarity is important for all team members.
	• In particular, team leaders should be clearly empowered by their supervisors to act as the clear leader of the team. This enables greater clarity for all team members and establishes clear responsibility for coordination. This can be especially important for ad hoc teams when an employee at the same (or sometimes lower) hierarchical level than others is selected to be a team leader. See *7.6 Leadership Theory*.[11]

Team action processes

The team action phase is dominated by team processes. In Table 7.5, I highlight key lessons from the literature about the impacts of team processes on team effectiveness.

Table 7.5 *Key team action processes and their influences on team outcomes.*

Processes	Key lessons
Leadership (see 7.6 *Leadership Theory* for more detail)	• Team leadership serves many critical functions, including creating an overall vision for the team, overseeing coordination, communication, motivation, conflict resolution, task completion, securing and distributing resources, identifying and diagnosing problems, managing both internal and external relationships, and monitoring and evaluation.
	• Teams with strong leadership consistently outperform teams with weak leadership. When teams are created from horizontal work structures, external supervisors may need to explicitly empower team leaders to direct the activities listed above in the presence of team members.
	• While *shared leadership*, or leadership that is dispersed among team members, can be helpful for subtasks, research suggests that the designation of an overall leader is important to ensure clear responsibility for team performance. Other leaders may emerge to lead specific tasks or portions of a project.
Boundary spanning	• Boundary spanning bridges the team environment with entities outside the team. Boundary spanning activities may be undertaken by both team members and team leaders to gain knowledge and build support for team efforts.
Coordination	• Coordination refers to efforts to organize and/or synchronize the interactions of team members in completing tasks. Teams with high interdependence typically need high levels of coordination, as members are dependent on each other for information, materials, and reciprocal inputs. High levels of coordination mean that team members work more closely together throughout the team's life cycle.
	• High degrees of coordination show positive effects on team performance for tasks that require flexibility or innovation. Low levels tend to be preferable (more efficient) for routine or predictable tasks.
Communication	• Frequent, informal, direct, and open communication among team members enhances team performance. Working separately and later combining work has been shown to be less efficient in contexts with high complexity or uncertainty.[12]
Monitoring	• Creating a system for team members to mutually monitor each other's work and provide non-threatening feedback on ideas, changing contexts, and performance can enable greater reflexivity. Moreover, it can identify needs for back-up or helping behavior and additional coordination.
Evaluation	• Rewards for performance should accrue at both the individual and the team level. Focusing on only the individual can promote opportunistic behavior at the cost of the team. Focusing only on the team can dampen individual performance. Focusing on both enables attention to both overall task achievement and individual contributions.

(Continued)

Processes	Key lessons
Balancing contributions	• Social loafing (or free riding) can occur in teams when members are not held accountable or otherwise lack motivation or ability to complete team work. Setting compelling goals with inherent value, designing smaller teams, enhancing team identity, increasing intra-team coordination and communication, and leadership actions to balance workloads can combat this issue.
Turnover	• While personnel changes may often be necessary, and sometimes desirable,[13] turnover most commonly has a negative influence on team performance. In particular, team cohesion and TMS can be negatively impacted.

Applications

When to use it

Elements of *Team Effectiveness Theory* can be helpful in any situation involving two or more people interacting to solve a common problem or to achieve a common goal.

How to use it

Research findings and associated theory suggest certain actions may enhance team performance. I divide suggestions into specific categories for easy navigation and to aid in trouble-shooting when specific deficiencies might arise.

How to use it: Team establishment

- Is a team necessary?
  - Simple tasks that don't require diverse inputs and are unlikely to generate disagreement amongst stakeholders are often best left to individuals.
- The following team member traits have each been linked to enhanced team effectiveness. Selecting team members with as many of these traits as possible may help to improve a team's chances of success.
  - Emotional intelligence (self-awareness of emotions; ability to communicate tactfully and empathetically).
  - Emotional stability.
  - Functional competence (being good at the tasks associated with the team's work).
  - Willingness to work collaboratively with others.
  - Flexibility.
  - Reliability.

    – Extraversion.

    – Experience working in teams and positive professional or social relationships with other team members.

    – Adequate time allocation for the tasks required, especially in projects that require high degrees of coordination.

- Team structure considerations should include:
  - The clear empowerment of a team leader who is generally well-liked and/or well-respected by team members.
  - Clear designation of who is on the team and who is not. In larger teams, sometimes designating a smaller "core" team can clarify roles and further support identity development and commitment to team tasks in this core group. This can also enable more effective boundary spanning by clarifying the team's assets and deficiencies.
  - Clear roles and performance expectations should be developed, monitored, and regularly updated as needed for all team members.
  - Some functional redundancy (overlap in expertise) can enhance the likelihood of helping behavior, especially in less predictable or more complicated situations.
  - Consider breaking teams larger than ten members into smaller sub-teams.
- Goal-setting:
  - Clearly defined goals for the team are critical, as are performance expectations. Involving team members in defining these team elements can enhance commitment.
  - Leaders should provide a clear explanation of the importance of the team's work to the broader mission or a larger goal.
- Establishing team culture:
  - In general, the more time spent upfront establishing expected norms for performance and communication among team members, the better the team is likely to perform. High performing teams have members who communicate frequently about how to improve team function, task accomplishment, and goal achievement. This often involves asking questions across areas of expertise, which can spur innovation.
  - At the outset, additional time spent developing a shared purpose, shared preliminary mental models, and a team spirit of working together to achieve something perceived by members to be important yields greater team cohesion and performance over time.

How to use it: Training

- Training for team members should address both the requisite skills for technical tasks as well as interpersonal skills for teamwork.

- Explicit communication training of team members on the differences between productive conflict and unproductive conflict can be particularly helpful. Productive conflict involves questioning and deliberation about knowledge, operations, and goals (see also "Separating people from the problem" in *6.2 Principled Negotiation Theory*). Unproductive conflict includes personal accusations and criticisms.
- Research suggests that cross-training, which involves training team members on other members' tasks, roles, and responsibilities, can enhance teamwork in various ways, including increasing the likelihood of the development of shared mental models, helping behavior, and enhanced coordination. Cross-training has been found to be particularly valuable in unpredictable task environments where creativity and flexibility are demanded.

How to use it: Leadership (see also 7.6 Leadership Theory)

- Team leaders coordinate team activities, motivate team members, secure and distribute resources, manage team member relationships, identify and diagnose problems, ensure adequate reflection and adaptive management, and serve as translators and liaisons between the team and external stakeholders, including organizational superiors.
- Research has identified a number of leadership styles that appear to be effective for team leaders. These styles are not mutually exclusive. Many leaders exhibit multiple elements of each.
  - *Transformational leadership* is most strongly and consistently associated with positive team performance. Transformational leaders spend time building a shared vision for the team that aligns organizational tasks with individual interests and values, convincing team members of the importance of their task outcomes, empowering team members to be creative, and leading by example with passion for their work.
  - *Empowering leadership* has also commonly been found to be effective, especially in projects involving the need for flexibility due to uncertainty or changing conditions. Empowering leadership aims to transfer power and responsibility to team members and involves team members in decision making.
  - Elements of *supportive* and *directive leadership* have also shown positive relationships to team effectiveness. Supportive leadership includes demonstrations of respect for team members' ideas, concern for team members' well-being, warmth and friendliness, and efforts to reduce time and task burdens of team members. Elements of directive leadership linked to enhanced team performance include establishing clear goals, tasks, and standards for performance.

How to use it: Boundary spanning

- Important boundary spanning activities of team members include seeking external help when specific knowledge is not held by team members.
- Team leaders may engage in boundary spanning activities to (1) secure financial, material, or knowledge resources; (2) protect team members from demands of other supervisors; (3) scout external networks to identify and diagnose potential problems or opportunities; (4) help to manage competing account-abilities of external stakeholders (see *7.3 Accountability Theory*), (5) manage communications with superiors (see *7.5 Nonaka's Theory of Organizational Knowledge Creation*); and (6) advocate for the team's causes within a wider network, building general support for the team's activities.
- Each of these boundary spanning activities can enhance team performance.

How to use it: Managing team relationships and performance

- Intra-team trust is critical. In an organizational setting, trust may often emerge from the establishment of common goals and agreed upon procedures, which might often require upfront meetings and collaborative planning work to set ground rules and team direction (systems-based trust); displays of, or peer-to-peer communications about, competence and reliability of team members (rational trust); active listening, informal social interactions, team-building exercises, shared positive experiences, and training that enables each team member to understand the tasks and challenges faced by each other (affinitive trust): and general organizational principles and climate that explicitly value and demonstrate trusting relationships between employees (dispositional trust). See *6.1 Trust Theory* for more detail on building trust and *6.2 Principled Negotiation* for ideas about promoting productive task conflict and avoiding unproductive relationship conflict.
- Balancing workloads, both between team members and between team-related tasks and other outside work, can help to maintain a positive work environment and interpersonal relationships on the team.
- Establishing agreed upon monitoring systems to enable collaborative reflection can enhance team coordination and performance. Focusing discussion on task achievement and improvement rather than critiques of individual team members (unless the latter is absolutely necessary) can help to maintain team spirit.
- Team identity can be created, enhanced, and maintained through (a) collab-oratively defining team goals, (b) developing shared mental models through reflexive communications about tasks, coordination, context, and improve-ment, (c) establishing and maintaining interpersonal trust, (d) maintaining perceptions of the importance of the work, and (e) broadly acknowledging and celebrating team work and accomplishments.

- Providing team members with more complete understandings of the roles and constraints of other team members can lead to better outcomes through enhancing communication, coordination, and cohesion, especially in less predictable or more complicated situations.
- Turnover of personnel can be challenging in multiple ways. Teams should consider developing explicit procedures for sustaining transactive memory systems (TMS) and team cohesion when new members replace others. Procedures for introducing new members to established team norms, both formal and informal, and for building trust (see *6.1 Trust Theory*) should also be considered.
- Evaluation and rewards should focus on both individual and team performance. Focusing on only one can hinder performance of the other, leading to overly individualistic behavior or to "free riding" on the team. Celebrating team successes as well as the individual contributions of members can help to avoid these consequences.

Key references

Barczak, G., F. Lask, and J. Mulki 2010. Antecedents of team creativity: an examination of team emotional intelligence, team trust, and collaborative culture. *Creativity and Innovation Management* 19(4): 332–45.

Hoegl, M., and H.G. Gemuenden 2001. Teamwork quality and the success of innovative projects: a theoretical concept and empirical evidence. *Organizational Science* 12(4): 435–49.

Hulsheger, U.R., N. Anderson, and J.F. Salgado 2009. Team-level predictors of innovation at work: a comprehensive meta-analysis spanning three decades of research. *Journal of Applied Psychology* 94(5): 1128–45.

Kozlowski, S.W.J., and D.R. Ilgen 2006. Enhancing the effectiveness of work groups and teams. *Psychological Science in the Public Interest* 7(3): 77–124.

Mathieu, J., M.T. Maynard, T. Rapp, and L. Gilson 2008. Team effectiveness 1997–2007: a review of recent advancements and a glimpse into the future. *Journal of Management* 34(3): 410–76.

Mathieu, J.E., S.I. Tannenbaum, J.S. Donsbach, and G.M. Alliger 2014. A review and integration of team composition models: moving toward a dynamic and temporal framework. *Journal of Management* 40(1): 130–60.

Robbins, S.P., and T.A. Judge 2011. Organizational Behavior. Fourteenth edition. Upper Saddle River, NJ: Prentice Hall.

Sivasubramaniam, N., S.J. Liebowitz, and C.L. Lackman 2012. Determinants of new product development team performance: a meta-analytic review. *Journal of Product Innovation Management* 29(5): 803–20.

Stern, M.J. and S.A. Predmore 2012. The importance of team functioning to natural resource planning outcomes. *Journal of Environmental Management* 106: 30–9.

Stewart, G.L. 2006. A meta-analytic review of relationships between team design features and team performance. *Journal of Management* 32(1): 29–54.

7.3 Accountability Theory

Uses: Organizational management, evaluation, inter-organizational communication, planning, outreach, community engagement

> How can we set ourselves up to better understand and manage competing accountabilities in our work?

Have you ever felt overburdened by onerous reporting requirements? Have you ever struggled with how to meet the demands of different stakeholders? We can often feel pulled in so many directions at once that our most important goals seem out of reach. *Accountability Theory* provides insights into managing these challenges and their associated implications, particularly in an organizational context.

In its most general sense, ***accountability*** refers to an individual, group, or organization being answerable to others for their actions. Ways to achieve accountability are called ***accountability mechanisms***, which can be formal or informal. Formal accountability mechanisms include monitoring, evaluation, reporting, membership requirements, term limits, or voting. Informal mechanisms include feelings generated by relevant norms, including responsibility, fairness, commitment, moral obligation, or general beliefs about right and wrong.[14] Both formal and informal accountability mechanisms can be powerful and can compete with each other.

In their broadest sense, accountabilities can be conceptualized as upward, lateral, downward, and personal. ***Upward accountability*** typically entails formal mechanisms of monitoring and reporting to funders, bosses, or other authorities. ***Lateral accountability*** refers to accountability that doesn't cross clear hierarchical levels or power differentials. It can involve answerability to co-workers or to professional peers outside of one's own organization. ***Downward accountability*** typically refers to answerability to clients or the populations being served by an organization. For example, a conservation worker might feel responsible to answer to a local community in which she is working, an elected official might feel answerable to his constituency, or an engineer might feel responsible to the local population associated with a water project. Downward accountability can also refer to accountability within an organization to one's subordinates. ***Personal accountability*** entails answerability to one's own morality. We may often find ourselves pulled by each of these accountabilities to different degrees in different situations (see Figure 7.2).[15] Tensions may exist within a single box in Figure 7.2 or

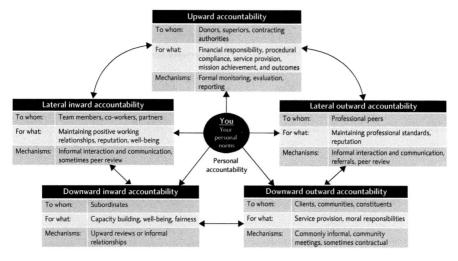

Figure 7.2 Mapping competing accountabilities.

between boxes. For example, multiple entities within a single category may want different things. Meanwhile, balancing upward vs lateral vs downward account-abilities can involve difficult trade-offs.

Competing accountabilities

An overemphasis on addressing any one type of accountability could come at the expense of addressing another. Because upward is where most power is concentrated, upward accountability mechanisms often receive the most attention within an organization. In a for-profit organization, this may involve an emphasis on meeting specific targets, such as sales figures. In non-profit organizations, upward accountability regularly involves reporting to donors. In governmental organizations, upward accountability commonly involves documenting compliance with procedural requirements in addition to meeting specific performance targets.

Over-emphasizing upward accountability has numerous consequences. While procedural requirements are typically created to ensure transparency and high quality work, adhering too strictly to pre-conceived notions limits practitioners' flexibility in the field, which can be critical to getting the job done well in many situations. Over-burdensome reporting requirements may limit the time and re-sources spent on actual mission achievement as well as attention to the rights and desires of other stakeholders.[16] In some cases, employees come to see procedural requirements and reporting as ends (direct goals) of their job rather than as the means by which they can achieve their organizational mission.[17]

Donors, superiors, or contracting authorities typically require information on inputs, processes, and outputs. **Input accountability** involves a careful accounting of the resources, financial or otherwise, spent on a project. **Process accountability** involves how faithfully grantees, contractors, or employees adhere to procedural requirements or a statement of work. **Outputs** are the tangible and countable services or products created or provided (e.g., the number of seeds planted or people reached). **Output accountability** often entails meeting pre-determined targets for such outputs.

Mission achievement, however, is best reflected in **outcomes**, rather than inputs, processes, or outputs. Outcomes are measures of the impacts the outputs create. Outcomes are notoriously more difficult to measure than inputs, procedural compliance, or outputs. While it is easy to count the number of seminars held and the people who attended, it is more difficult to determine the long-term impacts of those engagements. As a result, outcomes are less frequently measured directly.

Those working in the sustainability arena can feel tremendous pull downward from outward constituents as well. Environmental planning processes are often imbued with competing desires of various constituencies that result in conflict and/or legal challenges to planned actions. These challenges, of course, threaten upward accountabilities as well, particularly performance targets set by superiors, conservation goals, or other desires of funding agencies. Recent research suggests that the pull of these competing accountabilities can also lead to the neglect of lateral accountabilities, lowering agency morale and overall performance and causing defensive, rather than collaborative, engagement (see also *7.4 Project Risk*).[18]

In other cases, too much focus on upward accountability has come at the expense of local stakeholders, particularly in international conservation and development work, where donors' desires don't always align with the desires of local people.[19] Insufficient attention to these constituencies can doom projects to failure.[20]

Applications

When to use it

Accountability Theory is relevant in nearly any interaction with more than one relationship involved. In a general sense, accountability can encourage an individual to act in accordance with agreed upon social norms relevant to a situation (see the discussion of accountability in *5.3 Haidt's Social Intuitionist Model of Moral Judgment*).

In an organizational sense, the more complex the network of actors involved and the greater the differences in the real or perceived power of each of those actors, the more important it is to carefully map and consider how to manage competing accountabilities.

How to use it

Creating an accountability map can enable deliberation about the specific obligations and priorities of an individual or organization.

- Create a list of all stakeholders involved and their potential interests in your efforts. **Stakeholders** are entities who might be affected by an initiative as well as those who have the power to influence its outcome. Typical stakeholder analyses entail identification of specific interests, degree of involvement or importance, and relationships between stakeholders.[21]
- Using this list, consider all of the potential accountabilities in Figure 7.2. How might each be addressed sufficiently and efficiently? Including members of each stakeholder group in the conversation can ensure more effective accountability mechanisms (see *6.1 Trust Theory*).[22]

Carefully consider how reporting requirements can affect performance and mission achievement. Is it worth receiving a $500 grant that will require 20 hours of reporting? Can you negotiate with a granting or contracting agency (or your boss) to adjust reporting requirements, such that they enhance your ability to do your work?

While upward accountability mechanisms can promote certain behaviors within an organization, they can also constrain creativity, innovation, and responsiveness to changing conditions on the ground or to the rights and desires of stakeholders. Many practitioners merely adopt a "don't tell" stance when they work outside of standard procedures as a result.[23] This, however, can preclude an opportunity for organizational learning and adaptation.

I was once fortunate enough to be in a meeting with a top executive of Toyota Motor Company. Toyota considers *Kaizen*, which means continuous improvement, one of its core principles. The executive explained it this way, "If you don't have a problem, you have a problem." Within this philosophy, upward accountability can be viewed as an effort to ensure organizational learning rather than an effort in policing the activities of employees, contractors, or grantees. In addition to developing upward accountability mechanisms that ensure transparency and adherence to a set of acceptable moral principles, organizations can develop reporting requirements such that the information collected ensures learning relevant to mission achievement. In this way, all those involved can take a genuine interest in reporting. For example, in one research study, employees loathed spending time painstakingly cataloguing the specific materials donated to refugee families. Meanwhile, they relished weekly qualitative reports about the families' challenges and well-being as opportunities for learning, improving, and tracking their progress toward achieving their organizational mission.[24] Orienting reporting requirements toward demonstrating learning rather than pre-determined static outputs can make evaluation and upward reporting more enjoyable, meaningful, and useful, and diminish apathy, fear, and insecurity (see also *8.4 Collective Impact*).

Focusing reporting requirements on outcomes (in addition to learning), as opposed to inputs, processes, and outputs should also enhance mission achievement. For example, counting pounds of trash removed from a wetland (an output) may be meaningless if the trash continues to accumulate after the clean-up. The most effective measure in a case like this might be the community's long-term commitment to work on the problem. After all, what happens when a hurricane comes and undoes all the good work of the clean-up? Select only those inputs, processes, and outputs that are necessary to (1) understand the achievement of outcomes (or lack thereof), (2) ensure due diligence and ethical use of resources, and (3) generate learning about what is working well and what is not. This may often entail somewhat less detail at these levels, freeing up time for group reflection and qualitative discussions relevant to enhancing mission achievement and stakeholder satisfaction.

In organizational contexts with high levels of agreement on organizational goals and high staff capacity, greater discretion and flexibility can lead to better outcomes. This is especially the case when explicit efforts to consider appropriate degrees of accountability to all stakeholders have been undertaken and agreed upon collectively. In conditions of low agreement, low commitment to shared goals, or low capacity, additional accountability mechanisms may be warranted (see *7.4 Project Risk* and *7.6 Leadership Theory*).[25]

Key references

Bovens, M., R.E. Goodin, and T. Shillemans (eds.) 2014. *The Oxford handbook of public accountability*. Oxford, UK: Oxford University Press.

Stern, M.J., S.A. Predmore, M.J. Mortimer, and D. Seesholtz 2010. From the office to the field: Areas of consensus and tension in the implementation of the National Environmental Policy Act within the U.S. Forest Service. *Journal of Environmental Management* 91(6): 1350–6.

Tenbensel, T., J. Dwyer, and J. Lavoie 2013. How not to kill the golden goose: Reconceptualizing accountability environments of third-sector organizations. *Public Management Review* 16(7): 925–44.

7.4 Project Risk

Uses: Organizational management, planning, teamwork

What are the key sources of risk to a project and what can we do about them?

Planning and implementing environmental or sustainability-related projects is no easy task. While we may aim to bring people together to enhance environmental health and human well-being, lots of things can go wrong. Many well-intentioned projects have resulted in negative impacts to people or the environment, public protest and other forms of conflict, or just plain failure to effect change or successfully disseminate an idea. These failures can have long-lasting impacts not only on the environment or people they intended to serve, but also on those who attempted to implement them. Understanding the primary sources of *Project Risk* and planning with them in mind can help to lessen the likelihood of project failure.

Risk has two key components: (1) the probability of something undesirable happening (likelihood) and (2) how bad the resulting outcome would likely be (severity). *Project Risk* considers these elements with regard to specific projects or initiatives, and can be characterized in terms of risk outcomes and risk sources.

Project risk outcomes

Project risk outcomes can be classified into four overarching categories, based on an answer to the question, "Risk to what?"

Resource risk: Risk to natural resources or other key foci of the project emerging from different decisions, actions, or inactions. In projects not dealing directly with natural resources, this might alternatively be termed, **project goal risk**.

Process risk: Risk that the planning or implementation process will fail for any number of reasons.

Personal risk: The risk an individual involved in the project feels to his or her own position, reputation, or well-being.

Organizational risk: Risk to an organization involved in the project resulting from their actions and the responses of others, including future public relations challenges, cost escalation, fluctuating morale, reputation, or future risk aversion.

Each of these risk outcomes is interconnected. For example, making compromises between parties can assuage process risk but could increase resource risk in some cases. Meanwhile, failing to compromise effectively could cause the entire project to fail. Perceptions of personal risk can impact process and resource risk in multiple ways. To demonstrate these impacts, the organizational psychologist Edgar Schein identified two forms of anxiety felt by individuals within an organization.[26] *Survival anxiety* motivates a behavior when an individual feels that unless he or she changes, something bad will happen. Meanwhile, *learning anxiety* works in the opposite direction, inhibiting change, innovation, or other actions, as an individual fears the potential consequences of failure or going against organizational inertia or group norms. In each case, the fate of resource and process outcomes could be powerfully influenced. Resource, process, and personal risk can have ripple effects on prospects for an organization's future projects and relationships as well.

Sources of project risk

Examining different sources of risk[27] can help to identify strategies for mitigating each. These answer the question, "Risk from where?"

Programmatic risk: Risk stemming from the project's preliminary design and the pre-existing social and political climate in which the project is proposed, which each influence uncertainty, complexity, and controversy. These conditions set the baseline from which other types of risk emerge. For example, a large, complicated project in a politically active community is likely predisposed to greater risk than a small, simple project in a community with a history of similar successful projects.

Structural risk: Risk stemming from the availability, or lack thereof, of resources necessary to carry out the project effectively, including staff time, materials, meeting space, and financial resources.

Technical risk: Risk stemming from technical (in)competence and individual and group performance on project-related tasks.

Relationship risk: Risk stemming from both external and internal relationships relevant to the project. **External relationship risk** involves conflicts between organizations or individuals from different stakeholder groups. **Internal relationship risk** arises from conflicts within an organization or team.

Risk management

Risk management generally involves three steps: (1) risk identification; (2) analysis; and (3) response. The categories of risk outcomes and risk sources above can provide a useful checklist for identifying potential risks in a project, especially if multiple stakeholders are involved in their diagnosis. Once risk sources are identified, we need to decide what to do about them, if anything. Analyzing the ***controllability*** of each source of risk becomes helpful. Controllability refers to the degree to which we can influence the probability of the occurrence of an unwanted outcome.[28] If a risk has high controllability, we can work to minimize the likelihood of its occurrence. In cases of low controllability, we may rather choose to focus on minimizing the severity of the damage of the occurrence.

Some people might alternatively choose to ignore, or to not communicate to others, an identified risk. For low likelihood and low severity risks, this might be a reasonable approach to avoid lowering team morale or wasting energy on an unlikely scenario. In other cases, managers have been found to hide risks to avoid exposing their probable deficiencies in dealing with them. Risks may also sometimes be dismissed due to a lack of agreement about them within a team, purposeful denial, expected uncomfortable situations their acknowledgment would cause, declaring them as "outside the scope" of a project, or other forms of over-simplification.[29] In each of these cases, failure to address an identified risk will typically increase the severity of its impact should it occur.

Applications

When to use it

Risk management is particularly useful in the planning stages of a project. However, actively re-assessing risk at regular intervals or as conditions change is highly advisable. The categories of risk sources and risk outcomes can help to identify, rank, prioritize, and formulate plans for addressing *Project Risk*.

How to use it

First, identify all possible risks to a proposed or ongoing project. Use the *Project Risk* categories to ensure that each potential source of risk is considered. For each possible risk, identify (1) the potential outcomes of the risk's occurrence, (2) the likelihood of its occurrence, (3) the likely severity of its impact(s), and (4) its controllability. A simple rating or ranking system for each risk's likelihood and severity can enable a prioritization of which risks are most urgent and important to address. An assessment of controllability enables a consideration of whether efforts would be better spent trying to prevent the risk's occurrence or lessening its negative

Type	Source	Outcome(s)	Likelihood	Severity	Controllability	Potential responses
Programmatic						
Structural						
Technical						
External relations	*Be sure to consider and evaluate responses in terms of any new sources of risk they might create.*					
Internal relations						

Figure 7.3 *Project Risk* analysis worksheet.

impacts. See Figure 7.3. Note that potential responses can also create new risks, which should be assessed as well.

Different sources of risk typically entail different risk management strategies. I provide some common strategies and considerations associated with each below.

Programmatic risk is typically greatest in large, complex, and high-profile projects in politically charged social environments. Common strategies to address programmatic risk (and other forms of risk stemming from it) include making projects smaller, narrowing their scope, or attempting to "fly under the radar," limiting public involvement as much as possible. Each of these strategies, however, can have meaningful drawbacks in terms of organizational performance. Oftentimes, narrowing a project's scope can be seen as a means for avoiding conflict between stakeholders (external relationship risk). In environmental or sustainability-related contexts, this often means breaking down larger projects into smaller pieces, eliminating the treatment of highly contested areas, or simply pursuing less ambitious projects. While sequential implementation of smaller projects can often make sense, it can preclude efforts at more holistic ecosystem management. Sustainability problems often stretch beyond convenient social, political, or jurisdictional boundaries. Breaking a large project into smaller pieces endangers whether subsequent aspects might be implemented in a timely manner or at all.[30] A thorough risk assessment that weighs process risk vs resource (or project goal) risk can help make decisions in this regard clearer.

When projects, regardless of their size, are deemed necessary in a specific time or place, programmatic risk is more appropriately considered a baseline from which other forms of risk emerge.

Structural risk is particularly common in mission-based and governmental organizations, where funding sources can be inconsistent, turnover of personnel can be common, and over-burdened staffs struggle to balance competing tasks. A common source of structural risk, particularly for small non-profit organizations, is spreading the organization's resources too thin by pursuing too many projects at once or beginning projects before sufficient resources are in place. Each can lead to increased relationship risks, as internal staff are strained and external stakeholders perceive a lack of achievement or broken promises. Structural risk management strategies include:

- Balancing efforts across an organization such that the most important projects are prioritized and thus granted sufficient staff time and resources to do the job well.
- Ensuring an appropriate balance between efforts expended on upward accountability mechanisms and mission achievement (see *7.2 Team Effectiveness Theory* and *7.3 Accountability Theory*).
- Delineating clear roles for all employees involved in the project.
- Making explicit plans for knowledge transfer and relationship development in the case of staff turnover.

Technical risk emerges from a shortcoming in skills or performance on specific tasks. Addressing technical risk thus involves choosing the right people for the right tasks, ensuring common understandings of those tasks, assessing the capacities of team members, providing additional training if needed, and considering appropriate mechanisms to coordinate the work—in particular, finding an appropriate balance between worker discretion and standardization of work processes. Simple, routine tasks with low uncertainty may benefit from having standard operating procedures in place to maximize both accountability and efficiency. However, tasks that entail considerable uncertainty may be managed through multiple approaches, including (a) enhanced discretion for workers to solve problems as they emerge, (b) additional layers of hierarchy, in which a supervisor or team leader helps to resolve uncertainties that emerge, or (c) purposeful deliberative processes among team members to mutually address uncertainties that arise.[31] Enhanced worker discretion is typically most effective when clear goals are defined for the process and all team members share the organization's prevailing norms of appropriate conduct. Purposeful deliberative processes between interdisciplinary team members have been shown to enhance both process efficiency and the quality of process outcomes.[32]

External relationship risk emerges from conflicts between the organization and any number of external stakeholders. Perceptions of external relationship risk can look quite different in different contexts and can lead to multiple strategies. In government agencies, external relationship risk may often manifest through threats of litigation from various environmental, industry, or special interest stakeholders. In non-governmental organizations, it might involve disagreements with foreign governments, local domestic government officials, private organizations, or local communities. In private, for-profit organizations, external relationship risks might also include client perceptions or relationships with regulatory agencies, among others.

In short, research has shown that efforts to limit or contain public involvement or inter-organizational communications in environmental planning processes typically turn out badly. Rather, intensive public outreach and work with partners usually provide better options for managing external relationship risk.[33] See the theories in *Chapter 6 Trust, negotiation, and public involvement* as well as *5.1 Identity Theory*, *5.2 Self-Affirmation Theory*, *5.5 Moral Foundations Theory*, and *5.6 Frame Theory* for advice on how to address these relationships directly.

Because external relationship risk can feel especially intense in environmental or sustainability-related situations, particularly in formal public involvement processes associated with government initiatives, employees often enter a defensive mode, in which they may: (a) narrow the project scope of the project; (b) attempt to limit the influence of various publics; or (c) focus on strict procedural compliance to ensure a legally "bullet-proof" process.[34] Not only can these steps make public relationships worse, but they can also damage the morale of staff by: (a) limiting the perceived meaningfulness of the work; (b) setting up or perpetuating unproductive conflict between interested publics and the organization; and (c) limiting the discretion and creativity of staff to do their jobs in the ways they see fit. While more collaborative approaches with external stakeholders require more proactive energy (and often additional training of staff), they can save time and energy spent later in a process responding to ongoing conflict and suffering from lowered morale.[35]

Internal relationship risks involve repercussions of the displeasure of team members. Negative sentiments can emerge from multiple sources, each of which highlight the importance of balancing upward accountability with discretion and managing relationships within an organization. People tend to be most motivated at work when they feel competent, trusted, and autonomous (see *4.6 Self-Determination Theory*). Generating these feelings generally entails: (a) sufficient training, appropriate task assignments, and positive feedback; (b) the creation of safe spaces for open deliberation and the development of mutual respect among co-workers (see *6.1 Trust Theory* and *7.2 Team Effectiveness Theory*); and (c) freedom from excessive standardization of work processes (see *7.3 Accountability Theory* and *7.5 Nonaka's Organizational Knowledge Creation Theory*). In addition to curtailing adaptability and innovation, excessive standardization has been linked to strained inter-personal relationships and reduced job satisfaction and organizational commitment.[36]

Relationships within teams and between levels of hierarchy within an organization are crucial to managing internal relationship risk. Interdisciplinary teams of employees focused on complex tasks have become commonplace within federal agencies, non-governmental organizations, and private firms. Recent studies have shown that teams that openly deliberate various aspects of their projects tend to be more successful than others, in terms of both outcomes and efficiency. Also, projects in which team leaders feel clearly empowered to facilitate team processes and influence decision making (which is often higher up in the agency) tend to have better outcomes (see also *7.2 Team Effectiveness Theory*).[37] Time spent clarifying roles, building positive relationships, and creating transparent and consensus-based ground rules for debate is thus highly worthwhile (see theories noted earlier in this section). Disgruntled employees with low morale often underperform in their tasks. Moreover, their negative sentiments can bleed out into external stakeholder communities.[38]

Addressing any one category of risk in isolation of considering the others could expose your project to being blindsided. For example, an over-emphasis on managing external relationship risk can create new strains on internal relationships. Review risk management plans with this in mind. Will your proposed strategies create new risks? Risk planning should be an iterative process that not only entails predicting and planning for its own ripple effects, but also enables periodic revisitation as conditions change throughout the life of a project.

Key references

Project Management Institute 2013. *A guide to the project management body of knowledge.* Fifth edition. Upper Darby, UK: Project Management Institute.

Stern, M.J., C.A. Martin, S.A. Predmore, and W.C. Morse 2014. Risk tradeoffs in adaptive ecosystem management: the case of the United States Forest Service. *Environmental Management* 53(6): 1095–108.

7.5 Nonaka's Theory of Organizational Knowledge Creation

Uses: Enhancing organizational learning, building appropriate organizational structures for innovation

> **What practices best encourage learning and innovation within an organization or network?**

Organizations that do not learn and adapt eventually fail. The work of Ikujiro Nonaka and his colleagues over the past two decades has focused on how to build organizations that both create and apply knowledge in ways that enhance their performance over time.[39]

Learning theorists distinguish between information and knowledge. While information may refer to data, facts, or observations, *knowledge* requires some level of *justification* of the truthfulness of these data and some ideas about their meanings and potential applications. In other words, knowledge implies that information has been processed in a way to make it useful. Knowledge helps a person (or group) define situations and problems and act accordingly. Nonaka identified two forms of knowledge: tacit and explicit.

Tacit knowledge refers to knowledge that is so ingrained we find it difficult to articulate. It includes the skills we have developed through personal experience, such as mastering practical activities or performing common routines. It also includes our implicit mental models, paradigms, perspectives, intuitions, beliefs, or rules-of-thumb that we generally take for granted. When we examine our own tacit knowledge, we may sometimes not immediately know why we hold these beliefs. As a result, this knowledge is more difficult to justify or convey through language to others.

Explicit knowledge involves facts, figures, instructions, principles, or other forms of knowledge that can be communicated in images, symbols, or language. It lives in the rational, conscious part of our brains and is the type of knowledge authors attempt to share in practical books like this one. It can be disseminated in multiple forms.

In an organizational environment, tacit knowledge is built through experience and must be converted to explicit knowledge to be disseminated to benefit the larger organization (and others). One of the key premises of Nonaka's theory is that knowledge needs to be converted in four ways to become broadly useful at the organizational level (see Figure 7.4). These knowledge conversions are referred

From	To	
	Tacit knowledge	Explicit knowledge
Tacit knowledge	Socialization	Externalization
Explicit knowledge	Internalization	Combination

Figure 7.4 Nonaka's forms of knowledge conversion.

to as socialization, externalization, combination, and internalization (the acronym SECI depicts a full cycle of these conversions).

Socialization involves the sharing of tacit knowledge among individuals. The key to developing tacit knowledge is personal experience. Socialization thus involves sharing personal experiences and perspectives. For example, an apprenticeship in which one learns by watching and imitating or teamwork in which individuals share active experiences may each enable common elements of tacit understanding to develop between people. Socialization typically entails empathizing, which can be helped along by both personal relationships and storytelling.

Externalization is the process through which tacit knowledge is articulated into explicit knowledge. Interactive dialogue helps to make mental models and skills explicit, often through the use of dialectic approaches and the presentation, refutation, and fine-tuning of metaphors. Through these practices tacit knowledge becomes clearly describable (explicit) and can then be shared and justified to others.

Combination is the process of improving and transferring explicit knowledge by comparing it (and combining it) with the explicit knowledge of others. This creates more complete explicit understandings, which can then be further disseminated and combined with other explicit knowledge.

Internalization transforms explicit knowledge into tacit knowledge. As new explicit knowledge is received, individuals put it to work and expand their tacit learning by doing.

Promoting individual learning

Learning is both an individual and social enterprise. Regardless of the type of knowledge or methods involved, the act of building knowledge benefits from a number of conditions that can be enhanced (or diminished) in an organizational context. These conditions mirror the concepts of autonomy, competence, and relatedness in *4.6 Self-Determination Theory*. However, they manifest somewhat differently when considered specifically in light of the goal of organizational learning.

Autonomy for learning is enhanced by avoiding over-specification of tasks and encouraging the development of context-specific creative solutions. Throughout a learning organization, leadership is often dispersed, as different individuals are tapped to lead different projects or processes. ***Knowledge activists*** (see next section) work to connect team leaders to others and share lessons learned.

Competence for learning is enhanced by providing a variety of meaningful tasks (see also *7.1 Herzberg's Motivation–Hygiene Theory*), sharing information across work units, and promoting the dissemination of successes and lessons learned. Meaningful task variety, as well as broad information-sharing across the organization,[40] can provide an individual with multiple perspectives for approaching a problem. Meaningful task assignments that contribute to learning involve experiencing multiple aspects of a complicated process, exposure to multiple viewpoints, or explicitly following an idea from beginning (conceptualization) to end (implementation). Information sharing across functional units within an organization further provides opportunities for people to understand the causes and consequences associated with their own specific tasks. Promoting the sharing of lessons learned further enhances this cross-functional learning and also contributes to feelings of competence, as ideas are validated throughout the organization.

Building feelings of ***relatedness*** for learning involves establishing mutual trust and creating safe spaces for openly sharing perspectives. Widespread and transparent information-sharing within an organization again may help to establish these conditions. See *6.1 Trust Theory* and *7.2 Team Effectiveness Theory* for more on establishing conditions for trust development as well as the discussion of ***ba*** below.

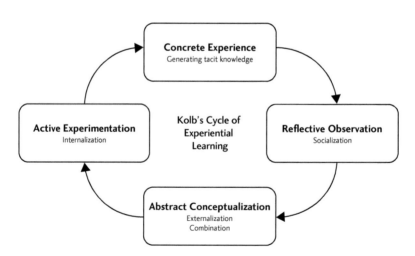

Figure 7.5 Linking Nonaka's Organizational Knowledge Creation Theory to Kolb's Experiential Learning Cycle.

In summary, individual learning within an organization is promoted by providing people with a variety of meaningful experiences, ensuring broad information-sharing, encouraging autonomous or collaborative problem solving, and promoting active reflection and lesson sharing. These processes mirror other familiar and well-tested learning theories. For example, Kolb's Experiential Learning Theory[41] also relies on converting tacit knowledge into explicit knowledge and back again (see Figure 7.5). *Organizational Knowledge Creation Theory* specifies that certain elements are best conducted collaboratively with other people, especially reflective observation and abstract conceptualization.

Promoting knowledge creation on an organizational scale

Nonaka and his colleagues use the term **ba** to refer to the physical, virtual, social, or mental space in which knowledge is created and have identified four *bas* (Table 7.6). *Bas* provide the context in which different forms of knowledge creation take place. Each *ba* may exist at different levels within an organization or between organizations or other networks. Specific bridging employees may serve as "knowledge activists" to help direct and connect the various *bas* into more coherent organizational learning.

Learning organizations can be conceptualized as **hypertext organizations**. Hypertext organizations have three virtual systems that operate simultaneously (Figure 7.6). The **business system** is where routine tasks are carried out and is typically rather hierarchical and bureaucratic. The **project system**, on the other hand, is heterarchical, meaning assets, talents, and leadership are dispersed, communication is often horizontal, and coordination is often less formal. The project system consists of project teams engaged in knowledge creation. The third system is called the **knowledge system**. This system captures and disseminates the organization's global learning. It also contains knowledge management systems for information-sharing and provides key linkages between the other two systems. The new ideas of project teams in the project system layer must be judged against (justified with) the accumulated knowledge within the knowledge system prior to being integrated into the business system. Knowledge activists can be instrumental in making all of this happen.

Knowledge activists act as boundary spanners that can avert common problems within the *bas* and catalyze dissemination of ideas to the broader organization or network. Boundary spanners link otherwise disconnected groups (see also *8.3 Diffusion Theory* and *8.4 Collective Impact*). As teams interact in knowledge conversions, they sometimes suffer from groupthink or lack creative energy. Even in successful teams, new knowledge doesn't necessarily diffuse beyond the team

Table 7.6 *The four bas, their functions, and operations.*

Ba/Purpose	What happens	Tips
Originating ba/ Socialization	People meet face-to-face to share emotions, feelings, experiences, and mental models.	• Organizationally relevant creative dialogue occurs when participants have broad access to organizational information and individuals have been exposed to a variety of meaningful tasks and granted autonomy to solve problems encountered.
	This can happen in project teams, purposefully arranged meetings or workshops, or informal gatherings.	• Understanding emerges best when individuals share their original experiences, which are the fundamental sources of their tacit knowledge.
		• Groups should be kept small while still capturing an appropriate range of expertise relevant to the problem.
Interacting (dialoguing) ba/ Externalization	Through dialogue, individuals probe and analyze each other's mental models and skills to convert them into common concepts and terms.	• Using metaphors and dialectic questioning exercises can identify fits and misfits in common understanding between members.
	This can happen in teams, meetings, or workshops.	• Groups should be kept small while still capturing an appropriate range of expertise relevant to the problem.
Cyber (systemizing) ba/Combination	Newly created explicit knowledge is combined with pre-existing knowledge to generate new explicit knowledge and figure out how to communicate it throughout an organization.	• Groups can be large; can be done virtually. • Explicit knowledge is discussed, evaluated and revised.
	This can happen in meetings, workshops, retreats, conferences, or even in online forums.	
Exercising ba/ Internalization	Focused training with instructors and colleagues establish new patterns of behavior.	• Building explicit reflection into new work patterns can enable new knowledge creation and initiate new learning conversion cycles.
	This also happens informally as workers employ new knowledge on their own.	

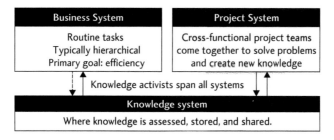

Figure 7.6 The systems of the hypertext (learning) organization.

without a little help. Knowledge activists can energize the *bas* and ensure their connection to the organization's knowledge system.

Knowledge activists can originate from multiple positions within an organization or network. Sometimes, they are the middle managers who translate between the visions of executives and the realities faced by work teams. Sometimes, a specific individual (or group of individuals) might be hired or a specific coordinator might be designated from within. Other times, an organization can serve this role within a broader network (see the concept of the "backbone support organization" within *8.4 Collective Impact*). Whatever their position, knowledge activists serve numerous important functions for knowledge creation and dissemination:

1. As outsiders to a team or a *ba*, knowledge activists provide new input for knowledge creation, which can help teams break out of groupthink or routine behavior.

2. By spanning organizational or network boundaries, knowledge activists can ensure the dissemination of their results throughout an organization or network.

3. Through observing multiple teams or *bas*, knowledge activists can identify and enable new opportunities for sharing and using knowledge across units. For example, knowledge activists can help to identify gaps in a team's knowledge and ascertain how those gaps might be addressed by the work of other teams. This might involve direct communication or collaboration between teams or the knowledge activist packaging one team's information appropriately for another team's consumption.

4. Maintaining a bird's eye perspective and a strong connection to the organizational vision and direction, knowledge activists can articulate future prospects for knowledge creation and coordinate teams to move toward a coherent overall direction. In essence, by translating between multiple levels of an organization, they create a ***knowledge vision*** to accompany the ***organizational vision***

of its desired future. The *knowledge vision* encompasses clear learning goals deemed necessary for achieving the organizational vision.

Applications

When to use it

In any organizational or network context in which learning is critically important, this theory is highly applicable. However, it might look quite different in small organizations vs large ones. Nonaka's work has focused mostly on larger for-profit corporations. However, many lessons will apply to other contexts.

How to use it: Building a knowledge vision

First, consider where learning is most important and urgent within your organization or network. This typically involves meetings between the leadership team and middle managers in large corporations. In smaller organizations, these meetings might include program managers, field agents, and sometimes key partners or stakeholders. Articulate a *knowledge vision*, which identifies clear learning goals deemed necessary for achieving the organizational or collective vision. What don't we know? Where are we not meeting our goals and why? What problems do we have? What do we need to know to do better? These questions can provide good starting points for articulating a knowledge vision.

Within knowledge visioning, and all other brainstorming processes, consider that originating and interacting *bas* are being created. Recognizing this should call attention to the acts of *socialization* and *externalization*. We are often tempted to jump straight to explicit rational explanations. Allowing for a socialization period, in which participants share the original experiences upon which their knowledge is based, allows for empathizing, trust-building, and a wider knowledge base. Socialization enables people with different points of view to learn about the realities of others and ask questions prior to forming conclusions. It also minimizes our tendency to jump too quickly to conclusions (see *Chapter* 2).

How to use it: Creating and managing bas

In traditional stereotypical top-down organizations, learning tends to be oriented toward enhancing efficiency of pre-existing operations rather than toward broader innovation that could contribute greater gains. While this may be sufficient for many routine activities within the business system, it can limit an organization's responsiveness to environmental fluctuations, or changes in the context in which an organization works. Middle managers can work to translate the vision of the executive team to on-the-ground workers and the needs of on-the-ground workers to the executive team. However, a lack of cross-functional or interdisciplinary learning spaces, or *bas*, typically limits learning. Creating cross-functional spaces for learning, either associated with the project system (as specific project teams are created) or with the knowledge system (as diverse groups are purposefully brought together to build new knowledge), can enhance organizational creativity and resilience.

Originating bas involve bringing people together to share tacit knowledge. While storytelling may be commonplace in informal gatherings, many organizations, especially in Western cultures, view this as a waste of time. The work of Nonaka and his colleagues demonstrate that sharing tacit knowledge through storytelling about work (socialization) can play a critical role in enhancing an organization's explicit knowledge and building positive, trusting relationships between staff. Socialization can take place in informal work groups, project teams, or intentionally designed working sessions to address specific problems or to set specific goals or visions within a group. Small groups (generally less than ten people[42], though no consistent "ideal" number has been identified in the literature) tend to work best. Participants should be encouraged to share their original experiences and to ask clarifying questions without judgment.

Interacting bas turn tacit knowledge into explicit knowledge and ideally follow soon after socialization processes. Participants are encouraged to propose metaphors to which they can compare their experiences and to use dialectic approaches which question the fit of those metaphors and emerging propositions with participants' experiences. The goal is to build knowledge that fits the combined experiences of those involved with shared concepts and terminology. Again, small groups are ideal.

Cyber bas build on the knowledge that emerges from *interacting bas* by expanding the number of participants and, effectively, the amount of knowledge under consideration. The broader group considers new knowledge in light of pre-existing knowledge and further fine-tunes the emerging ideas to fit a broader set of situations or circumstances. While some degree of combination inevitably takes place in the *interacting bas*, this expansion might be seen as the equivalent of testing an idea in a new market or with a broader audience. Groups can be larger at this stage and managed in various ways, ranging from interactive open dialogue to the analysis of online survey input.

Exercising bas aim to internalize new knowledge throughout an organization once it has been effectively incorporated into an organization's knowledge system. Learning here typically involves training or capacity-building workshops with employees. As employees begin to internalize (or act upon) this new information, they build new tacit knowledge and commonly face new challenges. Building explicit reflection exercises (see next section) into the suggested applications of new knowledge and avoiding over-specification (micro-management) of tasks can begin new cycles of knowledge creation.

How to use it: Institutionalizing organizational learning

Nonaka and his colleagues have identified a number of conditions that can enable more effective and creative organizational learning:

- In general, for any tasks that don't require exact specification of techniques, allow employees freedom to try their own approaches. In areas of high concern or risk, providing guidelines rather than specific step-by-step instructions can enable experimentation within an acceptable set of parameters.
- Provide workers with opportunities to experience a variety of meaningful tasks. See the discussion of job enrichment vs job enlargement within *7.1 Herzberg's Motivation–Hygiene Theory*. From a learning perspective, a broader view of more complete processes can enable a wider array of perspectives to address more holistic problems. Compartmentalization of employees, or confining them to a specific set of discrete tasks, limits these opportunities.
- Widespread sharing of knowledge and information throughout the organization can similarly enable workers to acquire a broader understanding of their roles and the interconnectedness between their work and the work of others. With this broader understanding, organizational visions and knowledge visions may come into clearer focus, and individuals may be able to see improvements in processes outside their own typical area of work.
- Create a culture of care and trust. Within *bas*, this can mean developing clear ground rules for sharing and asking questions. Within the broader organization, sharing information across functional units, encouraging informal social gatherings, assuring adequate resources for all teams, and providing appropriate recognition for work well done can create the conditions for greater trust. See also *4.6 Self-Determination Theory*, *4.9 Maslow's Hierarchy of Needs*, *6.1 Trust Theory*, *7.1 Herzberg's Hygiene–Motivation Theory*, and *7.2 Team Effectiveness Theory* for additional insights on building a positive and trusting organizational environment.
- Institutionalize reflection. Create expectations for constructive reflection on completed projects and processes. Focusing this reflection, at least in part, on the issue of problem identification and definition can enable a complete SECI cycle. Including learning outcomes as specific evaluation measures can further mainstream productive reflection and reduce fears of failure. This

effectively can enable and formalize learning from mistakes, rather than trying to hide them from superiors (see *7.3 Accountability Theory*).

• Consider how to fill the roles of knowledge activists. In larger organizations, middle managers, internal consultants, or cross-functional coordinators often fill these roles. In smaller organizations, the role of the knowledge activist may be fluid, with different people assuming the role at different times. Alternatively, the responsibility may fall on the shoulders of the chief executive. Knowledge activists:

  – Ensure that a knowledge vision for the organization (or for specific units) is clearly articulated and translated into appropriate terms for those at different levels of the organization and serving different functions.

  – Help to organize appropriate work teams or other *ba* to accomplish either general periodic or specific project-based learning.

  – Monitor the different *ba* within an organization to catalyze effective learning within them, using the principles above.

  – Communicate between *ba* and translate knowledge as appropriate throughout the organization.

  – Help to maintain the knowledge system of the organization and keep the knowledge vision up to date through serving as a liaison between work teams, upper management, and sometimes external stakeholders.

Key references

Nonaka, I. 1994. A dynamic theory of organizational knowledge creation. *Organization Science* 5(1): 14–37.

Nonaka, I., R. Toyama, and N. Konno 2000. SECI, *ba*, and leadership: A unified model of dynamic knowledge creation. *Long Range Planning* 33: 5–34.

Nonaka, I., G. von Krogh, and S. Voelpel 2006. Organizational knowledge creation theory: Evolutionary paths and future advances. *Organization Studies* 27(8): 1179–208.

7.6 Leadership Theory

Uses: Influencing others, coordinating collaborative efforts, motivating team members, enhancing the work of others, managing within networks, teams, or organizations

What is leadership and how can I become better at it?

Similar to other organizational topics, no single theory can holistically answer this question. In fact, *most* of the theories in this book provide guidance on how to become a better leader. Here, I focus on leadership primarily in organizational, network, and collaborative contexts in which you might find yourself responsible for leading other people toward a specific goal.

Leadership theories typically focus on specific aspects of leadership—most commonly the traits of successful (or unsuccessful) leaders, leadership styles and behaviors, issues of power, and contingency theories of leadership, which aim to match appropriate leadership approaches to different contexts. Rather than providing individualized summaries of dozens of leadership theories (which would surely require an entire book itself), I highlight here what I believe to be the most useful and validated claims of each of these approaches. If you are interested in tracing the history of these ideas, Table 7.7 provides a summary of some seminal studies and theories upon which most modern leadership theories are based.

Defining leadership

Leadership, in its simplest sense, is the process of influencing others to work towards achieving a goal. While we might often think about leadership involving formal hierarchies, a person can lead from any position. However, the source of their power to influence followers might be quite different depending upon their standing within a social group or organization.

Evolving leadership theory has begun to place less emphasis on traditional hierarchical leader/follower relationships in favor of a more functional view. In this view, leaders are those who can create *direction*, *alignment*, and *commitment* within a group of people toward a specific goal.[43]

Direction: Agreement within a group on overall goals.
Alignment: The organization of work and knowledge toward pursuing an agreed upon goal.
Commitment: The willingness of members to subsume their own interests in pursuit of the collective interest.

Table 7.7 *Some influential leadership studies and theories.*

The Ohio State Leadership Quadrants and University of Michigan Studies[44]	Drew clear distinctions between task-oriented leadership and relationship-oriented leadership.
Rensis Likert's Management Systems[45]	Identified four different systems of management, ranging from authoritarian through consultative to participatory. Research revealed that systems closer to the participatory end of the spectrum tended to sustain higher levels of productivity, while those reflecting more authoritarian systems typically yielded lower productivity.
Tannenbaum and Schmidt's Continuum of Leader Behavior[46]	Following on Likert's work, this descriptive theory draws a continuum between leader-centered leadership vs follower-centered leadership. The former is more directive and the latter is more empowering and participatory. The middle of the spectrum can be described as consultative.
The Managerial Grid[47]	Provided a characterization that leaders can be both task-oriented and relationship-oriented at the same time (or can display any combination of these characteristics).
Theory X and Theory Y[48]	Suggested that motivations may be different for different followers, ranging from extrinsic rewards (Theory X) to intrinsic motivation (Theory Y). Cautioned against over-reliance on extrinsic rewards.
Path-Goal Theory[49]	Highlighted the importance of responsiveness of leaders to the context-specific needs of followers.
Fiedler's Contingency Theory[50]	Fiedler defined the most favorable situations for leaders as those in which the leader is well-liked, has a powerful position, and a well-defined task. The theory contends that task-oriented leaders perform best in either very favorable or very unfavorable situations, while relationship-oriented leaders perform best in situations of intermediate favorableness.
Vroom–Yetton Normative Decision Model[51]	The model suggests how involved followers should be in decision making based on the nature of the problem and intra-team relationships. In situations of greater complexity and importance of follower buy-in, greater involvement of followers in decision making is suggested.
Hersey and Blanchard's Situational Leadership[52]	Matches task-oriented and relationship-oriented leadership behaviors with different degrees motivation and ability of followers. In cases of low motivation and ability, task-oriented (directive) leadership is most effective. In cases of low ability and high motivation, a mixture of high task and relationship-oriented leadership is desirable. In cases of low motivation and high ability, more relationship-oriented approaches are preferable. When followers are highly capable and motivated, delegation and empowerment are best.

Effective leaders create direction, alignment, and commitment and achieve goals in a way that is durable and does not damage the relationships of those involved.

Leadership tasks

Leaders can perform a wide variety of tasks, which can be categorized in multiple ways (see Table 7.8, see also *7.2 Team Effectiveness Theory*.). One of the most important distinctions involves relationship-oriented vs task-oriented leadership. Leaders decide how much emphasis to place on each. See **Contingency Theories of Leadership** below for more on the implications of this distinction.

Power

Power is the potential to influence others. Table 7.9 provides a summary of common bases of power available for use by leaders to influence followers. Power is based on perceptions, not necessarily actual behaviors. Power can be lost if not used judiciously (if power is abused) and consistently (if promises are not kept). The bases of power are not mutually exclusive.

Research suggests that expert and legitimate power tend to be the most predictive of general compliance within an organization. Expert and referent power, however, are the most consistent predictors of follower performance and satisfaction.[53] Relying on different sources of power may be more or less appropriate in different circumstances. See **Contingency Theories of Leadership** below.

Table 7.8 *Common categories of leadership tasks.*

Category	Definition	Specific behaviors
Task-oriented leadership	Focus on the tangible work that needs to be done to accomplish goals.	Clarifying; planning; directing; organizing; monitoring
Relationship-oriented leadership	Focus on people and their relationships and well-being.	Supporting; developing; recognizing; empowering; mentoring; encouraging
Change-oriented leadership	Leading a group toward a new vision or goal.	Envisioning and advocating change; encouraging innovation; facilitating collective learning; coalition-building
Boundary spanning leadership	Managing external relationships.	Networking; external monitoring; representing; advocating; protecting from external disturbance; bridging

Table 7.9 *Bases of power.*[54]

Power	Basis
Coercive power	Perception that the leader has the ability to create negative consequences for failing to perform. These consequences could come in various forms, including reprimand, pay cut, public shaming, or dismissal.
Reward power	Perception that the leader has the ability to provide rewards, which could include praise, public recognition, promotion, or compensation.
Legitimate power	Perception that the leader is justified in making decisions or demands based on their title, role, or position. The legitimacy of the position can be based on democratic election or consensus or on the support of others higher up in a hierarchy.
Referent power	Perception that the leader is a good person, worthy of putting forth meaningful effort. This can emerge through the development of positive interpersonal rapport and affinitive trust (see *6.1 Trust Theory*).
Expert power	Perception that the leader is competent in ways that matter to the follower. These perceptions can emerge through direct demonstrations of expertise, reputation, or through persuasive communication, and serve as a strong basis for rational trust (see *6.1 Trust Theory*).
Information power[55]	Perception that the leader has access to useful information. This differs from expert power in that the leader need not know how to expertly use that information.
Connection power[56]	Perception that the leader is connected to other people whom the follower considers to be important.

Leader traits

While researchers and theorists have long sought specific traits that all leaders should demonstrate, their work has identified relatively few traits that apply consistently across contexts. Table 7.10 displays some of the most common traits associated with successful and unsuccessful leaders. Most studies on leadership traits have focused upon formal leaders within organizations.

Leadership styles

Studies of organizational leadership have a long history of defining different styles of leadership, which are typically comprised of leaders' attitudes and actions. Table 7.11 provides a sampling of some of the most commonly discussed leadership styles in the vast literature on the subject. Most leaders employ a mixture of styles.

Only transformational leadership has demonstrated a consistent relationship with better outcomes across contexts. Aversive forms of leadership are rarely successful, especially over longer periods of time. The success of each of the other

Table 7.10 *Traits of successful and unsuccessful leaders.*[57]

Successful leaders	Unsuccessful leaders
Trustworthiness	Untrustworthiness
• Ability, benevolence, and integrity (see *6.1 Trust Theory*)	• Lack of ability, benevolence or integrity (see *6.1 Trust Theory*)
Genuine concern for followers	Abrasiveness or insensitivity to others
Good listening skills	Arrogance
Self-confidence and emotional stability	Over-ambitiousness
Systems and creative thinking, nonconforming	Rigidness, inability to adapt
Flexibility and adaptability	Overdependence on an advocate or mentor
Ability to clearly articulate goals and meaningfulness of work	Neuroticism (poor emotional adjustment resulting in anxiety, insecurity, or hostility)
Ability to make decisions with limited data	
Extraversion	

Table 7.11 *Leadership styles.*

Leadership style	Details
Directive	The leader focuses on setting clear goals and defining tasks for achieving them.
Supportive	The leader emphasizes personal relationships and creating an appreciative, friendly, and protective work environment.
Aversive	The leader motivates primarily through fear and/or punishments.
Empowering/ participatory	The leader delegates or shares decision-making authority with others and sets goals collaboratively, encouraging innovation and cooperation.
Transactional	The leader provides (primarily extrinsic) rewards in exchange for performance.
Transformational	The leader (1) sets a positive and consistent example (walking their own talk); (2) motivates and challenges others by clearly communicating the meaningfulness and importance of the work; (3) encourages innovation through creating an open environment where questioning assumptions, reframing problems, and considering new ideas are safe and valued activities; and (4) provides learning opportunities and a supportive climate to enable individuals to reach their full potential.

forms of leadership depends upon the quality of its application and its particular context. For example, transactional leadership can speed the accomplishment of short-term tasks, but extrinsic rewards alone rarely inspire long-term commitment (see *4.8 Motivation Crowding Theory*).

Contingency theories of leadership

Contingency theories of leadership focus on matching appropriate leadership styles to different situations. Hersey and Blanchard's Situational Leadership Model, which is based on prior contingency theories of leadership,[58] focuses on the performance readiness of followers, defined as followers' ability, confidence, and willingness to perform a task. They contend that conditions of low performance readiness tend to benefit from more directive leadership approaches, which entail higher task orientation and lesser relationship orientation. In cases where followers' exhibit high degrees of performance readiness, more empowering and participatory leadership are likely to be more effective. When followers have high levels of capability but low motivation, more attention needs to be placed on relationships than tasks. In the opposition condition, more emphasis needs to be placed on task specification (see Table 7.12).

Different power sources can also impact followers' motivations in different situations. For example, Hersey and colleagues suggest that coercive power is only typically effective for followers at the lowest level of performance readiness. Reward, connection, and legitimate power are more appropriate at moderate levels, and expert and information power are most effective at higher levels of performance readiness. Referent power is likely important at all levels of performance readiness, though it might be more difficult to develop at lower levels. These claims are primarily theoretical, however, as only limited targeted research has been conducted across contexts to validate the claims.

Legitimate power has been found to be particularly important in non-hierarchical teams, in which one person (or group of people) has been selected to lead a group or team without a formal promotion or hierarchical title or position. In these cases, legitimate power comes from the explicit support and formal charge of a superior in an organization or a clear public articulation of roles and responsibilities in a network. For example, a study I conducted with Andrew Predmore on the performance of interdisciplinary project teams in the US Forest Service revealed that directive, supportive, and empowering leadership styles could each contribute to positive outcomes. However, teams in which team leaders did not feel clearly empowered to direct their teams consistently underperformed.[59] In the same study, we also found that projects with greater complexity, uncertainty, or

Table 7.12 *Summarizing Hersey and Blanchard's situational leadership model.*

Performance readiness	Leadership style	Positive leadership actions	Negative leadership actions
Unable and insecure	High task/low relationship	Breaking tasks into smaller pieces, reducing fear of mistakes, instructing, guiding, structuring	Demanding, demeaning, attacking, dominating, controlling, coercing, harassing
Unable and unwilling	High task/low relationship	Telling, directing, informing, establishing rewards and consequences	
Unable but confident or willing	High task/high relationship	Persuading, mentoring, coaching, teaching, convincing, explaining, training	Manipulating, deceiving, preaching, entrapping, deluding, rationalizing, defending, cornering
Able but insecure	High relationship/ low task	Participating, encouraging, supporting, facilitating, involving, empowering, troubleshooting	Patronizing, condescending, placating, ensnaring, wavering, stalling
Able but unwilling	High relationship/ low task	Sharing, involving, empowering, focusing on results, communicating meaningfulness	
Able and confident and willing	Low relationship/ low task	Delegating, observing, listening, monitoring, entrusting, tracking, attending, empowering	Avoiding, dumping, relinquishing, abandoning, withdrawing, ignoring, overloading

controversy benefited from more participatory leadership styles that encouraged collaborative deliberation amongst team members throughout the process.

Applications

When to use it

Leadership Theory can be useful in any context in which you wish to create direction, alignment, and commitment in other people to move collectively toward a common goal. While many other theories in this book are also highly applicable to these situations, *Leadership Theory* provides specific ideas for situations in which formal or informal groups or organizations exist or emerge to address a collective challenge.

How to use it

Across contexts, a few consistencies about effective leadership hold. These consistencies can be useful for selecting appropriate leaders or being a more successful leader yourself.

1. Leaders with certain traits (see Table 7.10) tend to be more successful than others in the long run.
2. The most favorable situations for leaders tend to be those in which they are well-liked, possess power, and have well-articulated goals.
3. In general, leadership styles that lack concern for personal relationships and fail to empower followers to any degree over time rarely sustain high performance.[60]
4. Being attentive, flexible, and responsive to the needs and situations of followers enhances the likelihood of sustaining high performance across contexts.

How to use it: Developing positive leadership traits and practices

The most important trait influencing the long-term effectiveness of a leader is his or her trustworthiness. In this context, trustworthiness is typically related to perceptions of the leaders' ability, benevolence, and integrity (see *6.1 Trust Theory*). These traits can be developed through practice and dedication. There are countless manuals and self-help books on leadership development. Most point to the importance of being proactive and continually learning, demonstrating genuine concern for followers and others, staying positive and motivated, and adhering to a set of ethical principles in all decision making and behavior. I recommend Stephen Covey's work on the subject in particular.[61]

Trust can be further created through establishing procedures for decision making and workload sharing that are perceived as fair by followers and creating environments in which people feel heard and comfortable to express risky ideas. See *6.1 Trust Theory*, *7.2 Team Effectiveness Theory*, and *7.5 Nonaka's Organizational Knowledge Creation Theory* for more specific recommendations.

How to use it: Creating favorable leadership situations

Leaders are who are viewed as trustworthy, highly capable, energetic, and positive are most commonly well-liked (see *6.1 Trust Theory*). While other elements of charisma and attractiveness can also drive favorable dispositions toward certain leaders, they may be less easily learned.

Different bases of power may be more or less relevant in different situations. In informal leadership situations, where no official title has been bestowed upon the leader, trustworthiness and goal alignment may be the most important factors in creating influence. If I meet a potential leader who is trustworthy and can help me achieve a goal I care about, I am more likely to follow. This is especially the case if our shared goal is clearly defined and agreed upon. While coercive, reward or information power can create short-term alliances, they rarely create lasting leadership relationships, especially in the absence of a formal hierarchy. Rather, referent and expert power, which entail affinitive and rational trust, are stronger drivers of long-term performance. This underlines the importance of being a consistent performer who demonstrates genuine care for followers.

Oftentimes, leaders might be officially designated or chosen from an otherwise non-hierarchical group, such as a member of a team being selected to lead a particular project. In these cases, their "position power" is enhanced if supervisors or others explicitly and publicly articulate the leadership role. If you find yourself in the role of being designated a team leader within an organization, it is worth the effort to solicit public endorsement from a superior to clarify your role as leader for team members. If you are a superior creating a team at a lower level, providing this public empowerment can enhance team performance. If you find yourself elected or otherwise designated a leader of an informal group, spending time to clarify the roles and responsibilities of you and others is likely also a worthwhile endeavor.

How to use it: Follower-centered leadership and adapting to different contexts

Successful leaders can adapt to the needs, desires, and situations of their followers. This requires developing skills and habits that direct attention to followers' motivations, constraints, willingness, security, and capacity. Hopefully, reading and reflecting on the theories in this book provide powerful insights into many of these skills and habits. Paramount among them are listening and empathizing with followers, providing situations and opportunities for growth and self-actualization, plugging into followers' intrinsic motivations, and maintaining a trusting environment for collaborative learning, risk-taking, and performance. Particularly useful theories in these regards include *4.1 Social Norm Theory, 4.2 Norm Activation Theory, 4.6 Self-Determination Theory, 4.9 Maslow's Hierarchy of Needs*, and *6.1 Trust Theory*.

Different contexts will demand different approaches. Table 7.12 can be a useful guide for interacting with people at different career stages or levels of performance readiness. Strategies should adapt as followers change or develop. As people's willingness and capabilities change, so should leadership styles.

How to use it: Maintaining a wide angle view

Successful leaders are typically good boundary spanners. Effective boundary spanners regularly scan their group's external context to identify and secure information and resources; to build support for their group's work and link their work synergistically to that of others; to protect or defend group members from unproductive external controversies or demands (see also *7.4 Project Risk*); to identify potential problems or opportunities; to help manage competing accountabilities of external stakeholders (see also *7.3 Accountability Theory*); to ensure the group's work stays current and meaningful as contexts and conditions change; and to be able to refresh group members' motivation by communicating the meaningfulness of their work within the broader context.

How to use it: Leading from where you are

While this section has focused primarily on leadership within organizations, teams, or networks, the rest of this book clearly demonstrates dozens of ways to exert influence to accomplish goals outside of traditional leadership contexts. A formal title bestows but one source of power (legitimate power). Other power sources of influence are widely accessible to people in almost any context.

Key references

Bass, B.M., and R.E. Riggio 2006. *Transformational leadership*. Second edition. London: Laurence Erlbaum Associates.
Hersey, P., K.H. Blanchard, and D.E. Johnson 2008. *Management of organizational behavior: Leading human resources*. Ninth Edition. Upper Saddle River, NJ: Pearson Education, Inc.

8
Systems theories

Introduction: Social-ecological systems, resilience, and adaptive governance

The theories in this chapter are most relevant at the scale of the *social-ecological system*. Social-ecological systems contain natural resources, users of those resources, and the interactions between each. Because these systems typically cross social, political, cultural, and other jurisdictional boundaries, it is rare that any single entity, organization, or agency can adequately manage them on their own. Rather, social-ecological systems require effective *governance* (as opposed to government). The concept of governance encompasses the structures, processes, and traditions through which people in a society share power and make decisions.[1] Thus, governance challenges stretch beyond the purview of government agencies or single private landowners or organizations to include a wide array of stakeholders.

The concept of *resilience* has become central to the way in which researchers and managers consider social-ecological systems and their governance. While the traditional concept of sustainability implies persistence and continuity, the resilience concept stresses that systems are in constant flux. Resilient social-ecological systems are able to bounce back after shocks and maintain some semblance of the valuable functions and services they had previously provided, such as clean air or water, habitat, or other resources. In this view, the value of social-ecological systems is embedded in their functions, rather than in their specific forms. The relative importance of those functions, and the services they provide, may be hotly debated by different entities, making their governance extremely complex. Moreover, the maintenance or transformation[2] of different aspects of social-ecological systems are central topics of conflict and debate for those involved in their governance.

Environmental governance scenarios involve incomplete, uncertain, and sometimes inaccurate information, as well as changing, and often conflicting, human values. Effective environmental governance thus inevitably requires negotiation,

Social Science Theory for Environmental Sustainability: A Practical Guide. Marc J. Stern, Oxford University Press (2018). © Marc J. Stern 2018. DOI 10.1093/oso/9780198793182.001.0001

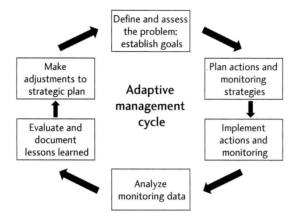

Figure 8.1 A general depiction of the adaptive management cycle.

monitoring, collaborative learning, and connectivity across organizations and institutions at various scales in both the definition and pursuit of desired states for social-ecological systems.[3] ***Adaptive capacity*** refers to the ability of a resource governance system to collectively learn and respond to changes in ways that maintain valued functions and services. It thus builds upon the well-known concept of adaptive management (see Figure 8.1) through acknowledging the importance of building enough ***social capital***[4] between the actors involved so that the system can benefit from diverse talents, knowledge, and perspectives at each stage in the cycle. If actors feel safe enough to honestly share their concerns, debate their ideas, co-generate strategies for action, and learn together, each can contribute to effective ***adaptive governance***.[5]

The theories in this chapter address issues relevant to resilience and adaptive governance at systems scales. While there is a vast library on these themes in the literature,[6] I have chosen four specific theories that help to explain each at this larger scale of consideration, the social-ecological system. Because this book is centered on how people can work together to address environmental sustainability, I take a somewhat anthropocentric view by focusing on theories that relate to directing these systems toward desired states that may serve diverse human values about them.

8.1 Commons Theory

Uses: Making decisions about how to develop systems to manage or govern resources that are not privately owned, designing conservation or development projects

How can we appropriately manage resources that nobody owns?

Garrett Hardin's classic 1968 *Tragedy of the Commons* article explained how resources that are either publicly owned (by everyone in a community) or unowned become depleted. Because the benefits of exploiting such systems accrue individually, while the costs are spread over the whole population, individuals choose to use as much as possible while the resource lasts. This leads to its eventual overall degradation as each user makes the same decision.

Hardin viewed this outcome as inevitable without either government ownership or privatization of the resource. This prediction is based on an assumption of all resource users as selfish, norm-free individuals aiming to maximize their own short-term take of the common resource.

Scholars studying these challenges, however, have found that local institutions can sometimes emerge to effectively address the *Tragedy of the Commons* problem without privatization or government ownership. Moreover, Hardin's proposed solutions are often wrought with their own problems. Government intervention requires reliable and stable funding, monitoring, and enforcement mechanisms, each of which may not always be available. Privatization may often exacerbate resource degradation, as individuals often maximize short-term profits over long-term sustainability for numerous reasons.

The historical work of environmental sociologist Walter Firey revealed that long-lasting resource systems have always contained aspects that are not economically gainful to individual users, demonstrating that individuals do not always aim to maximize their take of common resources. This is largely because people are influenced by each other in non-economic ways through formal and informal contracts of reciprocity, trust, and acting for the good of the group. Conformity to group norms emerges from both self-interest (in the long-term sustainability, or resilience, of the resource) and moral consciousness, which develops through relationships with other community members. In these cases, the primary threats to sustainable resource use involve external influences, such as the injection of new technologies, new markets, and new individuals or groups.

Table 8.1 *Ostrom's eight design principles for long-enduring common pool resources management institutions.*

Design principle	Explanation
1. Clearly defined boundaries	Clear boundaries between legitimate users and non-users of clearly defined resources, such that legitimate users may regulate and/or defend them from external appropriators.
2. Congruence	1. Resource use rules about time, place, technology, and quantities fit appropriately with local conditions. 2. Rules ensure that the distribution of benefits of resource use is roughly proportionate to the investment required to use the resources.
3. Collective-choice arrangements	The majority of resource users are sufficiently empowered to participate in modifying the rules when necessary.
4. Monitoring	Monitors, who audit both user behavior and resource conditions, are accountable to the users.
5. Graduated sanctions	Resource users share a common understanding that graduated sanctions (which vary depending on the severity of the violation) will be imposed by other users if they violate the rules.
6. Conflict-resolution mechanisms	Resource users have rapid access to low-cost local arenas to resolve conflicts within the group.
7. Minimal recognition of rights to organize	The rights of resource users to devise their own institutions are not challenged by external government authorities. In other words, there is some external recognition of the legitimacy of the group to govern itself.
8. Nested enterprises	In complex systems (those with fuzzier geographic or social boundaries, in particular), resource use rules, monitoring, enforcement, conflict resolution, and governance activities are organized in multiple layers of nested enterprises. In other words, rules and appropriate activities are considered and linked at multiple scales (e.g., local, regional, national).

Elinor Ostrom, who received a Nobel Prize for her work on solutions to the *Tragedy of the Commons* in 2009, identified eight key principles shared by long-enduring local institutions managing *common pool resources*. Common pool resources are defined as resources where exclusion of potential users is costly and exploitation by one user reduces availability for others (see Table 8.1).

Each of these principles is predicated on (1) the existence of a shared recognition of a generalized "community," regardless of its scale, (2) a widespread general concern for the community's well-being, and (3) intra-group norms of trust and reciprocity. **Community**, in this sense, could be defined in multiple ways.[7] In its most general sense, community refers to a group of people who are knowingly dependent upon each other in some way to ensure the continued availability of important resources and recognize the potential for collaboration.

Ostrom stresses that users of a common pool resource system can include (1) those who always behave based on narrow self-interest and refuse to cooperate ("free riders"); (2) those who are unwilling to cooperate unless they can be assured that they won't be exploited by free riders; (3) those who are willing to cooperate in hopes that others will return their trust; and (4) a few genuine altruists who are committed to higher returns for the group. Successful management of the commons depends on having a low proportion of those who occupy the first group. Otherwise, external intervention may be necessary to sustain the resource.

Applications

When to use it

Commons Theory applies most directly to the development or maintenance of institutions that might effectively govern resource use, particularly in the case of common pool resources. Common pool resources include publicly owned or unowned terrain, such as a park, a river, or a coral reef, or globally important unowned resources, like air, water, and weather. *Commons Theory* can apply at multiple scales, from considering potential projects in local communities for sustaining natural resources to addressing climate change as a global community.

How to use it: On a local scale

Perhaps the most important use of *Commons Theory* is to recognize when external intervention may negatively influence local cultural norms that support and nurture a sustainable, or resilient, resource management system. Examples abound in which external agents, such as national governments or aid agencies, have introduced new management regimes or technologies that disturbed previously healthy resource management systems. When national parks in some parts of Nepal replaced local forest management systems, massive deforestation ensued, as local cultural norms broke down (Stevens 1993). The introduction of genetically engineered rice crops and prescribed growing practices during the Green Revolution conflicted with traditional practices that maintained healthy landscapes in Bali for centuries, leading to deterioration of the resource (Lansing 2006). Ostrom's design principles provide a basis for assessing the health of local institutions for resource management and thus reveal cases in which certain forms of external intervention might be more damaging than helpful.[8]

Ostrom's design principles can also help to manage external threats. Changing external conditions can sometimes threaten otherwise healthy local management systems. For example, the expansion of market economies, such as tourism or resource extraction, can quickly shift local power dynamics, as some people benefit more than others and foreign cultural norms are introduced.[9] The design principles stress the importance of maintaining the rights and autonomy of legitimate resource users and the strength of collective action over individualistic pursuits in maintaining a healthy resource base. The work of external agents who wish to support these endeavors is strengthened when they can work together with local people to validate and endorse existing cultural norms that promote the notion of interconnected social and ecological health. External agents can also serve as boundary spanners that mediate and translate between the local and the extra-local to help local institutions to preserve components of successful local governance arrangements as they adapt to external pressures (see *8.3 Diffusion Theory*).

Ostrom's design principles also help to explain why certain common conservation strategies often backfire: new economic incentives can often disrupt local norms, as inequities develop and new motivations are introduced into a system.[10] Moreover, externally imposed management systems can disrupt social structures that maintain social norms, sometimes effectively re-organizing local and regional power structures.[11] Unless specific protections are guaranteed or economic incentives are directly linked with maintaining intact natural resources in perpetuity (both rare cases), a lack of broadly supported local institutions in which all members participate can undermine effective resource management.[12]

Alternatively, the design principles can be used to diagnose, design, or shore up existing resource management systems. Table 8.1 can serve as a checklist in this sense. Diagnoses may often reveal that the conditions for effective community-based common pool resource management don't exist. In these cases, Hardin's original theory suggests that government intervention and enforcement or working to privatize ownership (through land purchases by conservation agents, for example) might best serve to protect natural resources. These strategies tend to work best in the long run when local stakeholders are involved in their design and execution and consulted in decisions about their management.[13]

How to use it: On a global scale

Although issues such as the protection of the open seas, air pollution, and climate change clearly involve common pool resources, Ostrom's design principles have been difficult to apply at this scale due to the lack of a coherent self-aware global community that could realistically embody the principles. The problem of free riders is currently exacerbated by nationalistic rhetoric, and realistic means for applying meaningful sanctions are elusive due to unequal distributions of global power. Perhaps the most obvious lesson of *Commons Theory* and the large body of research it has generated is the need for resource users to be able to see themselves as a community with common interest in maintaining its resource base. I personally see hope in many of the theories in this book, collectively, holding promise for moving the world in this direction.

Key references

Firey, W. 1960. *Man, mind, and land: A theory of resource use.* Glencoe, IL: Free Press.

Hardin, G. 1968. The tragedy of the commons. *Science* 162(3859): 1243–8.

Ostrom, E. 1990. *Governing the commons: The evolution of institutions for collective action.* New York: Cambridge University Press.

Ostrom, E. 2005. *Understanding institutional diversity.* Princeton, NJ: Princeton University Press.

Ostrom, E., J. Burger, C.B. Field, R.B. Norgaard, and D. Policansky 1999. Revisiting the commons: Local lessons, global challenges. *Science* 284(5412): 278–82.

8.2 The Community Capitals Framework

Uses: Planning, project design, working in local communities, designing conservation or development projects, designing or managing governance processes

> How can we best marshal community assets to promote healthy and resilient social-ecological systems?

In its most general sense, a "capital" is defined as a stock which can yield a flow of valuable goods or services. Community capitals are assets that can be used to contribute to a community's overall health and well-being. Cornelia Flora and her colleagues have demonstrated the value of seven community capitals in contributing to healthy ecosystems, economic security, and socially inclusive (equitable) communities.

While each of these capitals can easily be translated to the individual level, in terms of ownership or traits of an individual person, I provide definitions below specific to the group or community level.

Natural Capital provides the raw resources upon which all other capitals depend. It includes the air, land, water, soil, wildlife, vegetation, landscape, and weather that surround us. The quality, quantity, and diversity of these forms of capital provide both opportunities and limits for human well-being.

Built Capital comprises all human-constructed infrastructure, including houses, bridges, roads, buildings, solar panels, wind farms, chemicals, schools, technologies, trains, planes, and automobiles, among other things. Depending on its purpose, use or neglect, built capital can have positive or negative influences on human well-being, sustainability, and resilience.

Financial Capital involves all assets once they become monetized. These assets tend to be the most liquid and fast-moving of all capitals and are typically measured in the form of cash, investments, and savings.

Political Capital is the ability of a group to turn its values into rules and regulations that can determine the distribution of resources. This involves organization, connections, and most directly, power, which can be formal or informal.

Social Capital refers to social networks, shared norms, trust, and reciprocity that enable people to live and work together. *Bonding social capital* describes these relationships within a specific group. *Bridging social capital* describes these relationships when they exist between socially defined groups, and typically involves boundary spanning individuals (see *7.5 Nonaka's Theory of Organizational Knowledge Creation* and *7.6 Leadership Theory*).

Human Capital encompasses the knowledge, skills, talents, abilities, health, time, and available effort of people that can facilitate learning and action.

Cultural Capital describes a shared worldview about what is taken for granted. First and foremost, it provides the lens through which cultural members make sense of the world around them. It can also include cultural artifacts, myths, festivals, ceremonies, or other traditions that symbolize a shared cultural identity.

Each of the capitals is linked to each other. For example, the creation of *built capital* typically requires *financial capital* and can be converted back into it. *Political capital* typically emerges from strong *bridging social capital*, whereas *cultural capital* typically grows out of the development of strong *bonding social capital*.

The seven capitals are increasingly used to measure the health, trajectory, and resilience of communities, with adequate stores of each contributing to overall positive community health.[14] I share additional insights from research within the conservation and development fields about the relative importance and positive and negative impacts of each below.

Lessons about each of the capitals in social-ecological systems

Particular attention has been given to *social capital* by social scientists studying social-ecological systems, dating back to long before Flora and colleagues coined "The Community Capitals Framework."[15] Research suggests that social capital may be the key catalyst for reversing trends of decline in social-ecological systems and for stimulating innovation, conservation, and development.[16] While adequate stores of other forms of capital might be necessary for sustained conservation action or community resilience, they are rarely sufficient without strong social capital to drive the process.

In a study I conducted with Nabin Baral on community-based conservation in Nepal, for example, we found that social capital, in particular intra-group trust (bonding social capital) and the ability to call upon outside organizations for help (bridging social capital) enabled certain governing bodies to continue to function throughout the Maoist insurgency (1996–2006), while others without strong stores of these forms of capital collapsed.[17] Human capital, in the forms of relevant experience and institutional memory of organizational members, also contributed to organizational resilience. Financial and built capitals were not significant predictors.

Natural capital is often more diverse than most communities realize. Boom and bust economies often rise and fall as a result of a failure to capitalize on the diversity of natural resources within an area. For example, mining communities have often collapsed when their ore is depleted. However, some have been able to diversify based on the beauty of their amenity-rich landscapes through various forms of culturally compatible tourism. Other communities, however, have perhaps placed too much faith in tourism to the detriment of the beauty or particular resources that attracted the tourists in the first place.[18] The island of Bali, Indonesia, for example, has developed an enormous trash problem resulting from its rapid tourism development and lack of public services, which is now beginning to threaten the island's tourism future.[19] Managing natural capital effectively relies on sound planning and a recognition of the diverse resources offered by a natural area.[20]

Similar to natural capital, *financial and built capitals* contribute best to resilient communities and landscapes when economies are diversified and investments are well-planned with broad societal input and a long-term vision. Financial and built capitals are typically the fastest-changing capitals, and therefore the easiest to manipulate. While investments in these capitals are often necessary, they are rarely sufficient on their own to generate long-term benefits without substantial social, political, or human capital to direct their impacts. Development projects have often fallen prey to investing dollars or building infrastructure that fails to produce meaningful long-term outcomes.[21] These failures often result from a lack of attention to simultaneously building social and human capital. Investments in financial and built capitals are thus best considered initial catalysts or barrier-removers, rather than long-term solutions to sustainability issues.

Cultural capital is rarely something that can be created anew. Rather, investments in cultural capital can renew or reinforce pre-existing traditions or norms. Heritage tourism provides one such example of using cultural capital to build economic prosperity. More commonly, cultural capital comes into play in environmental work in defining goals and appropriate means for achieving them. Working within culturally appropriate frameworks of communication, interaction, goal-setting, and strategy-planning enables social capital to grow and human capital to be invested. Cultural capital can become a liability when certain groups (cultures) might be privileged over others. This can create divisions among stakeholder groups if not carefully managed. In diverse settings, agreeing upon ground rules and procedures for accepting and valuing diverse viewpoints and establishing rights, responsibilities, and privileges within different decision-making domains can help to assuage potential conflicts.

Human capital is situated within human talents, time and energy available to do meaningful work, and is linked to the other capitals in multiple ways. For example, in areas with weak financial and built capitals, the outmigration of youth can be quite common, as they search for work elsewhere. This can create meaningful gaps in both human and social capital. Lack of investment in education, health care, and in protecting or enhancing healthy natural and social capitals can leave communities deprived of abilities, energy, and motivations necessary to thrive, not to mention an erosion of cultural capital as community pride diminishes.

Environmental work that addresses capacity-building, relationship-building, amenity enhancement, and overall quality of life can create synergies that enhance all community capitals and thus better promote community resilience.

Political capital is most directly about power and influence. Oftentimes in environmental work this means partnering with the right people to make things happen. Sometimes, this means working directly with formal elected leaders or hired bureaucrats who hold decision-making responsibilities. Often, however, developing or tapping into political capital involves identifying informal opinion leaders with the ability to make various connections and inspire or persuade others into collective action. See *8.3 Diffusion Theory* and *8.4 Collective Impact* for more detail.

Applications

When to use it

The Community Capitals Framework was articulated to help describe, understand, and monitor community-level economic development, particularly in rural communities. However, the concepts are broadly applicable to other contexts, including cases where external agents attempt to influence conservation behaviors or sustainable development within communities; where community members attempt the same within their own communities; or wherever individuals attempt to address environmental or sustainable development issues at the community (or larger) scale.

How to use it

Charting community capitals can be a helpful planning or assessment tool for a wide array of initiatives that aim to influence environmental action. In particular, predicting and monitoring which capitals can become assets or liabilities can lead to more effective strategic planning and adaptive management of projects. Crafting a table similar to Table 8.2 could prove valuable for evaluating existing capital stocks, weighing potential investments, and envisioning resulting asset growth or depletion, liabilities or conflicts. Tracking the influences of investing in one capital on other capital stocks may also be helpful. For example, investing in human capital through capacity-building for alternative agricultural practices, such as rotational grazing, can have the following outcomes:

1. Enhanced natural capital by limiting the need for additional forest clearing for livestock.
2. Enhanced financial capital through producing higher yields with less investment.

Table 8.2 *An example tool for incorporating consideration of the community capitals into planning and monitoring.*

Capital	Assets	Liabilities	Potential investments or other actions	Notes on barriers, feedbacks, adaptations, or problem solving
Natural				
Financial				
Built				*Multiple additional columns might be appropriate here—especially for understanding potential ripple effects of capital investments on other capital stocks (see the example in the text).*
Cultural				
Political				
Human				
Social				

3. Enhanced social capital *if* the training is designed to develop a community of practitioners who can rely on each other for help and expertise.
4. Potentially negative impacts on political, cultural, and social capital if some community members accumulate wealth from the practice while others do not.

Thinking through the ripple effects of one capital investment on other capital stocks can provide insights on potential synergies that might be achieved through thoughtful program design (item #3 above) and reveal potentially negative unintended consequences (item #4 above) that might be mitigated through more thorough planning and community feedback.

Key references

Fey, S., C. Bregendahl, and C. Flora 2006. The measurement of community capitals through research, *Online Journal of Rural Research and Policy* 1(1): 1–28. https://doi.org/10.4148/ojrrp.v1i1.29

Flora, C.B., J.L. Flora, and S.R. Gasteyer 2016. *Rural communities: Legacy and change.* Fifth Edition. Boulder, CO: Westview Press.

8.3 Diffusion Theory

Uses: Spreading ideas, designing conservation or development projects, working with local communities

> **How do innovations become adopted and how do they spread?**

Environmental work often involves spreading a good idea and encouraging its adoption through social networks. Examples include promoting more sustainable consumer choices, farming practices, or other conservation behaviors in target audiences. *Diffusion Theory* helps to explain this process and the factors that make adoption more or less likely.

Figure 8.2 summarizes the key factors that typically drive whether someone will choose to adopt a new practice or not. Some innovations may be imposed from above or through law. *Diffusion Theory*, however, better applies to optional choices made by individuals or groups. Adoption decisions are influenced by how and by whom ideas are communicated, by the social norms and social networks of target audiences, by the characteristics of the individuals making adoption decisions, and by their evaluations of both the innovation and its communicators.

Adopter characteristics: early vs late adopters

Figure 8.3 depicts the typical progression of the successful diffusion of an innovation. The earliest adopters are referred to as "innovators." They are followed by early adopters, early majority adopters, late majority adopters, and finally by very late adopters, or laggards. In Figure 8.3, the solid bell-shaped curve breaks down the percent of adopters typically falling into each category.[22] The dotted s-shaped curve depicts the cumulative number of total adopters over time. The exact length of different portions of this curve will vary, but the general "s" shape tends to be

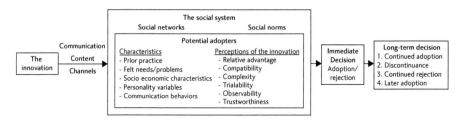

Figure 8.2 A summary of the innovation-decision process (based on Rogers, 2003).

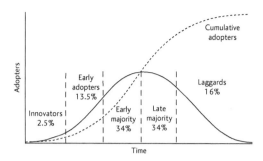

Figure 8.3 Categories of adopters based on timing of adoption. Adapted from Rogers (2003).

rather consistent, with slow adoption at first, followed by more rapid adoption, and finally a leveling off.

Innovators and early adopters typically share certain characteristics in common. They tend be more highly educated, have higher social status, participate more often in their communities, be more cosmopolitan (connected to the outside world), and have greater exposure to more channels of information than others.[23] This is because these people tend to learn about an innovation first and also tend to have a greater ability to take risks.

Other personal characteristics that influence potential adopters include their prior habits, their perceptions of social norms, whether they feel they have needs that are not being met, their general predispositions toward risk-taking behavior, their degrees of trust for different communication sources, their typical sources of information, and their perceived ability to experiment.[24]

Communication channels

People can learn about new ideas from various sources, including politicians, public officials, scientific experts, celebrities, advertising campaigns, relatives, co-workers, friends, and neighbors. Not surprisingly, the communication source makes a big difference on whether people receive the message and how they interpret it. Diffusion research has found that different communicators may be more or less influential at different stages in the diffusion of an idea. Mass media channels are typically very good at building general awareness of an innovation. However, interpersonal channels of communication are typically far superior for persuasion. Moreover, the earliest adopters tend to rely on different information sources than later adopters.

In the early stages of diffusion, communications from experts are typically most persuasive. In the later stages, friends and peers tend to be more effective. Across all stages of the diffusion process, credibility of the communicator is a powerful driver of adoption. In the early stages, this may often be associated with rational trust in experts. In the later stages, affinitive trust may become equally important (see *6.1 Trust Theory*). Diffusion research has found that higher degrees of **homophily**, or similarity between the communicator and the message recipient on attributes such as education, socioeconomic status, and political beliefs, typically enhance the likelihood of adoption. For the most part, interpersonal diffusion networks are largely homophilous. However, for diffusions to spread more widely, they must leap across homophilous networks. Herein lies the importance of social networks, and opinion leaders in particular.

Social networks and opinion leaders

Multiple aspects of social network theory deserve some attention when considering the diffusion and adoption of an idea or practice. **Social network theory** views social relationships as a system of nodes and ties. Nodes are individuals or groups, and ties are the relationships between them. Ties can be strong or weak, and direct or indirect. Strong ties exist between entities that interact directly and come to know each other in some meaningful way. Weak ties indicate little meaningful direct interaction between two entities. Nodes with indirect ties are only connected via their relationships with intermediaries. Network structures can vary tremendously.[25] While detailed mapping of social networks can be intense work, basic mapping can help to identify potentially effective means for diffusing a new idea. In particular, the concepts of opinion leaders and structural holes provide useful insights (see Figure 8.4).

Opinions leaders are people or groups who are able to influence others' evaluations of new ideas. Decades of diffusion research suggest that these people may occupy variable roles within communities. In many cases, they are key boundary spanners "who carry information across social boundaries between groups. They are not the people at the top of things so much as people at the edge of things, not leaders within groups so much as brokers across groups."[26] In other cases, they can be more centrally prominent and influential people within a community, such as formal or informal leaders or community role models.[27] As noted above, the most relevant opinion leaders may change over time, from experts early on in the diffusion process to peers later on.[28] Attention to pre-existing social networks and the early recruitment of appropriate opinion leaders generally accelerates diffusion processes.[29]

Structural holes[30] exist where there is an absence of direct ties between different clusters within a network (see Figure 8.4). Finding and filling these holes can be extremely valuable in promoting learning, diffusion, and adoption,

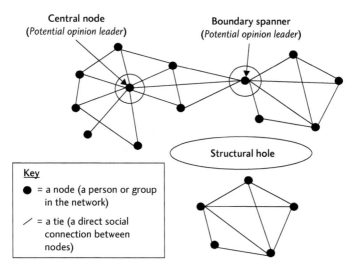

Figure 8.4 A simple social network map.

particularly when each group holds different knowledge. Brokering new relationships between these groups can facilitate the diffusion of innovations through providing potentially homophilous exemplars of a practice or through finding new potential opinion leaders. Many conservation projects have found it useful to introduce people in one place to similar people in another, often for demonstration purposes (to observe an innovation in practice). For example, some projects I've been involved with have brought fishermen from one island with depleted fishing stocks to another to observe the positive impacts of marine conservation efforts; others have brought agriculturalists from one village to another to observe the positive impacts of new irrigation systems or new farming techniques.

Elements of the innovation

When potential adopters view the messenger as trustworthy and perceive the following characteristics about the potential innovation, they are more likely to adopt it.

Relative advantage: The likely benefits of the new practice outweigh its costs and exceed the value of current practices.

Compatibility: The new practice does not conflict with dominant social norms, personal norms, past experiences, or needs of the adopter.

Complexity: The new practice is not overly difficult to understand or implement.

Trialability: There is opportunity to experiment with the new practice on a trial basis at low cost.

Observability: There is opportunity to easily observe the results of the practice, either through demonstration or observing neighbors.

Longer-term considerations

Numerous factors help to explain the longevity of an innovation—in particular, late adoption, persistence, or discontinuance. These may include:

- the confirmation, disconfirmation, continuance, or discontinuance of expected benefits;
- the social acceptability or rejection of the innovation by relevant reference groups (see *4.1 Social Norm Theory*);
- the development of new habits, routines, or norms associated with the innovation;
- changing ecological conditions or financial situations;
- the discontinuance of incentive payments (see *4.8 Motivation Crowding Theory*); and
- the introduction of newer innovations that may replace others.

Applications

When to use it

Diffusion Theory is relevant in any case where you might be trying to change the behavior of a group, community, or larger population. This includes implementing various forms of environmental or conservation projects, such as recycling programs, land conservation programs, ecotourism practices, or development initiatives. It may also involve new business practices or instituting natural resource management rules or governance regimes in which people are expected to adopt new forms of collective or individual decision making.

How to use it

You might consider the following a checklist of characteristics to promote the successful diffusion and adoption of new ideas or practices:

Relative advantage: Clearly communicate how the benefits of the new idea exceed the costs or risks of adopting it. This may entail covering (paying for) initial start-up costs to remove key barriers to implementation or experimentation.

Compatibility: Design innovations to match with the dominant social norms of target audiences. This means considering both pre-existing habits (descriptive norms) and cultural beliefs, practices, and taboos (injunctive norms). For example, providing ten gallon jugs to carry water from a newly provided clean water source will not work in a location where children are the primary collectors of water and have no means of transportation other than walking. Ten gallons of water weigh over 80 pounds (36 kg)! Even if exactly ten gallons of water is badly needed, the innovation cannot be adopted without a transportation solution that works with local norms.

Similarly, asking individuals to change their public behaviors is unlikely to be successful unless they believe others' behaviors will change as well (or at least not negatively judge them for changing their own). Letting lawns grow wild in a wealthy suburb is not a winning proposition to control water drainage or enhance habitats. Neither is asking rural pastoralists to get rid of their cattle to stop forest clearing for pasture. Cattle (and nice lawns) are commonly a sign of wealth and prosperity, a clear marker of socioeconomic status. A more promising effort to curb forest clearing for pasture might introduce the idea of rotational grazing, such that grazing plots can be re-used so additional forest no longer needs to be cleared. In the suburban example, developing attractive designs for greater water absorption might be a necessary first step.

Complexity: Ensure that the innovation is not overly complicated or difficult to understand or implement. Use local language, culturally relevant visual aids, and analogies to explain how new practices will align with pre-existing ones. Efforts to establish rotational grazing can be directly compared to the amount of effort involved in slash-and-burn forest clearing for new pastures. Start-up costs, materials, or labor can be provided to construct enclosures, easy-to-use tools can be provided to keep track of grazing schedules, and pastoralists' work hours can actually be reduced over time.

Trialability: Whenever possible, consider how a member of the target audience can experiment with the new practice on a trial basis at low cost. Is there a way to demonstrate its efficacy on a small scale? Can a small portion of a farmer's field be used to compare yields before converting the whole operation?

Observability: Develop an experimental demonstration site or take people to visit others who have already adopted the practice. Both observability and trialability help to reduce the perceived risks of adoption. Be sure to clearly report successes in terms that matter for potential adopters. For example, how have rice yields changed under the new system compared to traditional harvests? How much time did the pastoralist have to spend in his pastures compared to before? How fat are the cattle? What other benefits have been achieved?

A trustworthy communicator: Consider carefully who is communicating about the innovation. The complicated concept of trustworthiness can be best untangled through examination of *6.1 Trust Theory*, though lessons from *6.2 Principled*

Negotiation, 5.1 Identity Theory, 5.2 Self-Affirmation Theory, 5.5 Moral Foundations Theory, and *5.7 Meyer's Culture Map* will also apply in different settings. In short, communicators should exude benevolence (having the message recipient's best interest in mind), ability (being well-informed and capable), and *integrity* (adhering to a consistent moral standard that aligns with the moral system of the message recipient). Communications should acknowledge the merits of the viewpoints of the message recipient and provide opportunities for meaningful dialogue and flexibility in design based on that dialogue. When communicating within broader groups, trust is developed through rational, affinitive, and procedural means, reflecting competence and consistency, genuine understanding, listening and care, and fair and transparent procedures, respectively.

A social network approach to communication: Using a networked approach that taps into pre-existing social networks and facilitates the collaborative identification of a problem and potential solutions can have two benefits. First, solutions that complement local norms are more likely to be identified by insiders than by outsiders. Second, as ideas spread through a local social network, people can begin to see the likelihood of collective change, making personal change easier than would be possible through communication by outside experts alone.

Different communicators are likely to be more or less successful in different phases of a diffusion process. Most successful diffusion efforts involve external experts communicating with key opinion leaders early in the process. External expert communications alone will rarely, if ever, change dominant social practices. Rather, working first with individuals who are locally viewed as trustworthy sources of information or opinion leaders with strong social ties to multiple groups within the population enhances the likelihood of adoption. Key advice on selecting appropriate early adopters and communicators includes:

- If possible, choose initial communicators that share common characteristics (homophily), particularly cultural ones, with potential early adopters.
- Identify people who are widely respected within a target community. Be wary of selecting those who are most vocal at a community meeting too quickly. Just because someone is prominent or outspoken does not necessarily mean they are an opinion leader. Taking the time to gain at least a basic understanding of the social networks of target communities is well worth the effort.
- Identifying multiple opinion leaders can ensure more reflective design, enhance feelings of ownership over the idea, and provide access to a wider array of local networks.
- Include members of the target audience within the design and/or revision of the innovation to ensure compatibility with the local context.

- Connect potential later adopters with early adopters to provide demonstrations of the positive effects of adoption.

Seek to identify structural holes within target audiences for adoption. Consider bridging these holes with expert communication and/or filling them by creating new connections (boundary spanners) between groups. Take groups of non-adopters to visit early adopters to expand the power of the network and to build additional social capital (see *8.2 The Community Capitals Framework*).

The typical patterns of adoption (the s-shaped curve in Figure 8.3) also provide important lessons for those introducing innovations into communities. First and foremost, the widespread adoption of a new innovation may take a long time. Expert communication with early adopters should give way to peer-to-peer communications as adoption spreads. This undergirds the importance of selecting potential early adopters that are highly visible and respected within their communities. Early adopters typically are more cosmopolitan (connected to the outside world), more educated, participate more in their communities, and are of higher socio-economic status than others. This does not mean that selecting first contacts only on these characteristics is a good idea, however. Involving a wider array of highly socially connected people can ensure more inclusive design and better dissemination of the idea. As early adopters achieve early successes, change agents' roles may shift from persuaders to supporters. Maintaining close and supportive contact with communities of adoption can help not only to troubleshoot and improve innovations, thus limiting the risks for future adopters, but also to strengthen the trustworthiness of the innovation, as relationships are built and strengthened, and new reference groups are formed that may include the change agents (see *4.1 Social Norm Theory*).[31]

Key references

Fliegel, F.C., and P.F. Korsching 2000. *Diffusion Research in Rural Sociology: The record and prospects for the future*. Middleton, Wisconsin: Social Ecology Press.

Rogers, E. 2003. *Diffusion of Innovations*. Fifth Edition. New York, NY: Free Press.

8.4 Collective Impact

Uses: Structuring collective action on large-scale societal issues, establishing long-term collaboration

> **What do we know about tested strategies for building a coalition to solve large-scale societal issues?**

Some issues, such as making an entire coastal region more resilient to flooding or cleaning up a badly polluted river and its watershed, often lie well beyond the scope of a single organization, or even a small group of them. *Collective Impact* initiatives represent one promising strategy for taking on these challenges.

Traditional efforts to bring about conservation, environmental restoration, or nature protection typically involve grants to single organizations (or small groups of them), public–private partnerships between government and non-governmental organizations, or loose partnerships between various stakeholders, each primarily pursuing their own organizational goals and collaborating to leverage their impacts when opportunities arise. While these types of initiatives can achieve varying degrees of success, they often struggle to create the social change necessary to establish long-term impacts. Systemic change typically takes far longer than typical grant funding cycles of 1–3 years. Baral and colleagues (2007), for example, demonstrated that it typically took 5–10 years for regular conservation activities to become established within community-based conservation efforts in Nepal, despite heavy investments and capacity-building. Moreover, as organizations compete within a crowded landscape for limited funding, concerns for organizational survival can sometimes supersede the achievement of broader societal goals. Competition for limited funds can influence organizations to pursue projects with more predictable and easily measurable outcomes, so that they can demonstrate success prior to the next granting cycle (see *7.3 Accountability Theory*). This focus on short-term successes can drive piecemeal gains and an overemphasis on solving the simple problems rather than investing in the social learning and long-term relationship-building required to address more complex problems and influence long-term change.

Successful *Collective Impact* initiatives involve long-term commitments from a group of influential actors from different sectors working together toward the resolution of a specific social-ecological problem. Scholars have identified five factors commonly related to the success of these types of initiatives: a common agenda, shared measurement systems, mutually reinforcing activities, continuous communication, and a backbone support organization.

A common agenda. All participants must agree on the primary goals of the initiative. This requires that differences regarding desired futures be discussed and resolved.

Shared measurement systems. While individual organizations might have their own internal metrics for success, all participants need to agree on the ways success will be measured and reported at the community or landscape level. That is, participants develop a set of shared metrics that measure broader outcomes relevant to their shared goals. Successful *Collective Impact* initiatives employ continuous evaluation and reflection, rather than the more traditional episodic evaluations at the end of each granting cycle typical of short-term grants. This enables lessons about promising and failing strategies to emerge and new strategies to be implemented in a more timely fashion.

Mutually reinforcing activities. Each participant undertakes activities in which they excel, in a way that is coordinated with the activities of each other entity in support of the initiative's overall goals. This requires extensive communication and planning to coordinate activities such that they will complement each other in pursuit of the desired *Collective Impact*. *Collective Impact* does *not* involve all organizations conducting the same activities.

Continuous communication. Successful *Collective Impact* initiatives take years to develop, during which high level communication between participants is nearly continuous. Establishing trust enables the development of common vocabularies, the realization or creation of shared motivations, and the safe spaces necessary for collaborative learning in which lessons about successes and failures can be shared (see *6.1 Trust Theory*).

Backbone support organizations. Most organizations within a *Collective Impact* initiative do not have the time to effectively serve as coordinators of the group in addition to their regular activities. Effective backbone support organizations have their own staff dedicated to coordinating the *Collective Impact* effort. In particular, they (1) help to establish a common vision and provide overall strategic direction; (2) facilitate dialogue between partners, supporting the alignment of activities; (3) establish shared measurement and guide data collection, analysis, and reporting; (4) help to build public support; (5) advance policy; and (6) mobilize funding. Research suggests that the first three functions are critical early in the initiative, with the latter functions typically developing more fully over time.

To establish these conditions, *Collective Impact* initiatives typically require:

- An influential, well-respected champion who sees the value in enabling diverse viewpoints and strategies rather than promoting their own point of view about appropriate solutions.

- Adequate funding for at least two to three years to enable the establishment of a backbone support organization and to support initial planning processes.
- Some sense of urgency for change, brought about through a crisis, a new opportunity for substantial funding, or a broad recognition of shared frustration about current failures.

Applications

When to use it

Collective Impact initiatives may emerge in situations in which multiple organizations are working separately on a complex or wicked[32] problem. Opportunities to build *Collective Impact* may arise from a combination of factors: (1) the persistence of the shared problem, despite the best efforts of each organization; (2) recognition of synergies between these organizations; (3) an influential champion who brings groups together to explore those synergies; and (4) the availability of resources which could fund the development of a backbone support organization and initial brainstorming regarding how to tackle the problem collaboratively.

How to use it. By those interested in developing Collective Impact initiatives

Developing *Collective Impact* requires that organizations develop and commit to a shared broad vision and collective goals. As such, quite a few theories in this book can be helpful for enrolling partners, in particular: *5.6 Frame Theory, 6.1 Trust Theory, 6.2 Principled Negotiation, 8.1 Commons Theory, 8.3 Diffusion Theory,* and all of the organizational theories in Chapter 7. The *Collective Impact* framework provides an overarching structure in which to apply those theories to building broad and effective collaboration for large-scale problem solving (see Table 8.3). While these steps have been associated with numerous successful *Collective Impact* initiatives, their presence does not guarantee success. Rather, the likelihood of success may primarily depend upon the effective application of other social science theories within the broader framework.

How to use it: For granters hoping to support Collective Impact initiatives

Effectively supporting *Collective Impact* initiatives requires a change from the most common current forms of grant making, which entail funding single organizations to address discrete problems with easily countable outputs or short-term outcomes. Currently, typical grant cycles may last from a few months up to a few years with continued funding typically contingent upon recipients' achievement of the pre-determined outcomes or outputs listed in their grant proposals. Achieving

Table 8.3 *Phases of collective action.*

Phases	Activities
Phase One: Initiating action	**Problem identification:** Define the specific problem; collect and organize data into a coherent story to make a clear case for people and groups to come together to address it. **Team building:** Identify individuals and organizations with appropriate capacities, constituencies, influence, and potential shared interests. Reach across sectors and traditional boundaries and begin to build a group identity around a common desire to solve the problem. **Community involvement:** Engage the broader community to build awareness, solicit good ideas, and gain public support.
Phase Two: Organizing for impact	**Build collective infrastructure:** Use initial problem framing and group talents to seek resources to fund the effort. Create or identify an appropriate backbone support organization. **Establish ground rules for participation:** Co-develop procedures and ground rules for interactions and decision making with interested organizations. **Solidify a common agenda:** Re-visit and clarify problem identification collectively to further strengthen group identity. This includes marking boundaries around the scope of the specific problem. While efforts can shift or expand over time, an agenda that is too diffuse or broad at the outset can cripple the coordination of group activities and realistic accounting of success. **Develop an adaptive management plan:** Establish shared metrics for measuring success and reporting. Establish a system for group reflection, learning and adaptation. Evaluation should not involve a rigid theory of change, but rather a focus on tracking success and understanding the factors influencing outcomes. **Community involvement:** Engage the broader community to build awareness, solicit good ideas, and gain public support.
Phase Three: Implementation, adaptation, and impact	**Implementation:** The backbone support organization identifies opportunities, facilitates shared learning, and keeps the activities of individual organizations in alignment with achieving the broader shared goal(s). **Continuous communication:** Communication, which is facilitated by the backbone support organization, is consistent between high-level representatives of member organizations. Sending low-level representatives or skipping meetings can cripple collective motivation and efforts. **Adaptive management:** The backbone support organization collects and analyzes data to report on outcomes achievement and to identify and disseminate lessons learned. Success is defined both as the achievement of meaningful outcomes and as continual improvement based on collective learning. **Sustaining commitment and support:** The backbone support organization organizes and/or supports organizations' efforts in fundraising and educates potential funders on the importance of flexibility in how success is defined as conditions change and new lessons are learned. **Community involvement:** All members, and especially the backbone support organization, engage the broader community to build awareness, solicit good ideas, and gain public support.

long-term *Collective Impact*, as described here, is better served with longer-term commitments with different types of evaluation measures and accountability. This means re-defining measures of success to include those that assess the quality of relationships developed and the quality of learning and related adaptations. Continued funding could be contingent on demonstrations of continual learning and overall prospects for success rather than, or in addition to, meeting specific pre-determined targets. This approach would set organizations free to be more nimble and responsive to ever-changing contexts.

Funding *Collective Impact* also calls for investing in infrastructure and collaboration, in particular funding the backbone support organization, in addition to more traditional short-term project funding.

Key references

Hanleybrown, F., J. Kania, and M. Kramer 2012. Channeling change: Making collective impact work. *Stanford Social Innovation Review* January 26, 2012. https://ssir.org/articles/entry/channeling_change_making_collective_impact_workhttps://ssir.org/articles/entry/channeling_change_making_collective_impact_work

Kania, J., and M. Kramer 2011. Collective impact. *Stanford Social Innovation Review* 9(1): 36–41.

Kania, J., and M. Kramer 2013.Embracing emergence: How collective impact addresses complexity. *Stanford Social Innovation Review*. Blog Report, January 21, 2013. https://ssir.org/articles/entry/embracing_emergence_how_collective_impact_addresses_complexity

Turner, S., K. Merchant, J. Kania, and E. Martin 2012. Understanding the value of backbone organizations in collective impact. *Stanford Social Innovation Review* July 17, 2012. https://ssir.org/articles/entry/understanding_the_value_of_backbone_organizations_in_collective_impact_1

Part III

Putting the Theories to Use

9

Vignettes

Introduction: There is nothing so practical as an arsenal of good theories

The famous psychologist Kurt Lewin once wrote, "There is nothing so practical as a good theory."[1] In the title of this introduction, I offer a revision to this statement that recognizes the increased practical value of having multiple good theories to draw from. Applying diverse theoretical lenses enables us to better question our assumptions and avoid the comfortable trap of fitting a situation to our pre-conceived notions. As a result, we are able to see multiple aspects of a problem and imagine a wider array of potential solutions. Part III of this book is about demonstrating this practicality and providing some tangible examples of how to use theory to real world situations.

The vignettes that follow are all based on real world cases and contexts with which I have personally become familiar over the years. However, each has been adapted and fictionalized for the purpose of clearly demonstrating how to apply theories to real world problems, rather than maintaining fidelity to actual occurrences. In each vignette, a character is faced with a problem and uses multiple theories within the book to help him or her develop and execute a plan of action. There are certainly other theories that could be applied to each case. Moreover, the application of any theory might lead to a wide range of different actions and consequences, not just the ones I've presented here. I do my best in each vignette to summarize the key principles of the theories in use. Still, I recommend referring back to the original theory chapters in Part II if ever in doubt.

Using the theories in this book to think through problems by no means guarantees success, and I don't mean to imply that by sharing only happy endings within these vignettes. Rather, the problems we all face are likely to provide us with plenty of frustrations and surprises, no matter how we approach them. My hope is that the vignettes demonstrate the practical value of social science theories and of maintaining an adaptive mindset as situations change over time.

Social Science Theory for Environmental Sustainability: A Practical Guide. Marc J. Stern, Oxford University Press (2018). © Marc J. Stern 2018. DOI 10.1093/oso/9780198793182.001.0001

9.1 Managing visitors to a sensitive protected area

The problem

Beth works at Aloha National Park. She's been tasked with solving a difficult visitor management problem. There are seven natural pools along a series of beautiful small waterfalls that lead out into the ocean. The pools are home to multiple endangered species of plants and fish that are very sensitive to the impacts of hundreds of visitors swimming and wading in them each weekend. Moreover, they are a safety hazard—each month, at least one person seems to slip and get injured. The Superintendent would like to keep people out of these pools. She's considered staffing the area with more enforcement rangers, but the budget won't allow for that. Moreover, she doesn't think that would be very popular with visitors. She's now thinking about using educational signs to try to convince people to stay out of the pools. It is Beth's job to figure out how best to make this happen. Right now, there is only a single sign at the trailhead that reads, "Please do not swim in the pools." It is not effective.

After reading this book, Beth has decided that the following theories may help her to create a more convincing case for people to stay out of the pools:

- The Elaboration Likelihood Model
- The Theory of Planned Behavior
- Norm Activation Theory
- Value-Belief-Norm Theory
- The Extended Parallel Process Model of Fear Appeals
- Cognitive Dissonance
- Self-Determination Theory.

Applying the theories

Beth first considers the two pathways to persuasion delineated by the *Elaboration Likelihood Model*. She knows that she wants people on the central route to persuasion, which means they will actually be motivated and able to process her message. This means that her message should be attention-getting, relevant to the visitor, easy to understand, and interesting. She can use both the title of a sign and an attractive design to grab attention. She needs to use compelling language and make use of good persuasive theories to convince people to stay out of the pools.

Still, she knows that some people may not be motivated to read her entire message, no matter what is on the sign. For those who might only glance at the sign, she needs to convey the message succinctly, maybe just in the title or a subheading. She can also use peripheral cues on the pathway to the pools and possibly around them to further discourage people from entering the pools. She thinks small warning plaques or "no swimming" signs might help in this sense. That way, even people who don't read the sign or fully process her arguments might still be influenced to stay out of the pools.

Beth first considered trying to use a fear appeal to stress the dangers of swimming in the pools. The ***Extended Parallel Process Model for Fear Appeals*** tells her that fear appeals only work when there is a clear and easy way to avoid the risk. She feels she can make a good argument about the danger by citing all the injuries that have taken place, and she can tell people about other nearby more appropriate places to swim. She is a little concerned, however, that fear appeals don't work as well with "sensation seekers," or people who commonly take risks in search of adventurous experiences. Are these the types of people who typically swim in the pools? She decides to do a little research of her own to figure this out.

First, she sends some rangers into the area for three consecutive weeks to see if they notice any patterns in who enters the pools. The rangers report back that all types of people and groups are entering the pools, but the most common are teenagers, older solo travelers, and older groups of friends. They only saw one family with small children enter a pool. Beth would love to hire a social scientist to further examine people's motivations, but she doesn't have a budget to do so. Instead, she spends a few days talking to people exiting the area about why they did or did not go into the pools. It becomes apparent to her that most people entered the pools for the fun of it, with some indicating that they felt they were communing with nature by getting in the water. Many noted that they saw others having fun, so they decided to enter the pools as well. When she asked about dangers, most dismissed the idea quickly, even after hearing about prior injury reports, with the exception of a few families with small children. Some that didn't enter the pools suggested that they never even considered it to be a possibility. Only a few groups mentioned the sign.

Her research tells her that fear appeals may not work with the large numbers of "sensation seekers" she met. If it doesn't work with them, others who might not have otherwise ventured into the pools might be encouraged to do so when they see these people enjoying themselves. The ***Elaboration Likelihood Model*** suggests that this would serve as a peripheral cue to encourage entering the pools.

She considers instead focusing the fear appeal on enforcement practices, telling visitors that if they get caught by a ranger swimming in the pools, they will be fined. She knows, however, that rangers are unlikely to be able to patrol this area consistently. Trust between park management and visitors, especially local visitors, is extremely important to the park. If rangers can't be consistent in enforcement, this could cause distrust for park managers and lead to other problems, not to mention changing the fun nature of visitors' experiences altogether.

In the end, Beth concludes that fear appeals are unlikely to work effectively for a large portion of visitors who want to enter the pools. She thus turns her attention to crafting a persuasive message, making use of her knowledge of the *Elaboration Likelihood Model*, *Theory of Planned Behavior*, *Norm Activation Theory*, *Value-Belief-Norm Theory*, *Cognitive Dissonance*, and *Self-Determination Theory*.

- *The Theory of Planned Behavior* suggests that people form their behavioral intentions based on three types of evaluations they make about a specific behavior (see Table 9.1).
- *Norm Activation Theory* suggests that people may feel morally obligated to act pro-environmentally when they are made aware of the consequences of their actions and accept responsibility for them.
- *Value-Belief-Norm Theory* suggests that the activation of personal norms associated with environmental responsibility is most likely when people are reminded of pro environmental beliefs or values they already hold.
- *Cognitive Dissonance* suggests that people will act to keep their behaviors consistent with their attitudes and beliefs.
- *Self-Determination Theory* stresses the relative strength of intrinsic motivation vs extrinsic motivation and provides three bases for enhancing intrinsic motivation (see Table 9.1).

Beth makes the following table to help her consider how each theory might be put to use (Table 9.1). She is pleased to see considerable overlap between many of the theories as she carefully starts to think through how each might translate into action.

Implementation with an adaptive mindset

Beth develops multiple strategies that she thinks might work. In each case, she has decided to include a sign at the trailhead, another sign at the entrance area to the pools (to carry her main persuasive messages), small placards placed on the ground at the most common access areas to each pool (unobtrusive peripheral cues), and the addition of a small elevated walkway above one of the less-sensitive pools that enables a top-down view into the water to provide alternative means to achieve similar outcomes—partially addressing perceived behavioral control and competence

Table 9.1 Beth's efforts to brainstorm ideas based on theories.

Theory	Principles	Ideas
Elaboration likelihood model (ELM)	Central route processing creates more stable behavioral change. Central route processing, or the open-minded consideration of a new argument, occurs when the audience is motivated and capable to process the message.	• Capture attention with provocative title. • Use an attractive design. • Use simple language to make it easy to understand. • Make strong arguments using other persuasive theories. • Ask people to reflect (elaborate on their own beliefs relevant to the message).
	Peripheral route processing can serve as a back-up if central route processing doesn't work. The peripheral route involves contextual cues that don't require cognitive effort.	• Convey message on main sign quickly and obviously. • Small plaques and reminder signs on-site might help as well. • Consider using physical barriers.
Theory of Planned Behavior (TPB)	Attitudes toward the behavior: visitors will evaluate the likely outcomes (good and bad consequences for themselves) of entering the pools.	• Convince visitors that their experience will be better without entering the pools. • Find out visitors' most salient beliefs about the benefits and disadvantages of entering the pools and which of these elements they value most. Use these in communications (e.g., preserving the beauty of the area, respecting nature, saving wildlife, avoiding danger). • Consider mentioning enforcement.
	Subjective norms: visitors will evaluate how others with whom they identify (reference groups) would evaluate their actions.	• Reference how entering the pools negatively affects the experience of other visitors who are similar to them. • Reference the safety and experience of others in their group. • Ask visitors to set an example for others.
	Perceived behavioral control: visitors will do what they perceive to be within their control.	• Make it harder to go into the pools by considering physical barriers and/or mentioning potential enforcement. • Note the dangers of entering the pools (or make it seem difficult). • Convince visitors that they can still have a great experience without entering the pools. • Make it easy to attain their desires by identifying alternative places to swim.

(Continued)

Table 9.1 (Continued)

Theory	Principles	Ideas
Norm Activation Theory (NAT)	Personal norms more powerfully influence behavior when individuals are made aware of the consequences of their actions and accept responsibility for them.	• Use second person language to combat easy denial of responsibility. • Link consequences directly to visitors' actions. • Provide a simple solution to the problem.
Value-Belief-Norm Theory (VBN)	The activation of personal norms is more likely when individuals are reminded of pro-environmental values or beliefs they already hold.	• Evoke the most common pro-environmental beliefs held by park visitors—the value of the aesthetics and uniqueness of the place and the species it harbors.
Cognitive dissonance (CD)	When faced with dissonance (in this case internal discrepancy between an attitude or belief and a behavioral intention), people might change their behaviors to fit their attitude or belief.	• Try to arouse visitors' beliefs about nature protection, safety, and/or the enjoyment of other visitors; convince people that they hold these beliefs. • Link these beliefs to staying out of the pools.
Self-Determination Theory (SDT)	Autonomy: Visitors need to feel in control of their decisions.	• Stress that the visitor is in control of their own decision.
	Relatedness: Make it socially desirable to stay out of the pools.	• Tell visitors they can set an example for others. • Stress that other people like them want the pools to thrive in their natural state.
	Competence: Help people feel that staying out of the pools is easy and that it achieves meaningful outcomes.	• Stress how the pools, the park, and other visitors will benefit from their decision to stay out of the pools. • Provide other ways of enjoying the pools, like great viewpoints.

(TPB, SDT). She also considers opening up one of the pools to wading and swimming while keeping the others permanently closed, again so that visitors could achieve their goals through alternative means (TPB, SDT). In the end, however, she decides that this might weaken her main messages about protecting the pools if people see others swimming here. She rather decides to redirect visitors to the nearby Hikina Pools, which are far more resilient and present fewer safety risks. The management team also decides against the idea of constructing physical barriers to the pools, for fear of detracting from the natural beauty of the area.

In the end, the Park creates four different strategies, each with slightly different designs and configurations of signs. Beth's team tests them all by observing how

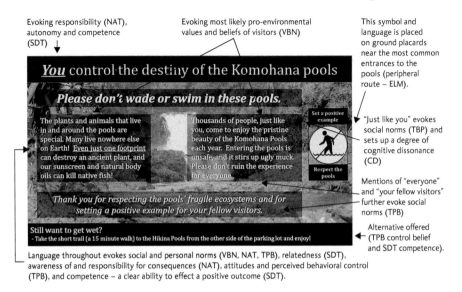

Evoking responsibility (NAT), autonomy and competence (SDT)

Evoking most likely pro-environmental values and beliefs of visitors (VBN)

This symbol and language is placed on ground placards near the most common entrances to the pools (peripheral route – ELM).

**You** control the destiny of the Komohana pools

Please don't wade or swim in these pools.

The plants and animals that live in and around the pools are special. Many live nowhere else on Earth! Even just one footprint can destroy an ancient plant, and our sunscreen and natural body oils can kill native fish!

Thousands of people, just like you, come to enjoy the pristine beauty of the Komohana Pools each year. Entering the pools is unsafe, and it stirs up ugly muck. Please don't ruin the experience for everyone.

Set a positive example

Respect the pools

"Just like you" evokes social norms (TBP) and sets up a degree of cognitive dissonance (CD)

Mentions of "everyone" and "your fellow visitors" further evoke social norms (TPB)

Thank you for respecting the pools' fragile ecosystems and for setting a positive example for your fellow visitors.

Still want to get wet?
- Take the short trail (a 15 minute walk) to the Hikina Pools from the other side of the parking lot and enjoy!

Alternative offered (TPB control belief and SDT competence).

Language throughout evokes social and personal norms (VBN, NAT, TPB), relatedness (SDT), awareness of and responsibility for consequences (NAT), attitudes and perceived behavioral control (TPB), and competence – a clear ability to effect a positive outcome (SDT).

Figure 9.1 One of Beth's theory-based signs. _Sign background photo credit: Nathan Reigner._

many visitors enter the pools while each combination of signs is in use. They interact with visitors throughout this time to get a better sense of which signs are most persuasive and which overall strategies, if any, may have detracted from the overall experience. Each of the interventions helps to reduce the number of people entering the pools, but using all in combination proves to be the most effective. Beth gets promoted and the pools remain intact for years to come!!!

Figure 9.1 is an example of one of the signs Beth created. It is surrounded by beautiful pictures and short natural history write-ups of some of the endangered plants and animals that inhabit the pool. Each of the smaller signs includes the words "Thank you for not wading into the pools."

9.2 Political communications

The problem

In the first ten days of the Trump Administration in the United States in 2017, a conservative congressman proposed the repeal of the "9B" regulations, which regulate oil and gas extraction in national parks in the United States. Environmentalists feared that this repeal would expand oil and gas exploration and extraction in the national parks and remove critical oversight, causing severe damage to their integrity.

Roberto is an avid outdoorsman who loves the national parks. He's been following the issue and is concerned that not enough people will take action to prevent the repeal from happening. Even though the national parks enjoy broad support in the United States, he's afraid that if only the liberal environmentalists speak up, the conservative majority of politicians in Congress will not listen. His internet searches reveal that the most common messages aimed to rally the conservation community against the bill are dry and factual. The few value-based messages he finds fail to address a wide array of moral foundations. He's worried that conservationists are only speaking to themselves. One of his best friends works for one of the major environmental groups fighting against the repeal. He's scheduled a lunch with her to talk about how her organization might better communicate to a broader audience and strengthen their coalition against the repeal.

Applying the theories

Roberto decides to consider the problem in light of the following:

- Haidt's Social Intuitionist Model of Moral Judgments (SIM)
- Cultural Cognition (CC)
- Moral Foundations Theory (MFT)
- Frame Theory (FT), in particular communicative framing
- Elaboration Likelihood Model (ELM)
- Theory of Planned Behavior (TPB).

Haidt's Social Intuitionist Model suggests that people who are already prone to feel one way or another are unlikely to be persuaded unless they can be prompted to consider the issue in an entirely new light. This might come from a particularly compelling argument or from inducing a feeling of accountability to relevant well-informed people whose views aren't entirely known. Roberto thinks the accountability idea might be particularly important for members of Congress who have to answer to their constituents. **Cultural Cognition** suggests that people evaluate information based on their prior cultural commitments. This means that information needs to be presented in a way that affirms, rather than threatens, people's cultural identities. **Moral Foundations Theory** suggests that communication will be more successful if it is based in the moral foundations that message recipients feel are most important to them. Arguments addressing other moral foundations are unlikely to resonate. He feels that **Frame Theory** will provide some further tools for crafting effective messages, as will the **Elaboration Likelihood Model** and the **Theory of Planned Behavior**. The *Elaboration Likelihood Model* stresses the importance of motivating people to cognitively process (or thoroughly evaluate) an argument. Roberto thinks that by using vivid imagery and morally charged language, he might have some success. If people are motivated and able to process the argument, then the *Theory of Planned Behavior* provides some additional guidance on how to make the argument effective. In particular, the benefits should outweigh the disadvantages of taking an action (in this case he wants people to contact their Congressperson), arguments should reference relevant social norms that affirm the desired action, and the action should be seen as easily within the person's control (it should be easy to do and the person should feel like the action will make a difference).

Roberto peruses everything he can find on the internet and in newspapers about how the issue is currently being communicated.

The typical communications coming from conservation groups read something like this:

> *Our National Parks are under attack. Republican congressmen propose to expand drilling in the national parks without proper regulations that protect park resources. The 58 national parks in the United States protect dozens of endangered species and provide recreational opportunities for millions of Americans each year. Oil drilling in the parks puts these values at risk.*

An expanded message might go on to discuss the economic values of parks (e.g., the monetary contribution to local economies from tourism), the endangered species they protect, or the ecosystem services they provide (such as clean air or water). The message typically might then call for some action. Call your congressman or donate to the (name your favorite conservation group here) today to help us protect our Parks.

Below is a statement by Nicholas Lund, Senior Manager of National Parks Conservation Association's Conservation Programs, made on January 31, 2017:

"These challenges are direct attacks on America's national parks. Each of these rules provides the commonsense protections for national parks that millions of Americans demand. If the Park Service's drilling rules are repealed, national parks across the country would be subjected to poorly regulated oil and gas drilling, threatening parks' air, water, and wildlife. These attempts to weaken protections put our parks at risk. And by using the Congressional Review Act process, Congress is forever tying the hands of the agencies charged with protecting America's favorite places. If Congress wants to protect national parks for future generations, it must reject these challenges."[2]

Roberto notes that neither message above hits the key conservative moral foundations. Each is primarily factual and presumes that any recipient of the message already has an underlying preference for protecting parks and will feel outrage at any threat to them. As such, he feels that neither is likely to convince any audience that doesn't already lean in the direction of the message.

Meanwhile, the Congressman proposing the repeal of the regulations used the following argument.

"The Park Service's midnight oil and gas regulation jeopardizes significant investments made by job creators, states, and private companies. The federal government has no right to impose job-killing regulations for private and state-owned oil and natural gas wells not owned by the federal government, especially when these wells are already subject to existing environmental regulations."[3]

The Congressman's statement focuses on government overreach that cripples the freedom of businesses to create jobs, addressing both the liberty/oppression foundation and the fairness/cheating foundation of *Moral Foundations Theory*. Similarly, President Trump campaigned on a promise to "unleash America's $50 trillion in untapped shale, oil, and natural gas reserves, plus hundreds of years in clean coal reserves," and accused prior President Obama of "denying millions of Americans access to the energy wealth sitting under our feet." Again, the language here, in particular the words, "unleashing" and "denying," speaks directly to the liberty/oppression moral foundation.

Having learned about *Haidt's Social Intuitionist Model* and *Cultural Cognition*, Roberto thinks that people can too easily dismiss the typical liberal conservation messages. He's convinced that they aren't based in the appropriate moral foundations. He also has a feeling that that conservative Congress people in favor of the bill can too easily dismiss accountability concerns, because most of them come from highly conservative districts. Unless their constituents can be activated in some way, they are unlikely to change their minds. Here are Roberto's notes on how he might use the theories to help his friend's organization build a better communication strategy (Table 9.2).

Table 9.2 *Roberto's efforts to brainstorm ideas from theories.*

Theory	Principles	Ideas
Haidt's Social Intuitionist Model (SIM)	Seek to understand the values driving emotional or intuition-based responses. Encourage exploratory thinking by enhancing feelings of accountability in decision-makers.	• Consider basing communications in different moral foundations that may be driving default responses. This can bring accountability to decision-makers by activating a broader constituency. • Enlist conservative constituents in asking questions and speaking up for parks.
	Present information in a way that affirms, rather than threatens, people's cultural identities.	• Don't attack or dismiss the underlying values of others' arguments. • Use *Moral Foundations Theory* to activate underlying morals and emotions in support of parks.
Cultural Cognition (CC)	Consider the identity of the communicator—ideally communicators mirror the values of the message recipient or are part of a pre-existing reference group.	• Try to find spokespeople who might cross traditional constituency groups.
	Focus efforts on people who aren't fully entrenched in their beliefs.	• Recent polls suggest that most Americans like the national parks. Thus, activating the right moral foundations has high potential for getting people involved.
Moral Foundations Theory (MFT)	Communication can be more effective if based in the moral foundations that message recipients feel are most important to them. Arguments addressing other moral foundations are unlikely to resonate.	• Conservatives associated with drilling in the parks in the United States tend to stress the following moral foundations: liberty/oppression; sanctity/degradation; authority/subversion; loyalty/betrayal; fairness/cheating • Craft messaging based on these moral foundations.
Frame Theory (FT)	Messages that are positively framed around the opportunity to avoid loss are more effective than those focused on achieving gains or on a likelihood of failure.	• Be sure to stress what is at stake and focus on the high likelihood that we can avoid losses, rather than the new gains we might achieve.
	Talking about collective efficacy ("we can do it") is more effective than talking about personal sacrifice.	• Stress the difference people can make together to avoid bad things happening.

(Continued)

Table 9.2 (Continued)

Theory	Principles	Ideas
	Focusing on local contemporary concerns is more effective than focusing on distant or future concerns.	• Provide tangible and personal examples of impacts, rather than broad generalizations. • Consider referencing nearby national parks in regionally specific communications.
	Past-focused messaging is more compelling to conservatives than future-focused messaging.	• Make allusions to a preferred past.
Elaboration likelihood model (ELM)	The open-minded consideration of a new argument can only occur when the message recipient is motivated and capable to process the message. Motivation can come from high relevance, a highly relevant messenger, or a novel or surprising message.	• Consider a provocative image to gain attention. • Use personal and highly descriptive language. • Enlist traditionally conservative spokespeople from outside the environmental movement.
Theory of Planned Behavior (TPB)	Attitudes toward the behavior: people will evaluate the likely outcomes (good and bad consequences for themselves) of performing a behavior	• Describe the tangible negative effects on recreation and other values commonly associated with parks. • Stress alternatives to drilling in the parks that might make more sense. • Argue that continuing to focus on fossil fuels sets us behind in the economy of the future.
	Subjective norms: people will evaluate how others with whom they identify (reference groups) would evaluate their actions.	• Use collective language and stress the value of parks to us collectively as Americans (this also addresses the loyalty/betrayal foundation—MFT).
	Perceived behavioral control: People will only act if they feel empowered to do so and feel they can make a difference.	• Stress collective efficacy and the ease of taking action. • Note that congress people are likely to listen if they call or send an email. • Note examples of when calling local congress people actually changed their behavior wherever possible.

Implementation with an adaptive mindset

Roberto uses the principles in Table 9.2 to draft some examples of how to address what he feels are the right moral foundations of the target audience. He also tries to incorporate what he's learned about *Frame Theory*, the *Elaboration Likelihood Model*, and the *Theory of Planned Behavior* (Table 9.3).

These phrases each feel a little unnatural to Roberto, but research suggests they will be more effective in activating those with different moral foundations who might otherwise sit on the sidelines. He knows that he isn't a communications expert, but he hopes that someone who is can take these ideas and craft even better

Table 9.3 *Roberto's efforts to craft theory-based messaging.*

Draft language	Theoretical justifications
Provide an image of oil derricks in front of a classic image of an iconic national park vista (see Figure 9.2). Caption possibility: "Are we ready to trade our sacred heritage for profit?"	ELM: This provides a striking and surprising view, hopefully inspiring central route processing of what comes next. MFT: Sanctity/degradation FT: Loss avoidance framing.
Our National Parks are the purest symbols of America—unspoiled monuments to the God-given beauty of this country. They stand as the last non-degraded sites of our nation's natural heritage, where brave pioneers and Native Americans alike were awed by their indescribable beauty, and millions of Americans visit each year for renewal and inspiration.	MFT: Sanctity/degradation; Loyalty/betrayal FT: Reference to past
Right now, some in our government wish to shirk their duties to protect our proud heritage in these parks, opening up them up to short-sighted, uncontrolled resource extraction that will forever tarnish their unique sacred beauty and wildness.	MFT: Sanctity/degradation; Authority/subversion FT: Loss avoidance framing
These efforts constitute an attack on all Americans. In effect, we, the taxpayers, would be paying for the profits of oil companies while they defile our national treasures.	MFT: Loyalty/betrayal; Fairness/cheating; Sanctity/degradation TPB: Norms
Opening up our National Parks to expanded resource extraction threatens the rights we've long enjoyed as Americans to witness nature's splendor unspoiled. It also corrupts the freedom reflected in the wild spaces of America.	MFT: Liberty/oppression; Loyalty/betrayal; Sanctity/degradation TPB: Costs FT: Past-focused
Let's honor the tradition of our nation's responsible stewardship of these amazing places. Let's be proud of our heritage. Don't sell our national treasures to the highest bidder. We owe it to our children.	MFT: Loyalty/betrayal TPB: Norms FT: Past-focused

(Continued)

Table 9.3 (Continued)

Draft language	Theoretical justifications
Contact your local representative (click here for a list by your zip code) so we can stand together against House Joint Resolution 46. It's simple and only takes 30 seconds. Below is a script you can use on the phone or in an email. Congress members regularly talk about how calls and emails make a difference in their voting. Together, we can surely avert this shameful threat to our most treasured places.	MFT: Loyalty/betrayal; Authority/subversion FT: Collective efficacy framing; Loss avoidance framing TPB: Control/ease
Our representatives need to hear from all of us that we want to save our precious heritage. If we want to stay competitive in the world, this isn't the way to do it. We can drill elsewhere. Better yet, we could win the race to developing alternative energy sources—which will unquestionably provide more jobs going forward than our finite supply of fossil fuels. Destroying our national pride won't get us anywhere. Be proud. Be smart. Protect our parks. Don't be duped by empty political moves that satisfy wealthy donors yet degrade our country at the same time.	MFT: Fairness/cheating; Sanctity/degradation; FT: Collective efficacy framing; Loss avoidance framing TPB: Attitudes toward the behavior (costs/benefits of drilling in parks vs alternatives); Norms

Figure 9.2 Roberto's idea for a provocative image. *Image courtesy of Boyd Norton.*

messages. He knows each will of course have to be supported by strong factual arguments as well, such as the relatively small amount of oil and gas available in these areas compared to other places and the promise of now affordable renewable energy sources, which again could be pitched in terms of national security (in terms of energy independence) or pride, each addressing the loyalty moral foundation, or another moral foundation.

When he meets with his friend, she is very interested in his ideas and sets up a meeting with their communications director. They find some traditionally con-servative spokespeople and develop a number of fine-tuned messages tailored to specific audiences they think could make a difference in specific Congressional districts. They track these messages through social media networks to see if they move any differently than the organization's more traditional messages, which are often based on the care/harm foundation (saving endangered species, providing for future generations, etc.). They find that these communications actually do travel in different patterns, moving outside their typical circles of members and likeminded environmentalists. They also find they receive greater coverage from traditionally conservative news media. They realize that their battle might last quite a while, but they recognize they are playing the long game. While they are not entirely confident they will win, they are optimistic about expanding their con-stituencies beyond the usual suspects.

9.3 Moving from traditional public involvement toward more collaborative engagement

The problem

Amy is the Forest Supervisor in charge of a National Forest in the United States. She's worn out by the controversies that surround nearly every decision she makes regarding how to manage the forest she oversees. Her plans have been litigated by environmental groups, industry groups, and recreational groups, each opposing actions that she sees as necessary for maintaining a healthy forest and meeting important management objectives. Public meetings have been hostile, with different groups shouting at each other, at her, and at her staff. Sometimes they are mad about timber harvest, other times about the lack of it. Groups argue about the construction of roads or the closures (or openings) of certain areas to motorized vehicles. Amy is well-trained in forest management and feels that she and her staff, which is made up of forest scientists, engineers, hydrologists, wildlife biologists, and other experts, know what is best for the landscape. Having read this book, however, she decides that it is time to try a new approach to public involvement.

U.S. Forest Service planning processes are governed by the National Environmental Policy Act, which requires federal agencies to disclose the likely environmental, social, and economic impacts of their proposed actions to interested publics. To accomplish this disclosure, the common practice is to designate an interdisciplinary team, known as an ID team, made up of experts in various disciplines relevant to the problem at hand. One person is designated the ID team leader. That person's job is to lead the team through a process that involves (1) developing potential alternative courses of action to meet a defined purpose and need on the landscape, (2) analyzing the potential impacts of each of those alternatives, and (3) involving the public to adequately disclose those analyses and to seek input for improving them. Amy serves as the supervisor of the entire process, maintains close contact with the ID team leader, and serves in a leadership role at public meetings. She is also responsible for selecting a final course of action at the end of the process.

Public involvement typically happens at various stages of the planning process. Public meetings begin once Amy and her team have defined a "purpose and need" for a potential project. In these early meetings, public comments are solicited to determine the appropriate scope of the analyses to be conducted (this is called "scoping"). Results of all impact analyses are shared in documents called an

Environmental Assessment (EA) or an Environmental Impact Statement (EIS). The public is consulted again after these draft reports are circulated to seek additional feedback on anything the agency missed or potential errors. Public meetings are publicized in the federal register, in local newspapers, and on email lists made up of individuals and groups who have asked to be notified of upcoming actions on the Forest. The public meetings most commonly involve a presentation by ID team staff followed by the opportunity for oral or written comments to be submitted for consideration by the public. Oral comments are limited to three minutes and are transcribed. The agency is required to respond to any comments they deem to be "substantive." This means that the comments are scientifically based or expressed in terms of the effects of potential agency actions. These comments require a written response in the EA or EIS. The agency is not required to respond to any comments that can be classified as mere conjecture, opinion, or position statements.[4]

Amy recognizes that traditional forms of public involvement amount to a series of one-way communications, rather than meaningful dialogue. People use their three minutes to make exaggerated claims or to fire up their co-sympathizers, rather than to think through reasonable alternatives or to understand the viewpoints of others (or the constraints under which she must make decisions). Many groups seem to think that the only way they can influence the process is to file a lawsuit. When this happens, the agency wastes valuable resources in litigation, and important actions are delayed. She's concerned that these delays are making the forest more susceptible to catastrophic wildfire, which no one wants to see. Furthermore, it just feels bad to constantly be yelled at and to wind up in court. She's worried about her staff's morale.

Applying the theories

Amy convenes a team of her employees with substantial experience in these conflicts to assess the situation and think through how to design new ways of working with these diverse stakeholders. After carefully considering the theories in this book, they decide that the challenge involves looking both externally at the ways in which they interact with the public and internally at their organizational structures and processes. Externally, Amy wants to find ways to create common understanding, build trust, reduce conflict, litigation, and stalemates, and ultimately make better decisions. She and her team recognize certain internal challenges that inhibit these external outcomes. In particular, they'd like to find ways to better manage internal team interactions, balance internal accountabilities with external ones, and better navigate the turnover of staff.

Amy and her team feel that the concept of *Project Risk* might best help them to identify problem areas and strategies for addressing them. They start by discussing *programmatic risk*, which in their case is risk that stems from trying to do big things that attract a lot of attention. In the past, they have tried to break up big projects into multiple smaller pieces in hopes that smaller projects might make for easier planning processes. Overall, this strategy has been ineffective. They have experienced cases in which one proposed project makes it through the process quickly, while another gets held up for one reason or another. As a result, they are unable to treat the ecosystem holistically. Moreover, multiple small projects seem to require more work than one larger project, and the work feels less meaningful to team members. They decide that moving forward, they should just accept programmatic risk and focus on addressing *structural*, *technical*, and *relationship risks* as best they can.

As they consider each form of risk, they quickly realize that other theories in the book will help them to formulate potential responses. They make two tables to keep track of key principles they think will be important: one summarizing key principles relevant to revising their internal processes (Table 9.4) and another for guiding engagement with external entities (Table 9.5). They use these principles to help them complete their project risk assessment (Table 9.6). The abbreviations of the theories in each of the tables will be used to guide readers through the subsequent text as Amy's team's plan unfolds.

After conducting their project risk assessment (Table 9.6), Amy and her team realize they have quite a lot of work to do, and that it might take a long time to make their hoped-for transition. Their brainstorming, however, has revealed some specific strategies they'd like to try. They continue to think of these in two ways: (1) internal strategies to enhance their teamwork and (2) external strategies that might improve the ways in which they work with external stakeholders. They feel that their project risk assessment exercise has identified most of the internal strategies they'd like to implement, particularly with regard to appropriate staffing, resource allocation, turnover management, knowledge management, intra-team communications, and finding appropriate trainings. However, they realize that their external strategies need much more extensive thought.

External strategies

After completing their project risk assessment, Amy's team collectively decides that conducting a diagnosis of *trust* among their most common stakeholders might be a good next step. They begin by assessing what they perceive to be their own trustworthiness in the eyes of external stakeholders, and they make some quick recognitions. They realize that they've made the assumption that people should trust them based on their technical competence alone. They hadn't really considered that perceptions of **benevolence** and **integrity** also play into trustworthiness. From the public's perspectives, these are highly questionable, as the Forest Service often goes against people's desires in their management decisions and doesn't always do a great job disclosing the reasons for choosing their prescriptions.

Table 9.4 *Principles to guide Forest Service ID teams in their planning processes.*

Theory	Principles
Self-Determination Theory (SDT)	People tend to perform better if they feel a sufficient degree of autonomy, relatedness, and competence.
Herzberg's Motivation–Hygiene Theory (HMHT)	Employee motivation is influenced by: relationships with others within their organization; working conditions; feelings of achievement; recognition; meaningfulness of the work; and opportunities for responsibility, advancement, and growth.
Accountability Theory (AT)	Agency culture and reporting requirements can create accountability mechanisms that can constrain innovation.
Team Effectiveness Theory and Leadership Theory (TET and LT)	• The collaborative development of goals by team members can help to create team identity and a sense of meaningfulness in the work, which each have positive effects on performance. • When employees are committed to clearly defined goals and share the organization's prevailing norms of appropriate conduct, they can be given greater discretion to solve problems and directly interact with external stakeholders with less risk. • More active deliberation between team members can lead to better outcomes. • Interpersonal relationship conflicts between team members are detrimental to team functioning. • Shared knowledge on the team about how to find information and who can answer which questions (transactive memory systems) is critical to efficient team functioning. Turnover threatens this knowledge. • Periodic internal assessment (reflexivity) promotes continual improvement. • Role clarity is important for team members to effectively coordinate their work. • Team leaders need to be clearly recognized as leaders to effectively lead teams. • Cross-functional training can enable team members to better understand each other's work and enhance communication and helping behaviors.
Nonaka's Theory of Organizational Knowledge Creation (NTOKC)	• Creating specific strategies for how to identify, store, and share useful knowledge can enhance team efficiency and learning.

Table 9.5 *Principles to guide collaborative engagement with external stakeholders.*

Theory	Principles
Trust Theory (TT)	Trust is based on rational, affinitive, and system-based foundations.
	• Rational trust involves demonstrating competence and building expectations of positive outcomes.
	• Affinitive trust involves building positive social relationships through demonstrating understanding, shared values, and/or caring for others.
	• Systems-based trust involves creating agreed upon procedures which help people to feel sufficiently empowered and protected from unwanted risk.
Accountability Theory (AT)	• Different individuals and stakeholders have different accountabilities. Balancing these accountabilities is often difficult.
	• Exposing these accountabilities to other stakeholders might help to generate better understanding of each other's interests and positions.
Principled Negotiation (PN)	Stakeholders should be encouraged to focus on interests, not positions; to separate people from the problem; to develop shared criteria for evaluating potential outcomes; and to look for win–win solutions.
The Co-orientation Model (COM)	Identifying areas of true and false consensus and dissensus can provide clear pathways forward for improving communication.
Identity Theory (IT)	When people feel that their core values are being questioned or misinterpreted, they can become hostile or defensive.
Self-Affirmation Theory (SAT)	Self-affirmation in a domain outside the one causing conflict can lessen the threats people feel to their self-concepts and enable them to have more open-minded and rational conversations and interactions.
Moral Foundations Theory (MFT)	Understanding the moral foundations of opposing parties can enable people to see merit in each other's interests and develop more inclusive communication.
The Reasonable Person Model (RPM)	Meetings go best when people have sufficient information to understand the subject matter and the process; when they feel their participation has a real impact on something meaningful; and when the process is varied and interesting.
Self-Determination Theory (SDT)	People tend to be more motivated when they feel a sufficient degree of autonomy, relatedness, and competence.
Commons Theory (CT)	People best work together in managing common resources when boundaries are clearly defined; when they feel empowered to impact decision-making processes; when monitoring enhances accountability; when rules are consistently enforced; and when conflict resolution mechanisms are available.

Table 9.6 *Project risk analysis for Forest Service planning processes.*

Type	Source	Outcome(s)	Likelihood	Severity	Control	Potential responses	Ripple effects and responses
Structural *Key theories:* TET, NTOKC, AT, LT. , SDT	Turnover of staff	Interruptions in analysis; lost information; trust gaps; need for re-training and re-establishing relationships (internally and externally); weakened transactive memory systems	High	High	Medium	• Limit turnover when possible. Provide opportunities for advancement in place. • Develop guidelines for transition memos. • Establish procedures for onboarding new members. • Create overlap between incoming and outgoing people. • Involve team members (or collaborators) in interviewing of new members. • Develop a clear system for knowledge management and retention. Designate two or more knowledge activists to collate relevant information and lessons learned.	Limiting turnover can sometimes curtail the infusion of new ideas (elevating technical risk) or perpetuate existing conflict. When turnover is necessary or deemed healthy, use other techniques to manage it better.

(Continued)

Table 9.6 (Continued)

Type	Source	Outcome(s)	Likelihood	Severity	Control	Potential responses	Ripple effects and responses
	Competing tasks	Lack of time or resources to focus on project-related tasks; deflated morale from being spread too thin; diminished responsiveness to stakeholders; inattentiveness to effective deliberation on the planning team—all leading to poorer decisions, lower morale, and increased external relationship risk.	High	High	Medium	• Clearly prioritize projects and staff time. • Stress the importance and meaningfulness of the work. • Allocate explicit scheduled time for intra-team discussion and deliberation.	This may strain other projects' timelines. However, it is likely to enhance overall efficiency by reducing risks to each project we can actually focus on. This may mean postponing or eliminating some projects altogether.
	Inflexible top-down mandates	Limits to creativity and responsiveness to external concerns; deflated morale from inability to influence decision making.	High	High	Medium	• Work with superiors to transform rigid measures of "success," such as specific targets for numbers of board feet, to more flexible statements of objectives that enable adaptive planning.	This could potentially cause problems with upward accountability and reporting. Extra work and upward relationship management will be required to demonstrate goal achievement if pre-determined targets are not met.

| Technical Key theories: TET, NTOKC, AT, LT, SDT | Lack of appropriate expertise on team | Insufficient analyses, which can lead to external relationship risk (e.g., litigation); common gaps in public relations expertise leading to poor public interactions. | Medium | High | High | • Hire and staff teams with disciplines and talents needed (ensure functional diversity).
• Prioritize projects and staff time (see above).
• Consider external partnerships to fill gaps. | Managing external entities can be challenging and can elevate structural and internal relationship risk. Be sure to include external partners in the establishment and/or review of team goals and guidelines (see below). This may require a longer timeframe. |
| | Failure to devote adequate time/effort to tasks | Insufficient analyses and responsiveness to stakeholders—leading to increased external relationship risk, as above. | High | High | Medium | • See structural risk comments above.
• Clearly articulate the importance and meaningfulness of the tasks.
• Agree upon clear goals and establish quality standards collaboratively as a team.
• Co-create explicit guidelines for team communications, internal reviews, and task completion.
• Create a plan for revisiting goals, standards, and guidelines on a regular basis. | Staff might feel anxious because of the additional time upfront spent establishing team norms. This may at first feel like a waste of time. However, it should help keep processes on track and create healthy lateral accountabilities. We may need to share evidence that this is a best practice that can enhance efficiency in the long run (e.g., Stern and Predmore 2012). |

(Continued)

Table 9.6 (Continued)

Type	Source	Outcome(s)	Likelihood	Severity	Control	Potential responses	Ripple effects and responses
External relations *Key theories:* *TT, PN,TET, IT, SAT, MFT, COM, SDT*	Identity threat	Stakeholders take adversarial or defensive positions resulting in a hostile process.	High	High	Low/ Medium	• Consider self-affirmation, principled negotiation, and other facilitated processes. • Expose shared moral foundations.	These exercises might feel forced or unnatural to some. However, if identity protective behavior can be diminished, more productive communication can follow, and conflict might be reduced.
	Rigid public involvement techniques	Lack of responsiveness to public input; inability to build trust; insufficient consideration of public concerns—all leading to additional conflict and unnecessary hold-ups at the end of the planning process (e.g., litigation) and deflated staff morale.	High	High	High	• Be more responsive to all comments, not just those deemed "substantive." • Shift to more collaborative approaches to public involvement. See "external strategies" below. • If possible, hire an external facilitator to help design and manage the process.	Many team members will lack skills or abilities to do this well. Consider specific trainings. Legally, the Forest Service cannot cede decision-making authority on any management decisions. To avoid misunderstandings, the role of the public must be very clear.

	Lack of staff willingness to engage the public in new ways.	Can result in staff relying on the rigid public involvement techniques noted above and external perceptions of disingenuous interactions, as staff go through required motions instead of genuinely engaging. False assumptions about stakeholders can lead to further conflict.	High	High	Medium	• Provide evidence of the importance of genuine forms of responsiveness to external stakeholders. • Find staff who are most capable and willing to serve as primary liaisons to external stakeholders. • Provide capacity-building. • Consider a reward system for excellent outreach.	Increased engagement with the public could burn out some staff, especially more introverted team members. This will be difficult and won't always yield positive outcomes. Staff need to have reasonable expectations and set long-term goals in this respect, rather than expecting short-term gains.
Internal relations *Key theories: TET, AT, PN, SDT, HMHT*	Task-related conflict	Disagreements about how to get the work done can slow down the process or turn into relationship conflict if not monitored.	Medium	Low	High	• Develop ground rules for resolving disagreements on the team at the outset of the process. • Encourage active dialogue and debate.	Teams may at first find these preliminary exercises awkward and even tiresome. Provide a clear rationale, citing research, for why setting clear team procedures at the outset of a process is helpful.

(Continued)

Table 9.6 (Continued)

Type	Source	Outcome(s)	Likelihood	Severity	Control	Potential responses	Ripple effects and responses
	Relationship conflict	Distrust or dislike between team members; personal attacks. Can result in sabotage.	Medium	High	Medium	• Same as above. • Develop ground rules for respectful communication and deliberation. • Consider providing some cross-functional training to build empathy and understanding between team members.	
	Competing account-abilities	Team members struggle to balance upward demands with the demands of each other and external stakeholders, resulting in paralysis, poor communication, or taking sides. This can lead to feelings of disempowerment and reduced motivation.	High	Medium	Mediurr	• Develop clear guidance for when team members should exercise their own discretion vs when they must follow specific procedures. Identify clear goals, rather than specific rigid procedures, wherever possible to enable flexibility and empower team members to solve problems on the spot. • Consider planned regular check-ins to spur open discussion about these tensions and joint decision making on their resolution.	There are likely to be many "gray areas," where the right thing to do might be unclear. Guidance should be developed for how to seek input from others on these tough decisions. Discretion can be dangerous in some cases, if clear goals are not established. Shared goals should provide principles that everyone should adhere to. This will enable team members to judge potential actions against whether they meet the intent of the guiding principles or not.

From a trust ecology standpoint, they're doing even worse! Technical competence only makes up one part of **rational trust**. If people don't see their actions as serving outcomes they care about, rational trust is unlikely. With regard to **affinitive trust**, the Forest Service has largely kept the public at arm's length, relying on formal public meetings and written correspondence. While individual employees have made friends with participants in public involvement processes here and there, the overall feeling is adversarial. They have made no collective effort to build responsive social relationships with external stakeholders. Moreover, stakeholders have little reason to have **systems-based trust**. While Amy's team knows that they regularly take public comments into account in their planning, they realize that they have fallen far short in reporting back to people how their comments have influenced their decisions. The team doubts whether most stakeholders understand how decisions are made and how to influence them. This is evidenced by the large number of non-"substantive" comments they receive, which they have readily dismissed. They realize that this dismissal likely further weakens both affinitive and systems-based trust. Each is further complicated by the presence of multiple stakeholders, each arguing for different desired actions and outcomes.

They begin to imagine a system where each of the three forms of actionable trust are better cultivated. First and foremost, they recognize that external stakeholders want more power to influence decision making. While the Forest Service cannot legally give away their decision-making authority, they feel they can be more responsive to these stakeholders and more transparent about how they choose their ultimate courses of action. To do so, they feel a wholesale change might be worth experimenting with. They'd like to move their public engagement toward multi-stakeholder dialogue, in which participants (including themselves) can better understand and respond to each other's interests and concerns. They begin by hiring a professional facilitator to help them turn their ideas into action.

They select their toughest, most comprehensive project, their upcoming decadal revision to the overall Forest Plan, to try something new. The Forest Plan sets management objectives for the next ten-year period for the entire forest. They expect it to generate tremendous interest (and disagreement) in their external stakeholders. The facilitator suggests that they invite stakeholders who would like to engage at a deeper level with the Forest Service into a specific arrangement in which everyone will have to agree to certain ground rules. They will also maintain regular, or improved, channels of providing public input for everyone else.

Improving traditional public involvement

They realize that not everyone will have the time, energy, or inclination to commit to a more collaborative process. For these people, the team agrees that they would like to at least move away from the traditional presentation followed by three-minute oral comments and provide additional means of receiving input—for example, breaking into smaller groups for actual discussion about issues of concern, summarizing those discussions, and providing more thoughtful feedback on how public concerns have factored into decision making. They recognize, however, that it might take time to sufficiently train staff to engage in effective dialogue with stakeholders in smaller groups at these meetings. In the short term, they commit to finding means to provide that training and to being more responsive to public comments. They decide they will summarize comments and provide responses within one month of the end of each public comment period. They will also respond to non-substantive comments by engaging with stakeholders to understand their underlying concerns outside of formal meetings through simple phone calls, emails, or conversations that enable the team to uncover substantive issues driving public opinions, or the interests underlying their positions (see *6.2 Principled Negotiation*). For example, perhaps people are angry because they believe that their favorite recreation area will no longer be accessible. Simple follow-up questions to opinionated tirades can enable the agency to actually respond in a meaningful way.[5] As employees receive training on facilitation, they will move toward new formats for these meetings.

Designing and initiating a more collaborative process

They decide they will send out an announcement of their intentions to develop an alternative process for the Forest Plan to all interested parties.[6] They will also make announcements at their traditional meetings. They realize that the collaborative process won't achieve their goals unless they have representatives of all major interest groups at the table, so Amy will be tasked with making the rounds to the usual suspects to encourage their participation and make sure that meeting times will be convenient.[7] She plans to reach out to a few key stakeholders from different interest groups (leaders of recreation groups, environmental groups, and industry groups) to begin discussions. Together, they will further brainstorm procedures they think might work for everyone in a collaborative process, based on the principles set forth in Table 9.5.

Amy's team's primary concern involves generating enough trust between participants such that communications can be open and constructive. The facilitator stresses the importance of developing a charter that all members of the collaborative group will sign if they wish to participate. This clarifies roles and should contribute substantially to systems-based trust. The charter should lay out the following:

1. Clear goals for the collaborative group.
2. Requirements and expectations of members.
3. Requirements and expectations of the Forest Service, including how group recommendations will be treated.
4. Rules of engagement—how members will work together and communicate with each other, including clear rules for how Forest Service representatives will engage with the larger group.
5. Guidelines for maintaining transparent decision-making processes.
6. Procedures for expressing dissent with the recommendations developed by the collaborative group.
7. Mechanisms for resolving disputes between members.
8. Transition planning for addressing turnover (the coming and going of members).
9. A plan that contains procedures for periodically evaluating the collaborative process and re-visiting the charter.

The facilitator stresses that collaborative members should develop the actual charter together. She will facilitate this process. Together, they develop specific principles they feel will be critical to abide by as the charter is written.

- The group needs to collaboratively develop shared goals. These goals must acknowledge the limitations of the group to influence Forest Service decision making to avoid unrealistic expectations. Primarily, the group will provide information and recommendations to the Forest Service.
- Members must commit to attending meetings on a regular basis. In this way, relationships can be built over time, and no party should feel left out of decision making. Also, the initial group should aim to identify all the key interest groups involved and make sure that as many of these groups are represented in the larger group as possible.
- The charter must include ground rules about open, honest, and respectful communication. These rules need to be enforced by the facilitator. Members should be educated about key elements of *Principled Negotiation*, and a specific process for resolving disputes must also be agreed upon.
- The charter can also document guidelines for how the overall work will be structured and tasks should be accomplished. For example, subcommittees may develop to investigate specific issues and provide background and recommendations to the larger collaborative group. A larger steering committee may develop to set agendas and manage the group's work more generally.

- The group should collaboratively develop procedures for how collective decisions will be made and how dissenting opinions will be forwarded to the Forest Service when they exist.
- Transition planning should include specific procedures for orienting newcomers to group norms, procedures, roles, and other important information—for example, developing a "welcome packet" that clearly outlines the rules of engagement and is updated regularly with current happenings for new members.
- Periodic evaluation should reflect on the quality of participation and communication between members in addition to the achievement of goals. Reflection should focus on lessons learned and potential improvements to the process.

Building on the systems-based trust they hope will be established through the writing of the charter and its enforcement by the facilitator, they consider how to enhance rational and affinitive trust between the stakeholders (TT). They feel that rational trust can emerge through demonstrations of competence, joint fact-finding, and in-depth discussions of where stakeholder interests may overlap (PN). The facilitator agrees that providing opportunities for all stakeholders to showcase their specific knowledge and dependability is important. She will design specific tasks and shepherd stakeholders through the process of completing them well and in a timely fashion—for example, collecting information on forest use or explaining to the larger group how timber harvests can enhance forest health. She also plans to facilitate joint fact-finding processes, in which groups of stakeholders work together to better understand an area of uncertainty.[8] This can serve to enhance feelings of meaningful participation and clear-mindedness as well as build shared mental models among stakeholders and (RPM). It may also enhance feelings of autonomy, competence, and relatedness, each important to keeping members motivated (SDT). By working through uncertainty together, groups can have more trust in the information they find. They might also develop stronger interpersonal relationships, and affinitive trust, as a result (TT).

In a similar vein, they'd like the group to commit to multiparty monitoring. Multiparty monitoring involves collaboratively determining how management activities should be monitored to see if they are achieving intended goals. Subsequently, multiple stakeholders actually collect the monitoring data. Multiparty monitoring should enhance transparency, lessen concerns about cheating or negligence, and enable adaptive management. It should thus contribute to both rational and systems-based trust (TT).

The facilitator is also skilled in leading groups through the process of ***Principled Negotiation.*** By setting up clear ground rules for respectful communication and helping stakeholders to express the interests underlying their positions, common ground often emerges that enables groups to develop shared goals that reflect each other's concerns. Amy's team is concerned, however, that they will be starting from a baseline of distrust and animosity between many of the stakeholders involved. They expect that some stakeholders will have difficulty letting down their guard enough to participate openly and honestly. They discuss ideas for reducing perceived threats and for enhancing the likelihood of finding common ground and building affinitive trust.

Based on *Identity Theory,* they are worried that stakeholders may focus more on defending their previously held beliefs than on engaging in exploratory thought around new information. They think that trying self-affirmations prior to active engagement might be helpful. If people can be reminded that their self-worth comes from domains outside the specific topics of debate of the group, *Self-Affirmation Theory* suggests they are more likely to approach deliberations with a more open mind. In experimental studies, self-affirmations typically involve short writing exercises in which individuals select a core value from a list and write about their own experiences in which they have embodied that value. The team is unsure about whether they can pull off the writing exercise with participants in these meetings, but they'd like to try. They also consider other "icebreaker" activities that might not only serve as self-affirmations, but also help participants to see each other as generally good people with common values. They like the idea of people sharing recent personal events that made them feel proud at the beginning of meetings (IT, SAT).

If feelings of risk can be diminished, seeking areas of agreement becomes more feasible. They collectively feel that there may be two levels at which common ground might be found: core values and specific ideas about management actions. They think that considering *Moral Foundations Theory* in light of the concept of affinitive trust (TT) provides insights about exposing core values.

Sometimes, people's interests regarding a specific management action don't align very well. However, there might still be opportunities for stakeholders to amicably disagree and respect each other's views enough to either compromise, accept a suboptimal solution, or keep working collaboratively until a better solution is identified. If people can come to see their counterparts as good people, even if they disagree, conflict can move from destructive to constructive. They brainstorm a number of ideas:

- Facilitated field trips, in which the facilitator drives conversations toward identifying common moral foundations and interests (MFT, PN).
- Openly discussing the concept of *Moral Foundations Theory.* The theory emphasizes that all people hold common moral foundations at least to some degree. If stakeholders can see each other as moral actors, working from their

deeply held moral convictions, then they might find more common ground than they expected. If the morality of former adversaries is made clear, it is harder to claim moral superiority and dismiss their concerns (MFT).
- Ground rules that involve specific listening techniques and responses that require participants to find and express merit in the ideas of others—even if they disagree (PN, TT).
- Informal social interactions. Finding ways to provide time and space for these, with food and possibly beer, wine, or some other treat, can help affinitive trust to emerge (TT).

Once it appears that sufficient trust is developed, and stakeholders better understand each other's interests, finding common ground about appropriate management actions might be easier. Following the guidelines of **Principled Negotiation** can help to identify it. Collaborative visioning of desired futures, in which stakeholders are encouraged to jointly envision what they would like to see the landscape look like at some designated date in the future, can also often reveal overlapping interests and spur meaningful discussions. The facilitator is skilled in these approaches.[9]

Even in the best conditions, however, Amy's team is concerned about the competing accountabilities of participants in the collaborative group. Even if agreement is reached within the group, some members' organizations might still decide to sue the Forest Service or otherwise try to stop proposed actions. In an effort to address the issue before it happens, they devise an exercise in which each stakeholder develops and shares their own accountability map (see Figure 7.2 in **Accountability Theory**). They feel this might help to build empathy between stakeholders for the challenges they each face and further the development of affinitive trust (TT). They hope that by making these accountabilities more transparent, members might help each other strategize how to best bridge the interests of the collaborative group with those of their home organizations or other constituencies. They also realize that managing their own upward accountabilities within the agency (see Table 9.6) will be critical to their ultimate success and that making them visible to others might have similar benefits for them.

They hope that all of these strategies together will help them to move from a place of adversarial conflict toward a situation in which open-minded deliberation and innovation can take place. With this hope, they embark upon their Forest Plan process using their new approach.

Implementation with an adaptive mindset

It takes quite some time to get all the relevant parties to agree to join their collaborative arrangement, and implementation proves to be a long and bumpy road.

After about a year of getting to know each other through facilitated processes that establish the charter and initial goals for the landscape, specific arguments begin to be more about scientific uncertainty and specific desired outcomes than about doubts concerning the honesty or intentions of counterparts in the collaborative group. Subcommittees are formed to engage in joint fact-finding tasks to address scientific uncertainty. Field trips take place in which different groups educate each other about their concerns for the landscape and about different management activities.

Some members drop out early in the process, but when they learn about the progress being made by the stakeholders who remain engaged, they rejoin—especially when they see that official Forest Service documents are clearly responsive to the concerns of multiple parties. Relationships begin to form between previously disconnected or adversarial stakeholders. They call each other up to ask about whether they might face opposition to different ideas. When they do, they enter into facilitated discussions to see if they might come to agreement.

People outside the collaborative group still maintain direct lines of communication with the Forest Service, but they now also can connect directly with collaborative group members who share their interests to advocate on their behalf.

The collaborative arrangement lasts beyond the Forest Plan process, as the Forest Service and others see value in this new way of interacting. Not everyone becomes the best of friends, and conflict still happens. In one case, the representative of an environmental group becomes convinced that some tree harvest makes sense on the landscape to re-establish more natural conditions following years of fire suppression. However, her organization's official position is to oppose any tree felling on public lands. Although she officially dissents from the consensus recommendations of the group, she manages to convince her home organization not to file a lawsuit in this case—particularly because they have managed to see their interests met in other areas (protecting sensitive habitat for a valued species) based on the collaborative arrangement.

Multiparty monitoring enables group members to trust that agreed upon outcomes are being met. When management actions fail to meet expectations, they reconvene to discuss adapting future management. The Forest Service remains responsive to suggestions of the collaborative group. In cases when Amy feels the need to go against a recommendation of the group, she provides a clear explanation of her reasons and makes an effort to incorporate underlying concerns as best she can.

As members come and go over the years, they manage turnover by welcoming new members with a semi-annual reception that enables social introductions to other members and also provides formal orientation to the established procedures, norms, expectations, and historical accomplishments of the group. When Forest Service staff change, a period of overlap enables the new person to adapt to the workings of the group. The group re-visits the charter and overarching goals on a regular basis. The facilitator keeps track of recommendations and lessons learned to share with the group during each of these revision periods.

Amy and her team continue to advocate upwards within the agency hierarchy for greater flexibility in their on-the-ground management. They have considerable difficulty getting the agency to let go of pre-determined performance targets that constrain their options—for example, the number of acres on which they must reduce fire risk each year. In some discussions, this proves to be a frustration for everyone. However, their openness to the collaborative group about their constraints through accountability mapping exercises helps to generate creative discussions about how to achieve their goals along with everyone else's. As they begin to produce more efficient processes with fewer subsequent lawsuits, they find more leverage in their upward communications within the agency.

In summary, the collaborative effort takes a tremendous amount of uncomfortable work upfront. However, after a couple years of operating in this new mode, no one wants to go back to the old way of conducting business. While participating groups don't always get what they want, they feel more satisfied with their participation. More often than not, they decide to look the other way and do not litigate or actively oppose resulting management decisions that don't fully align with their organization's positions.[10]

9.4 Starting up an energy savings program at work

The problem

Sofia has been working as an accountant at Bottrill Industries in the headquarters office for three years. It's a large transportation and logistics company with large offices in six countries around the world and dozens of packaging and transportation centers. There are about 400 employees at headquarters. Recently, she was invited to participate on a task force to help find cost savings across the company. Their group collectively identified a number of initiatives that would save the company hundreds of thousands of dollars on an annual basis by shifting their fleets to more fuel-efficient vehicles, re-locating some of their transportation hubs to more strategic locations, and revising procedures for taking and filling orders to ensure that each shipment maximized return on investment. As a mid-level employee, she enjoyed the rare opportunity the task force provided to interact with some of the higher-ups in the company. It gave her better insights into the company's overall operations and the organizational culture of the management team.

As she reflects on her experience, she realizes she is most excited that the cost savings they identified were also good for the environment, a personal passion of hers. She'd like to try to do more. She has noticed that her office wastes enormous amounts of energy. Lights and computers are left on all day and overnight, and there are certainly other things they can do to maximize their efficiency. She's convinced she can use the theories in this book to make Bottrill Industries a greener company.

Applying the theories

She realizes that she has at least two challenges before her. The first will involve convincing her superiors to let her try something new. The second will be designing a program that will get people on board and saving energy into the future. She decides that a number of theories might be helpful. Table 9.7 highlights her thinking about how these theories can help her to accomplish each task. As she thinks through the theories, she realizes the potential for an energy savings program to do much more than save energy. She feels like she has the opportunity to develop a program that could inject some new motivation into employees and create a game-like atmosphere that could enhance the overall tenor of the office. Instead of just changing bulbs or installing new technologies, she decides that involving everyone in some fun teamwork around energy savings would be worthwhile.

Table 9.7 *A summary of Sofia's thinking on how to reduce energy usage in her company.*

Theory	Key principles	Ideas
Challenge One: Convincing her superiors		
Trust theory (TT)	The management team will need to trust her to carry out the project successfully. This trust will likely be based on their belief in her competence to execute a program that will benefit the organization (rational trust); whether they like her or not (affinitive trust); and whether she creates a system that minimizes potential risks (systems-based trust).	She feels she has already built rational and affinitive trust with her superiors through their work together on the cost savings task force. She worked efficiently and was always responsive to all requests. She knows she contributed good ideas and made no effort to take personal credit for them. She realizes she'll still need to design a convincing program with little risk involved (systems-based trust).
Social norm theory (SNT)	Organizational norms are already shifting in her favor. There is a clear interest in saving money, and the company has already begun to use the cost saving strategies she helped develop to begin to market themselves as an environmentally friendly company.	She can pitch the idea as building on the great work they have already begun. She'll talk about empowering all employees to work together to contribute to the higher goals of the organization and to do what they can to contribute to society in general.
Theory of Planned Behavior (TPB)	The management team is likely evaluate the proposal based on: • Its ability to reduce costs and/or provide other benefits to the company's performance. • Its fit with the social norms of both employees and the organization's norms. • Its level of difficulty to implement.	She'll need to focus on each of these ideas in her program design. She's convinced the program can reduce costs. If she designs it well, it might also enhance feelings of team spirit and camaraderie as people work together to achieve energy savings goals. The program should be easy and fun, not requiring any drastic changes to daily workflows. Because her company has already begun to market themselves as "green," she's not concerned about going against industry norms. It should also require minimal oversight.
Challenge Two: Designing and implementing the program		
Social norm theory (SNT)	People are more likely to take action if they feel their peers will either take similar action or at least approve of that action.	The program should be a group effort in which energy savings are calculated based on group or team performance. Any rewards should primarily be contingent on group, not individual, performance.

(Continued)

Theory	Key principles	Ideas
Norm activation theory (NAT)	Personal norms influence behavior when individuals are made aware of the consequences of their actions and accept responsibility for them.	Most people agree that saving energy is a good idea. Messaging needs to stress that individuals can make a real difference. Monitoring data can provide a sense of direct connection to outcomes.
Theory of Planned Behavior (TPB)	People will participate if they see that the benefits of participating exceed the costs, if they think their peers look favorably on participation, and if participation is easy and well within their abilities.	If she can create a program that makes the benefits of saving energy clear, highlights the value of projecting a green image for the company, and convinces people that it is easy and fun, she'll have a good chance at sparking change. Easy tasks and fun collective rewards will be important.
Self-Determination Theory (SDT)	People's intrinsic motivation can be activated when the situation generates feelings of autonomy, competence, and relatedness.	There should be no formal penalties or punishments for not participating. Employees should receive regular feedback on their energy savings so they can see their impacts. Employees can be encouraged to work together and remind each other to save energy. This should be easy if they are working toward a common reward. All should be reminded that the goal is not to "police" each other, but rather to encourage each other. If employees can help to create the reward system, they may be even more motivated.
Elaboration Likelihood Model (ELM)	Providing immediate feedback can serve as reminders (or peripheral cues) of desired behaviors.	Conspicuous displays of daily energy use can remind employees of the challenge to save energy. Other simple reminders placed around the office could also serve as peripheral cues.
Identity Theory (IDT)	Working together toward a clearly defined and achievable goal can enhance feelings of group identity. This can further enhance performance and commitment.	Stress the meaningfulness of the impact of the activity, not only to the organization, but also to society. Celebrate achievements together in the hopes of creating pride in collective accomplishments.

(Continued)

Table 9.7 (Continued)

Theory	Key principles	Ideas
Motivation Crowding Theory (MCT)	Intrinsic motivations tend to be more powerful than extrinsic motivations. If incentives or other external rewards replace intrinsic motivations for energy saving, participation in the program may wane—especially if the value of external incentives is not consistent over time.	Rewards provided for energy savings should accrue collectively, not to individuals. This can enhance the influence of social norms and dampen the effects of motivation crowding. Rewards should be fun, but not so large that they can crowd out intrinsic motivation. They should demonstrate that these behaviors are valued.
Leadership Theory (LT)	Within an organization, the management team has legitimate authority to begin a new initiative.	Sofia feels poised to take advantage of her new relationships with key formal opinion leaders within the organization. She would like the management team to be the key communicators of the new initiative. She hopes that other opinion leaders will emerge as the initiative grows.
Diffusion Theory (DT)	Finding and energizing the right opinion leaders can hasten the adoption of new ideas.	

Sofia does some research to get a better sense of how much energy they are using and some ways they could reduce their consumption in meaningful ways. She does some quick calculations based on simple information she finds on the internet related to the costs associated with leaving lights, computers, printers, copiers, and other appliances on overnight. She stays late after work each day for a week to observe how many lights and other items are left on overnight and over the weekend. With this knowledge, and knowing that they pay roughly 10 cents per kilowatt hour (kWh), she can determine how much energy, and how much money, the company might be able to save if employees are willing to make some simple changes to their behaviors. She feels she'll need these numbers to convince her superiors to try something new.

Sofia figures out that each office in the building uses roughly 240 watts per hour for lighting. This means that leaving the lights on overnight (roughly 12 hours) uses about 3 kWh; leaving them on over a one-day holiday uses about 9 kWh; and leaving them on over the weekend uses about 14 kWh. While this doesn't seem like much, there are 300 separate offices in the building. On average, Sofia observed that the lights were left on in at least 60 of those offices each night, including the weekend. Over the course of a year, that equates to over $9,000 wasted. Lights in the common spaces (meeting rooms, bathrooms, break rooms, hallways) are often left on as well. From her walk-throughs, she calculates that these spaces are collectively burning at least 80 kWh on a typical weeknight; 240 kWh over a one-day holiday, and 400 kWh on a typical weekend. Together, that's roughly $12,000 wasted over the course of the year on lights alone. Even if they only turn half of these lights off, the savings would be substantial ($6,000!). She has also learned that leaving computers, printers, monitors, copy machines, radios, coffee makers, mobile device chargers, and other devices on, plugged in, or even in standby mode can add up to thousands of dollars over the course of a year. While she has a harder time counting which computers are on, in stand-by, or off, she suspects that they may follow a similar pattern as the lights. Coupled with her observations of copy machines, fax machines, and printers in common spaces, she calculates a probable additional loss of at least $8,000.

Sofia also observes that there are manual thermostats in every common space in the building and every office (or office suite).[11] She learns that switching to programmable thermostats, which enable employees to control the temperature in their own spaces and save energy while they are away, can save roughly 20 percent, or nearly $10,000 annually, on their overall heating and cooling bills.

All in all, she feels confident that she has identified at least $20,000 in easy savings, even if half the lights are still left on. While it's not a huge amount given the scope of their large company, she feels that the primary benefits aren't really the cost savings. Employees can feel good about their contributions, and the organization can further market itself as an environmentally friendly company interested in sustainability.

Sofia decides to ask for an initial investment of $10,000 to replace all old thermostats with programmable ones and to install energy use feedback monitors. She feels this is a reasonable request if she can clearly demonstrate the benefits of the program. The energy monitors will be installed in every office (or office suite) and all major common spaces to provide daily feedback on the amount of energy used in each space. This can serve as a reminder of the program and an opportunity for employees to learn about the key drivers of energy use and become competent in managing them (ELM, SDT).

Before pitching the idea to the management team, Sofia first establishes clear objectives (TPB):

1. Reduce energy usage at headquarters to further solidify the organization's identity as an environmentally friendly company.
2. Enhance the team atmosphere of headquarters to promote employee satisfaction and motivation.
3. Achieve objectives 1 and 2 at no financial cost to the company.

At first, she considered including cost savings as an objective as well. Upon further reflection, however, she realizes that the savings would be better used to enhance the company's image and contribute to a better working environment for employees. She feels this argument will work better with her management team, as the savings might not be big enough to have a major impact on the company's overall bottom line.

She decides to first pitch the idea to the Vice President of Operations. He is a clear opinion leader in the company (DT). He was a transformative leader of their earlier task force and has close personal relationships with the CEO and at least two of the other Vice Presidents (their kids play on sports teams together). He also regularly interacts socially with people throughout headquarters, sharing lunches and circulating throughout the building to make friendly visits. She's amazed at how well-liked and accessible he seems to be, and she heard the CEO ask his opinion about employee morale in one of their earlier task force meetings as if he was the resident expert on this for the management team. Before she talks to him, she designs the general structure of her proposed program. As she begins to design the program, she checks in with other people she knows are popular within the company to get their advice on what they think will work best (DT).

She decides that the program should begin with an internal information campaign that emphasizes the pride Bottrill Industries takes in its efforts to become more sustainable. These efforts make the company not only more competitive and efficient, but also a more trustworthy organization known for caring about its impacts on society (TT, SNT, NAT). The organization has already developed marketing materials they can draw on to further solidify this group identity, including a new green logo (IDT). All employees will be invited to participate in a friendly challenge to further the company's efforts in this arena. The challenge will be presented by the top management team in an all-staff meeting (LT, DT), which will be followed by regular email communication. These communications will share information about the program, its impacts, and tips for success. She makes a table to summarize the program's components (Table 9.8).

Implementation with an adaptive mindset

Sofia contacts the Vice President of Operations to share her idea. He agrees that it sounds promising and encourages her to develop it into a full proposal. He facilitates the scheduling of a meeting for the entire management team to listen to Sofia's proposal. They can clearly see that there is little risk in giving the program a try. In the worst likely case, they save a little money in energy costs and nothing

Table 9.8 *Theory-based planning for an energy savings program.*

Program component	Details	Theories
Initial invitation to employees	Initial communications will come from the organization's leadership team, stressing that the challenge will be fun, meaningful to the company, meaningful to the planet, and a team effort. Everyone can make a difference. Summary details about current energy use will be shared, as well as information on costs. The program and its reward system (see below) will be explained, and everyone will be encouraged to participate. We should stress that the goal is not to compete against each other, but rather to motivate each other to save energy. Everyone can decide for themselves how much they want to participate.	LT, DT, NAT, SNT, TPB, IDT, SDT
Ongoing communications	Short monthly emails will share progress on energy and cost savings, information on environmental impacts, and simple tips for further saving energy (e.g., turning off lights in unused rooms, powering down at the end of the day, unplugging charging devices, etc.). For example, one email can explain the concept of carbon dioxide and its contribution to pollution and climate change. It is easy to convert kWh saved into carbon emission reductions (1.21 lbs per kWh), and the impact of these reductions can be communicated in interesting ways. "This month, we saved 1.4 tons of carbon emissions, roughly the same amount as a forest of 700 mature trees over the course of a year."	SDT, ELM, NAT, TPB
Programmable thermostats	All regular thermostats will be replaced with programmable ones, which enable employees to control their own climates and ensure that heating and cooling energy is not wasted when they go home. I will set the common space thermostats to begin with, but employees who share those spaces can discuss and change the settings if they wish. All will be trained in how they work.	SDT, TPB
Labels for light switches	Not everyone knows where the light switches are in the common spaces. Simple small signs will be placed on the walls in high traffic areas with arrows, the company's green logo, and a simple message, "Lights switches this way."	ELM, SDT
An energy slogan	The management team should sponsor a simple competition to come up with a slogan for signs around the office to remind people about our new energy savings goals. These signs could then serve as reminders to all staff on a regular basis. See reward ideas for individual recognition below for the person who comes up with the slogan.	ELM, SDT, SNT
Energy monitors	Energy monitors will be installed in all offices and common spaces, tracking energy usage in that space. Employees can see their daily energy use and experiment with different strategies to lower it.	ELM, SDT

(Continued)

Table 9.8 (Continued)

Program component	Details	Theories
Rewards	The program will avoid monetary compensation as rewards to individuals. The big reward will be shared by everyone. I suggest that 50% of the cost savings (money saved over last year's energy bills) go into enhancing our already popular annual party. Based on the projected amount saved, employees will vote on options for the party's location and potential add-ons made possible by the savings. I suggest that the other 50% of the savings then be allocated to environmentally-focused charities. Employees should take part in suggesting and then voting for their favorite charities.[12] The money can be allocated proportionally based on the voting. Limited individual recognition will also be included. Each floor of the building, and the management team, will get to nominate up to two "energy heroes" at the end of the year. These will be people who exemplify team spirit in support of our conservation efforts. Each will be honored at the end of the year. The honorees will get to choose from a list of potential rewards. These will be small enough to avoid replacing intrinsic motivation, but fun and interesting enough to demonstrate that these behaviors are valued. Examples might include tickets to a sporting or entertainment event, a dinner with members of the management team, a series of in-office massages, or a gift certificate to the nearby pub. Going forward, we can slowly adjust the baseline from which we calculate our savings, rather than simply always using the prior year. It might be become difficult to find substantial new savings on an annual basis, and this could limit motivation.	SNT, IDT, MCT, SDT, TPB
Innovation fund	The program should promote innovation. The more we save, the better we meet our goals, the more we contribute to environmental health, the more we give to charity, and the better our annual party will be. We should set aside a small fund to enable investments in energy savings. For example, some employees might want to change bulbs or other appliances in their offices to more energy efficient models. If their ideas show energy and cost savings equivalent to the investment over a two-year period, they should receive funds for doing so, as well as recognition in the monthly emails. I will help to calculate projected savings if needed.	TPB, SDT, IDT

(Continued)

Table 9.8 (Continued)

Program component	Details	Theories
Safety net	To lessen the risk of failure, the housekeeping staff, who typically work in the building at night, will be instructed to turn off all unnecessary common area lights each night. The housekeeping staff will also be instructed to turn off individual office lights, but only on the weekends. When they do so, they will drop a slip of paper we will provide them on the employee's desk that says, "I turned off your office lights for you this weekend." The paper will include the company's green logo and a smiley face. This will provide a friendly reminder and a further guarantee of energy savings, but it will not remove all responsibility from employees.	TT, ELM, SNT
Growing the program	If the program is successful, we can share our process and our successes with the rest of the company. We'll need to consider cultural norms in each location to properly think through how implementation may differ in each place (we can consult *5.7 Meyer's Culture Map* for help). We can also expand on this work right here at headquarters by enhancing our recycling habits or reducing our waste or water usage using the same principles in the years to come. This could have huge impacts on our organization and for the environment if it works!	TPB, SDT, IDT, DT

else really changes in the office. In the best case scenario, they get their employees excited about a fun and easy challenge that has tremendous intrinsic value. Sofia agrees to spearhead the behind-the-scenes work but asks the management team to serve as the primary communicators of the campaign. As a result of their earlier meeting, the Vice President of Operations volunteers to take the lead. She's very happy about that.

There are a number of minor challenges regarding the installation of energy monitors and programmable thermostats, and a handful of employees scoff at the idea at first, thinking it is a waste of time and money. However, each agrees to set their programmable thermostats, and most employees find all of the associated tasks easy enough. After the first full month, the company has already saved $1,200 over the same month's energy bills from the prior year. This seems to motivate even those who weren't engaged in the beginning. Sofia notices people reminding each other to turn off lights and making playful jokes about energy saving in the hallways. She even overhears a conversation about how interesting it is to pay attention to the energy monitors.

Some employees come up with innovations on their own. One person decides to book the largest conference room in the building, which has huge windows, for "Lights Out Lunches." Normally, employees would eat lunch in the kitchen area, at their desks, or at nearby eateries, either alone or in small groups. He convinces the people who work in offices near him to shut their lights off during lunch time and join him in the sunlit conference room. At first, they do this just once per week. As others hear about the idea, more people show up each week. They begin to make it a daily routine, and even start to schedule specific topics of discussion and designate discussion leaders for each day. The news travels, and soon employees on each floor of the building regularly meet on their floor's naturally lit conference room at noon each day. They save energy, build social capital, and talk about their work and other topics of interest. Other employees use the innovation fund to change out light bulbs or lamps in their office. A small group emerges that wants to look into motion detector lights that turn off automatically when no one is around. Another starts to investigate the costs and benefits of solar panels.

Sofia is convinced that most of the benefits of the program would not have emerged if the company just decided to send the janitors around each evening to turn off lights. Employees seem to be more motivated and enjoying themselves at work more than ever. Come October, people are excited about a few new possibilities for their annual party and feel good about nominating their favorite charities to benefit from their simple shifts in behavior. The management team decides to match the amount saved by the program on a 2:1 basis to make the charitable donations feel more meaningful, in effect moving a portion of their typical charitable-giving budget into the hands of their employees at no net cost to the organization.

Overall, the program is a great success. The management team shares the program with other offices in the company with no requirements or mandates attached. In the first year, only a few offices adopt the practice. In the second year, the management team sends some of their most motivated employees to visit non-adopting offices, and the benefits multiply (DT).

At headquarters, they decide to improve their recycling program in the next year. While their revisions don't save them money, they find that staff are already motivated by the new social norms created by the energy savings program. They feel proud of their accomplishments and enjoy the new image the company is projecting publicly. The recycling program involves educating employees about where their waste goes and its impacts, placing conspicuous recycling bins in more convenient places throughout the building, and installing a companywide trash monitoring system that tracks the weight of their recyclable vs non-recyclable trash. Employees agree through a vote to use the cost savings from the energy program for the initial costs for the recycling program, and a friendly competition emerges between the main office floors to see which can achieve the best monitoring results in terms of overall trash and recycling rates.

9.5 Conservation under pressure from development

The problem

Maria has lived on the island of Bali, Indonesia for nearly 20 years. She loves the island, its beauty, its people, and its culture. She's concerned, like many others, about the rapid changes the island has witnessed since she arrived. When she first came to Bali from Australia, there were some resorts in the southern part of the island, but most tourism in the rest of Bali consisted of small lodges and homestays. The incredible landscape of terraced rice fields, water temples, and tropical forests was largely intact. The rivers and waterways flowed charmingly through the cultural landscape, diverted at the locations of intricate shrines into locally managed irrigation systems called *subaks*. Subaks are collective governance arrangements in which rice farmers make communal decisions about the timing of different water flows in consultation with religious leaders to ensure healthy rice harvests each year. The system has strong spiritual overtones, with detailed ceremonies taking place multiple times each day within each subak. A uniquely beautiful landscape supporting an amazing array of biological diversity has resulted from this system. Over the past 20 years, however, the landscape has changed dramatically, and the subaks are facing unprecedented challenges.

Mass tourism has crept north from the southern cities into the once quiet and peaceful area around Ubud where Maria lives. Ricefields are being converted at astonishing rates into vacation villas. To serve the burgeoning influx of tourists in these areas, hotel and villa builders have dug wells to ensure a consistent water supply. This has begun to drain enough water from the subaks in some areas to leave farmers' fields dry. It is difficult for local Balinese people to resist the unprecedented amounts of cash being offered for their lands. After they sell, however, their lives are forever changed, and not always in desirable ways. The socioeconomic structures of entire villages are changing rapidly. Some of those who have partnered with foreign investors have grown wealthy quickly. Others who have sold their land have been forced to move to the southern cities to work manual factory jobs once the initial cash outlay has been spent. Others have begun to work in the tourism industry, most commonly as hotel workers or purchasing a car and becoming drivers. Those who have maintained their traditional lifestyles are quickly becoming poorer than everyone else. The deeply spiritual feel of the island, which has always been rooted in a powerful religious connection to water and land, is changing.

Along with the influx of tourists has come a flood of new materials. When Maria first arrived in Bali, food was consumed on banana leaves and the waste was simply tossed into the forest, a nearby river, or burned. Unfortunately, the arrival of plastics and glass has not been accompanied by an effective disposal system. Government-led trash pick-up is woefully inadequate, and local people have not changed their habits of tossing waste in the nearest waterway or burning it. Waterways around Bali are clogged with massive barricades and flotillas of plastic waste, and health problems have increased exponentially associated with both air and water pollution.

The challenges feel overwhelming. Maria and a number of her friends have tried to petition the government on a number of these issues, but each effort has fallen on deaf ears. She decides that it might make more sense to focus more locally, where she might actually be able to make a difference. She frequently travels to a small village just outside of Ubud where she has a few close Balinese friends. She knows that the rice farmers there are likely to be receiving offers on their land before long. She and her good friend from the village, Ketut, have a long conversation about what can be done. He tells her that many farmers don't want to sell their lands, especially when they have seen what has happened to the South. They value their traditional way of life and are sad about the pollution and urbanization they have seen. However, as the prices for market goods go up with foreign money continuously flowing into Bali, it is hard for them to resist selling out.

Ketut tells her that rice crops have been failing in recent years. Ever since the Green Revolution, farmers have been using genetically modified rice and chemical pesticides provided by the government. While the seeds have produced reasonable harvests in most prior years, yields have been decreasing over the past few decades, and more chemical inputs have been necessary, especially in dry years. She learns that the genetically modified white rice is far less nutritious than traditional varieties and requires large amounts of chemical inputs to sustain. Soils have become degraded over the years from these chemically intensive practices. Some farmers seem ready to quit, and many in the younger generation view farming as an old-fashioned and difficult lifestyle compared to the possibility of purchasing a car or a van and becoming a driver for tourists or working in a shop or hotel.

Maria thinks that she might be able to help these farmers hold on to their lands and their traditions. One of Maria's best Balinese friends, Chakra, is an agricultural engineer, who spent years studying in England before returning home to Bali. She knows that he cares deeply about these issues as well. He tells her of an heirloom variety of rice grown in another village not far away called *mangkok* rice. This traditional rice is naturally resistant to pests, more nutritious, drought resistant, and requires no chemical inputs. As they talk more, she learns that Chakra has developed a large array of fascinating small-scale agricultural inventions that make traditional rice farming much easier. They have the potential to make it much more profitable as well.

Having read this book, Maria is getting excited about what she is learning. Ketut has told her that many rice farmers are intrinsically motivated to maintain their traditional farming practices. Chakra might have some technical solutions to make this lifestyle not only more profitable, but also less labor-intensive. Maybe the younger generation might be willing to continue the practice if it weren't so difficult? Could they do enough to enable intrinsic motivations to overpower large external incentives?

Applying the theories

The three friends get together to think through some strategies for how they might help this village resist the conversion of their lands to foreign-owned vacation villas and hotels. They'd like to re-introduce more hearty traditional rice varieties and offer some new practices to farmers that will enhance their yields and hopefully make their lives easier in a culturally sensitive way. If they can make a project work here, maybe they can use it as a demonstration site for other villages that would like to continue their traditional land stewardship as well. They use the theories in this book to brainstorm a path forward (Table 9.9).

Implementation with an adaptive mindset

Maria, Ketut, and Chakra use *The Community Capitals Framework* to begin to chart out their resources and some preliminary strategies (Table 9.10). They first acknowledge that they'll need some funding and perhaps some additional legitimacy to present their ideas formally to the subak's leadership. They decide to form a foundation, a *yayasan*, so they can begin to seek out funding for their work. They call it *Sawah Lestari*, which roughly translates to *sustainable rice fields*.

As they develop their plans to provide heirloom seeds and promote more sustainable farming practices, they write a number of grant proposals, and Maria uses her networks to seek funding to get them up and running. They need money to buy tools and materials and to pay for their time. By framing their solicitations within the idea of *Tri Hita Karana* (see Table 9.10) and using powerful imagery of what is happening to these beautiful spaces to South in their presentations (FT), they are able to drum up enough support to fund a small pilot project within the subak. While Maria is disappointed she wasn't able to raise more money, they move forward with what they have. Despite their best efforts in attending village meetings and visiting farmers in their rice fields, they only manage to get four

Table 9.9 *Applying social science theories for promoting agricultural innovations.*

Theory	Key principles	Applications
Maslow's Hierarchy of Needs (MHN)	People's basic needs must first be met before they are willing to take risks.	Any intervention must first guarantee that the risks of participation are low and that basic needs are met.
Social norm theory (SNT)	People are influenced by descriptive norms (what everyone else is doing) and injunctive norms (what they believe others think they should be doing).	Proposed techniques should not diverge too drastically from current practices. We need to be sensitive to religious beliefs and ceremonies. We need to convince a wide array of farmers to participate in order to develop social acceptance.
Theory of Planned Behavior (TPB)	People are most likely to act when it is clear the benefits outweigh the disadvantages, they feel their peers will approve, and it is within their control.	The system should be easy-to-implement, clearly beneficial, and fit with local customs.
Motivation Crowding Theory (MCT)	If incentives are only about money or other material benefits, they could crowd out intrinsic motivations—especially if they are large.	We can't compete financially with selling out, so we must focus on intrinsic motivations. The small incentives we can provide make it possible to continue a valued way of life.
Frame Theory (FT)	People will do more to avoid a loss than they will to achieve a gain.	Our communications should focus on avoiding the degradation of natural and cultural heritage and the dispossession of land by foreigners. We can draw upon examples of what has happened elsewhere to highlight the value of maintaining village traditions.
Diffusion Theory (DT)	People are most likely to adopt new behaviors that (1) fit with pre-existing norms, (2) address a known problem, (3) provide an observable relative advantage over prior practices, (4) are simple, (5) are communicated by a trustworthy person, and (6) can be experimented with on a limited basis.	Proposed innovations must fit with pre-existing rhythms of life rather than requiring drastic changes. People have seen their harvests decline. We need to show that our techniques can produce better yields. We may be able to start with a demonstration plot. We can't expect the entire subak to adopt new practices all at once, but we'll want the entire subak to understand what we are doing and open participation to everyone. We'll want to identify potential opinion leaders to be early adopters.

(Continued)

Table 9.9 (Continued)

Theory	Key principles	Applications
Community Capitals Framework (CCF)	Natural, financial, built, cultural, political, human, and social capital can all be invested in a project to potentially yield returns. Developing human and social capital is often the key to long-term success.	We should chart out our assets and liabilities, especially focusing on human and social capital. This might help us to see more options (see Table 8.2).
Commons Theory (CT)	The subak system currently operates as an effective governance system of a common pool resource—water. If members sell to external entities, however, that governance system would be threatened.	Our goal should be to keep the current community-based system in place and to not disrupt it with our proposed actions.
Self-Determination Theory (SDT)	People's intrinsic motivations are best promoted in situations in which they feel high degrees of autonomy, relatedness, and competence.	Our work should aim to provide capacity-building for those who want it, not to coerce people or make them feel otherwise obligated through contracts against their will (autonomy) We should do our best to be welcoming and friendly and look for opportunities to engage socially (relatedness). We need to show participants that their efforts are paying off by tracking success (competence).
Trust Theory (TT)	Trust will be based on pre-existing relationships and cultural norms (dispositional trust); personal relationships that change, develop, or remain the same (affinitive trust); beliefs about the likely outcomes of proposed innovations based on the team's demonstrated competence, honesty, and consistency (rational trust); and on the degree to which we can limit community members' perceptions of risk (systems-based trust).	We will need to be careful that we only make promises we can keep and commit ourselves to fulfilling them (rational). We should look for ways to strengthen our personal relationships with subak members, attending ceremonies, meetings, and social events (affinitive). We should consider ways to buffer participants from risks and enable them to track their yields compared to prior years. We'll need to build in some extra safety nets if our methods fail (systems-based).

farmers to agree to work with them in the first planting season of their project: Ketut's family and three others with rice fields nearby. It seems others want to see if it works first before risking their crops (MHN, DT). Two of the other early adopters are long-time friends of Ketut's family, and the third is a wealthier farmer who can afford to take the risk and is interested in modern farming techniques from his interactions with foreign travelers (DT).

Table 9.10 *Using the Community Capitals Framework.*

Capital	Assets	Liabilities	Investments/needs/notes
Natural	47 hectares of rice fields in the subak. Ketut's rice field (1 ha) for experimentation.	Everyone is using inferior seeds and harmful chemicals.	We need to collect heirloom seeds, provide them to farmers, and get them planted.
Financial	Grant-writing ability, some savings (Maria).	Lack of startup costs for tools, materials, salaries.	We need to find donors and apply for grants.
Built	Rice terraces are well-maintained. Ketut has a small shed we might be able to convert to some use in his rice fields.	We have no central headquarters in the village.	We can meet at the co-working space in Ubud and at each other's homes for planning. We can fix up the storage shed and look for other locations to use if we need more space.
Cultural	Our project fits perfectly with the spiritual basis of the Balinese culture, *Tri Hita Karana*, which focuses on creating harmony among people, harmony with nature, and harmony with God. Existing rituals are very strongly adhered to.	Farmers may not be convinced of the fit of our program with *Tri Hita Karana* and some rituals may conflict with our planting or harvest schedules.	Consider all strategies in light of *Tri Hita Karana*, and communicate in these terms. Respect local cultural rituals and concerns. Try to build new practices into these rituals directly whenever possible.
Political	Ketut's father is on the village council and an elder member of the subak.	We will need the blessing of the subak and village council.	We all need to spend time with Ketut's father and networking. Form a *yayasan* and prepare a formal presentation.

(Continued)

Table 9.10 (Continued)

Capital	Assets	Liabilities	Investments/needs/notes
Human	Chakra's extensive knowledge of sustainable small-scale agriculture and his ingenuity. Maria's ability to write grants. Ketut's local connections. One-hundred and thirty-five subak members who could potentially join the program.	Farmers currently use Green Revolution techniques and may be resistant to change (old habits die hard).	New techniques must be easy to implement (TPB). We'll need to demonstrate early returns and get our hands dirty working alongside the early adopters (TT). If we can create early success, others will follow (DT).
Social	Maria has some friends in the village, and Ketut lives there. Chakra has only visited once.	Chakra and Maria may both be viewed as outsiders, especially since Chakra spent so much time off island (a rarity for the Balinese).	Chakra and Maria need to spend time building local relationships. Ketut will inform them of social events and meetings. They will aim to attend as many as possible and be respectful at all times.

Chakra draws on the well-known System for Rice Intensification (SRI) to develop methods that work well for Bali. He's already tried them in his family's rice fields and increased his yield by 40 percent while lowering the costs of his inputs. In short, his system involves using heirloom seeds instead of the genetically modified Green Revolution seeds, planting seedlings earlier than the typical custom, planting fewer seedlings per bundle in a grid arrangement further apart than the typical custom, intermittent (as opposed to constant) flooding, rotary weed control with a simple-to-use tool Chakra has built from bamboo, and replacing all chemicals with organic fertilizer. The team also develops a careful accounting system to track their inputs and yields. In short, the system should be easy, beneficial, and fit with local customs, and results will be easily observable (TPB, DT).

Most of the implementation goes smoothly, but a few problems emerge. Chakra wants farmers to allow their cows in the uppermost rice fields to provide natural fertilizer that will flow down field to field (see Figure 9.3). However, farmers refuse, as the uppermost portion of the rice terraces is considered sacred and should be free of all livestock. They decide to start compost piles on the farmers' dry lands instead (SNT). It takes a bit more labor to move the compost into the rice fields. The composting efforts, however, give them another idea. They help farmers to

Figure 9.3 Balinese rice terraces. *Photo by Marc Stern.*

create organic gardens in these same areas, producing *moringa* and other simple crops with high market values. The gardens are easy to irrigate with small hose diversions from the rice fields. Even with this additional water need, their four farmers use 85 percent less water overall in the new system than they did in their conventional harvests the year before. With the absence of chemicals, they also are able to reinstate the older practice of having fish in the rice fields when they are flooded. This provides additional natural fertilizer and another source of protein for families. Other species return to their fields as well that had been long absent because of the pesticides and other chemicals in use over the past years.

While Chakra and Ketut focus on the farmers in the field, Maria focuses on finding markets to sell their crops. She also contacts her friends overseas to try to fundraise. The fundraising doesn't yield much, but her international friends help her to recognize the possibility of agritourism. She links up with a university in Australia to bring students to Bali to work in the rice fields. The students also help with marketing materials and other important tasks.

The demonstration year turns out to be a tremendous success for their farmers. While conventional farmers in the subak lost nearly 80 percent of the rice crop due to drought, none of the participating farmers lost any of theirs. Their farmers harvested 70 percent more rice than they did in the prior year. Moreover, the *mangkok* rice sells for three times the price of conventional rice, and the garden crops provide further income.

Their early successes enable Maria and her team to develop a glossy report to share with additional potential funders and to further promote their program at subsequent subak meetings. Their report helps to generate additional interest from funders but still not as much as Maria had hoped. Donations seem to be spread thin across dozens of sustainability initiatives in Bali. At subak meetings, people are still hesitant to join in, despite the obvious benefits they have demonstrated. Only three more farmers agree to join the program for the next planting season. The team holds a retreat with an external consultant to help them think through why their program isn't growing as fast as they'd like.

The retreat reveals a few important lessons. The consultant reminds them that changing the behaviors of an entire community typically takes a long time. From the consultant's point of view, they are doing great and are well on track to reach more meaningful system-wide outcomes within a few years. Together, they realize that their communications have focused solely on the program's financial benefits and highlighting their technical expertise. While they have become good friends with their participating families, they have been so busy that they have not really managed to build meaningful relationships with the rest of the families in the subak. They also realize that other families might look upon their participants, including Ketut's family, as somehow unfairly privileged by the program—despite their best efforts to be inclusive and welcoming. They feel they are suffering an affinitive trust problem (TT).

They decide to use the small amount of additional funding they have to open a small office in the village. They equip the office with a computer, internet access, and other simple amenities. They also further develop Ketut's shed in his rice field with a fire pit, a water filter, coffee pot, musical instruments, and other simple treats. Maria rents a room in a family compound to split her time between the village and her regular home in Ubud twenty minutes away. They invite villagers to use their office and internet access; they also invite farmers to Ketut's shed on a regular basis to demonstrate their work and for enjoyable social time. With more time in the village, Maria gets to know more people on a personal basis.

In their second year, the seven participating farmers again out-produce their neighbors, and the team faces another reminder of the challenges of changing social norms. A persistent monsoon threatens rice plants across the subak just prior to harvest. Chakra attends a subak meeting and offers an alkaline substance farmers can spread on their rice fields to protect their harvests. Only a few families take the time to do so. The rest claim that they are too busy preparing for an important religious ceremony. Nearly half of the subak members lose more than half of their crop as a result. The team learns that they need to account for important cultural norms in times of emergency as well. Maybe they should have asked permission for their volunteers to spread the crop-saving substance, rather than asking farmers to do it themselves. They worry, however, that doing it for them isn't a sustainable solution in the long term. They hope that norms might shift enough over time to enable important new farming practices to coexist with long-standing cultural traditions.

The most important successes of their second year involve the relationships they develop with a wide array of subak members, especially with the head of the subak, who they spent extra time with over the course of the year. In year three, they are able to enroll 50 percent of the subak members in the program.

As part of Maria's marketing efforts, she has been regularly attending workshops and conferences focused on sustainability around Bali where she has been learning about other great initiatives on the island. To further enhance their impacts on the village, she builds a partnership with the the Bali Village Tourism Organization (BVTO), a *yayasan* with experience in training local people to provide homestays for foreigners. Together, they work with interested local families to develop homestays for their visiting students. The BVTO shares a small portion of the profits from the fees the students pay. The rest of the profits stay with the villagers. Six families develop homestays, enabling them to bring in more volunteers and provide them with a more authentic Balinese experience. Each family only commits to hosting when they want to. No official quotas or obligations are made (SDT).

Over the next year, more families become interested in providing homestays. They expand the agritourism program beyond just their students to other tourists who are willing to commit to at least two weeks of work. They are hopeful that this revenue will sustain the program itself. It also provides some labor relief and fun exchanges for the farmers.

After three years, more than two-thirds of the subak is growing *mangkok* rice using SRI methods. Only one family has sold their land. The program appears to have activated pre-existing intrinsic desires to maintain the subak (SDT, MCT). While most families have diversified their incomes by having some family members working in the tourism industry or other jobs, they are now able to sustain their traditional cultural farming lifestyles as well. Some younger family members seem to enjoy the work more now that young tourists are visiting and their workload has been reduced.

Maria, Ketut, and Chakra begin to turn their attention to other villages. They bring farmers who are already enrolled in the program with them to share their experiences with others (DT). Simultaneously, they look to bring greater benefits to their participants (TPB). As they regularly see the same groups over and over again at workshops and conferences on the island, they are able to build meaningful collaborations that help in this respect. For example, they partner with another *yayasan* that specializes in trash management and recycling. They help to introduce their programs in the villages in which they are working. Similarly, other successful organizations make introductions for them in other subaks (DT).

Sustainability-related groups on the island begin working together toward collective impact. These organizations collectively decide to each make small contributions toward the development of a backbone support organization (see *8.4 Collective Impact*). This organization further catalyzes the sharing of information and networking. Together, they are more successful at fundraising. With more success to report and more resources, Maria, Ketut, and Chakra are able to slowly expand their organization and its impacts. Moreover, the wider network has contacts at all levels of government in Bali and is working on governmental approval to begin to collect a small fee at the airport to support their initiatives. While the plan has yet to come to fruition, the prospects are promising. After four years of hard work, she feels that together they are finally beginning to gain enough traction to make a real difference on the island outside of their individual smaller efforts. It's still too early to tell what they might be able to accomplish, but she feels all the pieces are coming together to help Bali balance its development with both environmental and cultural concerns to build a more sustainable trajectory.

10

Putting it all together

10.1 Navigating theories for environmental problem solving

It should be apparent to any reader at this point that no single theory neatly summarizes nor explains all of human behavior. However, it should also be apparent that certain principles seem to stretch across multiple theories, and others clearly build upon one another. There are hundreds of ways the theories in this book could be combined to aid in the understanding of social phenomena. I provide in this concluding chapter what I believe to be one useful approach.

Figure 10.1 depicts the role of the theories summarized in this book in charting pathways toward a more sustainable and resilient future. [1] In the figure, **collaboration** is posited as the most fruitful form of interaction leading to the greatest potential for long-lasting and resilient solutions to environmental problems. Collaboration involves people working together shoulder-to-shoulder to learn, take action, and continually reflect on, deliberate, innovate, and adapt appropriate pathways forward. These types of interactions, I believe, provide us with the best chance to capitalize on diverse talents, knowledge, and ideas to produce mutually agreeable solutions that can enhance the resilience of social-ecological systems. In their absence, we are often left with unproductive conflict, stalemates, and an absence of sufficient attention to our common future. **Persuasion** is often necessary along the way toward effective collaborative interactions and thus represents an intermediate outcome for building constituencies and making informed choices. The theories in this book provide strategies for helping people work together in more productive ways and persuading a larger portion of society to take up the challenge.

My purpose here is to make it easier to connect the dots between context and appropriate theories to make it easier to use the knowledge in this book to work toward solving today's most pressing challenges. Figure 10.1 provides two distinct starting points that represent the initial conditions in which you might find yourself.

Social Science Theory for Environmental Sustainability: A Practical Guide. Marc J. Stern, Oxford University Press (2018). © Marc J. Stern 2018. DOI 10.1093/oso/9780198793182.001.0001

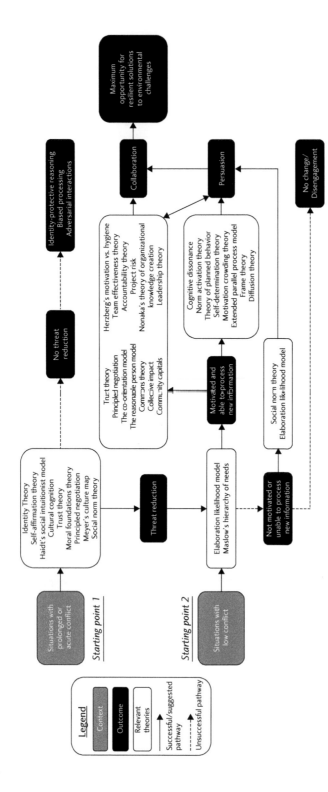

Figure 10.1 Using theory to move toward resilient solutions to environmental challenges. Gray squares represent two different starting points. The white squares contain recommended theories to apply to each. The black squares indicate potential outcomes from applying the theories. The arrows show potential pathways toward outcomes. The dotted arrows represent pathways in which the theories fail to produce desired outcomes.

Starting point 1 involves situations with long-standing or acute conflicts or highly politicized debates. In these situations, people often feel threatened in very personal ways, as their core beliefs about themselves and their values are called into question (see *5.1 Identity Theory*). These **identity threats** often cause people to shut down or respond defensively or irrationally. Without reducing these feelings of threat, people engage in **identity-protective reasoning**, which involves justifying pre-conceived notions rather than evaluating new information with an open mind. It also sometimes involves attacking the source of the perceived threat. Many of the theories in this book identify the sources of these threats and provide strategies for addressing them (see Chapter 5, in particular).

If we can't successfully reduce the personal threats people feel in these situations, we are often left with unproductive conflict or withdrawal from efforts to understand each other. Sometimes, adversarial interaction might be appropriate. Stoking the fires of identity threat can energize certain groups and spur courageous acts of protest. While this mobilization can bring short-term victories and even help to establish social movements, long-term solutions typically involve eventually engaging with the other side in reasoned conversation to find mutually agreeable paths forward. Ultimately, identity threats become a hindrance to long-term progress if not addressed sooner or later.

If personal threats are effectively reduced, we arrive in a similar situation as *starting point 2*, at least in terms of which theories most immediately apply next. Here, we face a different challenge: how to engage audiences who are simply not concerned with the things we care about. **Maslow's Hierarchy of Needs** suggests that we must first address people's most basic needs prior to engaging them in larger societal problems that might feel less urgent. The **Elaboration Likelihood Model** suggests that building personal relationships (see also *6.1 Trust Theory*), crafting provocative messages (see also *5.6 Frame Theory*), and drawing clear connections between a cause and people's regular lives can enhance the likelihood that they will actually listen to our message and consider its content.

If we are unsuccessful in applying these particular theories, we might still see small or short-term changes in people based on what is happening around them. People tend to go with the flow (*4.1 Social Norm Theory*) and follow cues if they are simple and easy enough (*4.4 Elaboration Likelihood Model*). If social norms or cues are stacked against us, and we haven't been able to make our issues salient or interesting, we're unlikely to affect any change.

If (1) identity threats are sufficiently reduced, (2) people's most basic needs are met, and (3) we've generated interest in an issue, we can use many of the theories in this book to help us make convincing arguments (persuasion) and to build collaborative spaces in which we might be able to work together toward solving bigger problems (collaboration). Here, re-hashing the key elements of each theory would be redundant. However, certain principles span across multiple theories. I summarize several below.

10.2 Extracting key principles

My hope is that you have found the nuances of each theory I've tried to share in this book useful to your work. Nevertheless, I recognize that the sheer volume of information contained in these pages could easily be overwhelming to the busy and engaged people most likely to read it. Here in this final chapter, I have therefore attempted to distill a short list of key principles. For each, I provide references to specific theories in the book (see the italicized notes under the bulleted principles). I imagine that every reader could easily add more to this list or see things differently. After all, that is one of many beautiful things about good theories; the possibilities for their application are nearly limitless.

Bias and humility: We are all prone to the former and in need of the latter

- Our expertise can blind us to things we are not trained to see.
- Learning to listen better and seek multiple viewpoints can enhance our problem-solving ability and uncover ways to dismantle social or political roadblocks on the way.
- Resist the temptation to rely too heavily on any one theory or metaphor.[2]

Cognitive biases and limitations; Haidt's Social Intuitionist Model; Cultural Cognition

Basic needs come before collective action

- Any effort to influence environmental stewardship or any kind of behavior change must first take into account the basic needs of target populations, including physiological needs, health, safety, and social belonging.
- People's beliefs about their own basic needs might differ from yours, but their perceptions are typically the ones that matter most.

Maslow's Hierarchy of Needs

Social norms matter

- Effective environmental solutions must link in some way with pre-existing social norms, even if the solutions require changes to common behaviors.
- Learning about and abiding by social norms and cultural customs enables easier communication. Violating them can inhibit it.
- Calling attention to positive behaviors is a more effective strategy than complaining that undesirable behaviors are common.

Social Norm Theory; Theory of Planned Behavior; Meyer's Culture Map; Diffusion Theory

Communications should be personally relevant and stress both positive outcomes and loss avoidance

- If people cannot see direct consequences for themselves or others they care about, communications are likely to fail.
- Storytelling is more effective than fact-sharing.
- While discussing positive outcomes of potential actions is critical, framing messaging in terms of how people can avoid a loss to something they care about tends to be more motivating.

Elaboration Likelihood Model; Theory of Planned Behavior; Frame Theory; Norm Activation Theory

Intrinsic motivation is typically more powerful than extrinsic motivation

- Avoid the urge to quickly provide monetary or other tangible incentives in return for action. First, consider whether intrinsic motivation might exist for taking action. If intrinsic motivation can be activated, it is typically stronger and longer lasting.
- External rewards can crowd out intrinsic motivations. In cases where intrinsic motivations can be activated, external rewards are best used to remove barriers, rather than to create new motivations.

Self-Determination Theory; Motivation Crowding Theory; Herzberg's Motivation-Hygiene Theory

When people feel empowered, they are more likely to take action, innovate, and collaborate

- Empowerment emerges from feelings of perceived behavioral control, self-efficacy, and response efficacy. This means that people feel like they have enough autonomy to make their own decisions, are capable of carrying out their intentions, and believe that their actions will make a meaningful difference to an outcome they care about.
- Empowerment involves helping people feel that their voices are heard; that they can actually influence decisions; that they have enough information to make informed decisions; that they have the resources and skills necessary to take meaningful action; that they do not feel coerced into action; and that they don't feel threatened by others in the process.

- Decision making should be as inclusive of participants as possible. Help key stakeholders feel they have a voice.

Norm Activation Theory; Theory of Planned Behavior; Self-Determination Theory; Extended Parallel Process of Fear Appeals; The Reasonable Person Model; Herzberg's Motivation-Hygiene Theory; Team Effectiveness Theory; Leadership Theory

There is a meaningful difference between productive and unproductive conflict

- Unproductive conflict involves personal attacks, defensive maneuvering, and often hiding true intentions.
- Productive conflict involves active deliberation about what is known and unknown, what is desired, and how to move forward.
- Designing interactions to minimize feelings of risk and maximize feelings of autonomy, competence, and relatedness can facilitate more productive conflict.
- Specific strategies include inviting all those with a legitimate stake in outcomes to participate; employing strategies designed to diminish identity threats; co-developing transparent procedures for deliberation and decision making; and empowering participants to collaboratively re-visit the rules as necessary.

Self-Determination Theory; Trust Theory; Principled Negotiation; The Reasonable Person Model; Identity Theory; Self-Affirmation Theory; Moral Foundations Theory; Team Effectiveness Theory; Commons Theory

Factual arguments alone are not persuasive in high conflict situations

- Finding and acknowledging merit in the perceptions, interests, beliefs, and arguments of others with whom we passionately disagree can create a space for meaningful conversation.
- People often shut down if they feel their identity is threatened by new information or people. Find ways to affirm the self-concept of others outside the domain of debate.
- Learn the language of others' moral foundations to better communicate across adversarial lines.
- Look for common interests underlying adversarial positions.

Identity Theory; Self-Affirmation Theory; Principled Negotiation; Frame Theory; Trust Theory; Moral Foundations Theory

Understanding the perspectives of others is difficult, but important, work

- False assumptions about others can derail collaboration.
- We often move through problem definition too quickly, failing to recognize the various ways in which others may view the issue and whether they agree a problem even exists in the first place. Not only might the means and ends of potential strategies be hotly debated, but also the definition of the problem itself. Without a common understanding of the issue at hand, strategies are extremely difficult to agree upon.
- More open and inclusive discussion up front can save years of conflict down the road.

Trust Theory; Identity Theory; Moral Foundations Theory; The Co-orientation Model; Principled Negotiation; Meyer's Culture Map

The power of positive interpersonal relationships should never be underestimated

- Trust between individuals can emerge from perceptions of competence, dependability, consistency, integrity, shared values, positive social interactions, or demonstrations of genuine caring. Each of these perceptions can be influenced by the settings in which people interact.
- Create safe spaces through joint agreement on procedures, guidelines for communications, and decision-making rules.
- Positive, trusting relationships reduce the risk people feel in their interactions and enhance the likelihood of win–win solutions.
- Building these relationships can take time. However, building them throughout a social network can be just as important as having a great idea to share.

Trust Theory; Diffusion Theory

Understanding social networks can reveal key leverage points for communications and constituency-building

- The adoption of good ideas happens faster if they are communicated by trusted opinion leaders.
- Boundary spanning activities across social, political, or geographically separated groups can (1) catalyze further dissemination of ideas; (2) identify problems and new opportunities; (3) mediate relationships; and (4) build support for initiatives.

Diffusion Theory; Nonaka's Theory of Organizational Knowledge Creation; Leadership Theory; Collective Impact

Integrating flexibility, learning, and adaptive management with accountability mechanisms can enable more resilient and responsive solutions to ever-changing social-ecological contexts

- Groups that do not learn and adapt eventually fail.
- Overly prescribed and rigid accountability metrics can constrain innovation and adaptation.
- Evaluation that focuses on learning, in addition to more traditional measures of success, can spur more successful and resilient initiatives.
- Designating specific individuals or groups as knowledge activists, who gather and share lessons learned in real time, can enhance organizational learning and performance.

Accountability Theory; Nonaka's Theory of Organization Knowledge Creation; Commons Theory; Collective Impact

Take on less. Do fewer things better. Deliver on commitments

- We often find ourselves overwhelmed with too much to do, too few resources, and too little time. Effective environmental problem solving requires significant time and energy. Over-committing leads not only to suboptimal performance, but also to trust breakdowns as we fail to meet our commitments. The ramifications can be long-lasting.
- One of the greatest risks to any project, group, or organization is a lack of time and energy to do the work well. As difficult as it may be, prioritizing the few projects with the most meaningful impacts and kindly saying "no" to everything else (or accepting a reduced role) pays dividends.

Trust Theory; Project Risk; Leadership Theory

Anyone can lead from anywhere

- Power, in its simplest form, is the ability to influence others or any particular outcome. Power can come from a title or the accumulation of resources, but it can also come from the ability to provide non-monetary incentives, the cultivation of a positive reputation, expertise, access to information, interpersonal relationships, or persuasive abilities. As such, every theory in this book is about how to find and use your own sources of power.

All theories, but most specifically: Leadership Theory; Self-Determination Theory; Team Effectiveness Theory; Commons Theory

This work is difficult, and it takes time

- It is easiest to invest in quick fixes, like building something or donating money to a cause. However, these capital investments are rarely the ones that make long-term differences. Rather, investing in more slowly developing social capital can build the coalitions necessary to work together over time, to learn and adapt as systems change, and to be resilient to emerging threats.
- Solving environmental problems involves playing the long game. Building collaboration and influencing broader change happen over years, not weeks or months.
- Setbacks are inevitable. People change, as do political and environmental contexts. Resilience often provides a better metaphor than sustainability. As conditions shift, so must our strategies, and sometimes even our goals.
- Commitment and perseverance are required to be successful in this line of work.

Commons Theory; Diffusion Theory; Community Capitals Framework; Collective Impact

I wish you all the best in your efforts.

Notes

Chapter 1

1. See, for example, Kellert (2014), Louv (2006).
2. These characteristics ensure what some scholars describe as *multiple-loop learning*, which involves experimenting with new ways of doing things and regularly questioning our underlying assumptions about how the world works and about the validity of our intended goals (Keen et al. 2005).

Chapter 2

1. A *heuristic* is an approach to problem solving that involves limited to no cognitive effort. In other words, it is a mental shortcut.
2. See Stern, Powell, and Hill (2014).
3. See, for example, Fernandez-Gimenez, Ballard, and Sturtevant (2008).
4. Stern and Powell (2013).
5. Maxwell and Dickman (2009).
6. See Gilovich (1991) and Haidt (2012).
7. The science writer Stephen Pinker (2014) calls this the "curse of knowledge" and attributes much of scientists' inability to communicate with broader audiences to it. It is often difficult to recognize the complexity of our own specialized languages, which we each develop in our own professional fields (whether coal-mining, physics, or accounting).
8. See Goldstein, Martin, and Cialdini (2008).
9. Thaler and Sunstein (2008).
10. See, for example, Vaisey (2009); Haidt (2012); Van Boven et al. (2012); Thaler and Sunstein (2008).
11. For ideas about how to address climate change denial in particular, see *5.4 Cultural Cognition*, *5.5 Moral Foundations Theory*, and *6.1 Trust Theory*.

Chapter 3

1. You'll find Figure 10.1 (in Chapter 10) also helpful in this respect.

Chapter 4

1. See Simon, H.A. (1997).
2. Formal norms, on the other hand, are standards for behavior that are backed by an established institution and typically associated with explicit sanctions or rewards. Written laws or rules are examples of formal norms.

3. In the case of personal norms, consequences take the form of expected emotional states, such as pride or guilt. See *4.2 Norm Activation Theory.*

4. See Schultz et al. (2007), for example.

5. See Heberlein (2012).

6. See Cialdini, Kallgren, and Reno (1991).

7. See Cialdini et al. (2006).

8. Here, the theory overlaps with the concepts of *competence* in *4.6 Self-determination Theory, perceived behavioral control* in *4.5 The Theory of Planned Behavior,* and *self-efficacy* and *response efficacy* from the *4.7 The Extended Parallel Process Model of Fear Appeals.*

9. Other studies have found that individuals with *collectivist* value orientations are more prone to environmentally friendly behavior than those with *individualist* value orientations. See *5.4 Cultural Cognition.*

10. See, for example, Barata, Castor, and Martins-Loucao (2017).

11. Onwezen, Antonides, Bartels (2013); Thøgersen (2006); Bissing-Olson, Fielding, and Iyer (2016).

12. For some great examples, see Heberlein (2012).

13. Cialdini et al. (1998).

14. Rosenthal and Jacobson (1966).

15. Tybout and Yalch (1980).

16. Goldstein, Martin, and Cialdini (2008).

17. See *2.2 Common cognitive biases* for additional guidance on crafting effective stories.

18. This strategy can also create normative pressure (*4.1 Social Norm Theory*) and trigger desires to maintain internal consistency (see *4.3 Cognitive Dissonance* and *5.1 Identity Theory*).

19. See Abrahamse et al. (2005); Heberlein (2012), and Thompson (2007), for example.

20. See Thaler and Sunstein (2008).

21. See Heberlein (2012).

22. This is why the theory refers to "planned" behavior and is also described by its authors as "reasoned action" (Fishbein and Ajzen 2011).

23. See also Cialdini (2006).

24. See the concept of *reference groups* in 4.1 *Social Norm Theory.* These are people to whom an individual feels (or wants to feel) attached.

25. In these cases, a sense of collective efficacy (that we can do it together) might help to counteract low self-efficacy.

26. See Murray-Johnson et al. (2001). See also *5.7 Meyer's Culture Map.*

27. This is largely due to the *availability heuristic.*

28. See Witte and Morrison (1995).

29. Brandon and Wells (1992).

30. Baral and colleagues (2007) suggest allowing five to ten years for such projects to succeed.

Chapter 5

1. Different emotions may also ensue from different forms of role confusion. For example, if someone is non-verified by a person in a position of higher power, it can result in fear, often leading to withdrawal (or sometimes subversion). However, when someone is non-verified by someone in a position of perceived lower power, rage might be more common. Moreover, if an identity is primarily contingent on one's own internal expectations (moral

norms), sadness, guilt, or shame may result from non-verification. When the relevant identity is imposed from the expectations of others (for example, when someone is elected leader of a small group), non-verification can lead to anger (Stets and Burke 2005).

2. Bryan et al. (2011).

3. Other theories, such as *6.2 Principled Negotiation*, provide a better basis for more directly seeking common ground *within* an argument or negotiation between multiple parties.

4. See Cohen et al. 2007 for a potential list.

5. Lerner and Tetlock (2003).

6. For a more thorough treatment on the sources of our intuitions, see *5.5 Moral Foundations Theory*.

7. See *7.2 Team Effectiveness Theory* for advice on how to build successful teams.

8. Lerner and Tetlock (2003).

9. In the United States, gerrymandering and the influence of money in politics pose serious challenges to convincing elected officials of the diversity of their constituents. Organizing in larger numbers, using the media (social media, print, radio, and television) effectively, and employing legal mechanisms are just a few strategies for addressing this issue.

10. Kahan (2010, p. 297).

11. Hastorf and Cantril (1954).

12. These distinctions are based on earlier work delineating what is known as the *cultural theory of risk*.

13. See for example, Geert Hofstede's cultural dimensions (Hofstede 1984).

14. See *5.5 Moral Foundations Theory*.

15. See Graham et al. (2011).

16. Feinberg and Willer (2013, 2015)

17. See Feinberg and Willer (2015) for complete messages.

18. Other values frameworks exist beyond *Moral Foundations Theory*—for example, Kellert's values of nature (Kellert 1996), Hofstede's cultural dimensions (Hofstede 1984), or egalitarian communitarianism vs hierarchical individualism (see *5.4 Cultural Cognition*). However, *Moral Foundations Theory* may be particularly powerful in this sense, as the foundations have been found to drive intuitive decision making across cultures.

19. See Walzer and Hamm (2012) for examples.

20. These are also known as valence frames or equivalency frames, depending on their specific nature.

21. See McCright et al. (2016), for example, who found that none of these frames were convincing in the face of counterarguments.

22. Kahneman and Tversky (1979)

23. Meyerowitz and Chaiken (1987)

24. Hine and Gifford (1996), Morton et al. (2011)

25. Levin and Gaeth (1988)

26. Gifford and Comeau (2011).

27. For example, see Scanell and Gifford (2013); Spence and Pidgeon (2010), and van der Linden, Maibach, and Leiserowitz (2015).

28. Benford and Snow (2000).

29. In Figure 5.3, one can also notice elements of moral foundations framing. The past-focused frame evokes loyalty (to our forefathers and founding fathers) and sanctity ("how

it was supposed to be back then"). The future-focused frame strongly evokes the care/harm foundations through its emphasis on future generations.

30. For deeper exploration of these ideas, some good sources include Hull (2006), Daniels and Walker (2001), and Lewicki, Gray, and Elliot (2003).

31. See *6.1 Trust Theory* for a more complete treatment of this scale.

32. E.g., Hofstede (1984), Hofstede, Hofstede, and Minkov (2010), and House et al. (2004).

33. Kroeger, Thuesen, and Rutledge (2002).

34. Widiger (2017); Ferguson (2014).

35. Daniels and Price (2009); Riso and Hudson (2003).

36. The GLOBE project, based on Geert Hofstede's work, also provides useful national-level trends that describe broad cultural norms (House et al. 2004).

37. See erinmeyer.com/tools. Last accessed December 1, 2017.

Chapter 6

1. Most environmental laws, such as the National Environmental Policy Act in the United States, upon which many other nations' environmental laws are based, set forth a substantive goal associated with public involvement.

2. Stern and Predmore (2012).

3. Stern and Predmore (2012); Wondolleck and Yaffee (2000).

4. Stern (2008b).

5. These objects are typically referred to as "boundary objects." Sometimes, shared trust in a boundary object can enable initial collaboration and the subsequent development of interpersonal trust (see, for example, White et al. 2010).

6. See Smith et al. (2013).

7. See Parkins and McFarlane (2015).

8. A great source for ideas on working with emotional aspects of negotiations is Fisher and Shapiro's (2005) *Beyond Reason: Using Emotions as you Negotiate.*

9. See Stern 2006; Susskind and Field 1996.

10. See Coleman, Stern, and, Widmer (2017).

11. Stern (2006).

12. For more detail on this specific case, see Brown (2000) and Stern (2006).

13. Multiple tools and manuals are available for guiding the facilitation of these types of processes. For example, see Creighton (2005); Daniels and Walker (2001); Gregory et al. (2012); Fisher and Shapiro (2005); and Susskind, McKearnen, and Thomas-Lamar (1999).

14. For more on concept mapping, mental modeling, and logic modeling, see: Knowlton and Phillips (2013); Lynam and Brown (2012); Margoluis et al. (2013).

15. Isaacs (1993, p. 25).

16. See also Lynam and Brown (2012).

17. See Kaplan (2001).

Chapter 7

1. See Eisenhardt (1989) for an overview.

2. See Baard, Deci, and Ryan (2004); and Hines (1973) for examples.

3. While others depict more complex frameworks of team life cycles (see Marks et al. 2001; Rousseau et al. 2006 for excellent examples), this simplistic division enables a practical and straightforward treatment of the drivers of team effectiveness.
4. Daspit et al. 2013.
5. Morgeson, DeRue, and Karam 2010.
6. Simons and Peterson 2000.
7. Hulsheger, Anderson, and Salgado 2009.
8. Maynard et al. 2012.
9. Stern and Predmore 2012.
10. See Kozlowski and Ilgen (2006).
11. See also Stern and Predmore (2012).
12. Stern and Predmore (2012).
13. Turnover can be desirable in cases of adding new energy and ideas or removing under-performers or non-collaborative team members.
14. See Romzek et al. (2013).
15. Although Figure 7.2 is based on the accountabilities felt by an individual, it could also be used at the organizational level to map the real and perceived accountability of entire organizations within a broader network of actors.
16. See Christensen and Ebrahim (2006) and Stern and Predmore (2011).
17. Merton 1968.
18. Stern and Predmore (2012).
19. See Brosius and Russell (2004), for example.
20. Brandon and Wells (1992).
21. For additional guidance on stakeholder analysis, see Brugha and Varvasovsky (2000), Candler and Dumont (2010), and Reed et al. (2009).
22. Having different stakeholders create and share accountability maps with each other also represents a potentially fruitful exercise for increasing transparency and potentially trust between them.
23. Christensen and Ebrahim 2006; Lipsky 1980.
24. See Christensen and Ebrahim 2006.
25. See Hersey, Blanchard, and Johnson (2008); Lipsky (1980). Wilson (1989).
26. See Schein (2010).
27. While numerous conceptualizations of the sources of project risk exist in the literature, these four classifications are more or less reflective and inclusive of all others.
28. Fan, Lin, and Sheu (2008).
29. Kutsch and Hall (2010).
30. Stern et al. (2014).
31. Mintzberg (1983).
32. Stern and Predmore (2012).
33. Stern (2008b); Stern and Predmore (2012).
34. Stern et al. (2014).
35. Stern and Predmore (2012),
36. Merton (1968); Mintzberg (1983).
37. Stern and Predmore (2012).
38. For example, in a study I conducted years ago, the sentiments of national park staff about their jobs were often cited by local residents to explain their active opposition to

the park (in the form of public protest, illegal resource extraction, and other infractions). In tracing the history of park–people relationships in these places, I found shifts in the general public's attitude to be strongly influenced by internal staff practices and morale. At one park, locals cited one particular time period as particularly harmonious between the park and local people. During that time period, the park superintendent would make it a point to spend at least a few hours talking with his locally hired maintenance staff before making any major management decisions that would affect the local community (Stern 2006; 2010). Long-time employees recalled the time period fondly and noted the sense of pride they felt in working for the park during that time.

39. I summarize only a small portion of Nonaka's extensive work and theoretical contributions. Those interested will find a far greater array of ideas in the key references listed at the end of section 7.5.
40. This intentional overlapping of information is commonly referred to as redundancy within Nonaka's theory (Nonaka, Tonna, and Konno 2000).
41. Kolb (1984).
42. Hoegl (2005).
43. Drath et al. (2008).
44. Stogdill and Coons (1957).
45. Likert (1967).
46. Tannenbaum and Schmidt (1973)
47. Blake and Mouton (1982).
48. McGregor (1960).
49. House (1996).
50. Fiedler and Chemers (1984).
51. Vroom and Yetton (1973).
52. Hersey, Blanchard, and Johnson (2008).
53. French and Raven (1959).
54. Raven (1965).
55. Hersey and Goldsmith (1980).
56. See Bennis (1984); Judge et al. (2002); and Kirkpatrick and Locke (1991) for additional significant works on leadership traits.
57. Hersey, Blanchard, and Johnson (2008).
58. Fiedler's Contingency Theory, Path-Goal Theory, and the Vroom–Yetton Normative Decision Model, in particular (see Table 7.7).
59. Stern and Predmore (2012).
60. Likert (1967).
61. Covey (1992; 2004).

Chapter 8

1. Folke et al. (2005).
2. *Transformation* occurs when a fundamentally new system (new forms, functions, and services) emerges after a major disturbance, rather than one that more or less resembled what was there before—for example, the development of an entirely new urban design for a waterfront after a major hurricane or the conversion of a grassland to a forest. Transformations

could be deemed desirable or undesirable by different stakeholders, depending on the new functions and services provided. Transformations can be brought about intentionally or unintentionally by individual actors, groups of stakeholders, broader governance regimes, or environmental disturbances, such as a catastrophic fire or weather event.

3. As such, theories of persuasion, trust, negotiation, public involvement, organizational effectiveness, and identity, each shared in prior chapters of this book, will also apply to these situations.

4. Social capital refers to the qualities of the network of relationships between those involved, especially regarding trust and stakeholders' willingness to honestly participate, listen, learn, and contribute. See *8.2 The Community Capitals Framework*.

5. Pahl-Wostl (2009).

6. For good overviews on the broader concepts of social-ecological systems, resilience, and adaptive governance, I recommend Berkes, Colding, and Folke (2008); Burch, Machlis, and Force (2017); Chaffin, Gosnell, and Cosens (2014); Collins et al. (2011); Walker and Salt (2012).

7. Agrawal and Gibson (1999).

8. See Ostrom (2005) and associated work on the "Institutional Analysis and Development Framework," in addition to the design principles listed here, for diagnostic tools.

9. See Butler (1980).

10. See Brandon and Wells (1992) for examples and *4.8 Motivation Crowding Theory*.

11. Brosius and Russell (2004).

12. McShane and Wells (2004).

13. Stern (2008a).

14. E.g., Emery and Flora (2006); Magis (2010).

15. Pretty and Ward (2001).

16. See Emery and Flora (2006); Pretty (2003); Pretty and Smith (2004).

17. Baral and Stern (2011).

18. See Butler (1980).

19. Breaux et al. (2015).

20. Ban et al. (2013); Groves et al. (2002).

21. Robinson and Torvik (2005).

22. Of course, some never adopt. Figure 8.3 depicts adopters only.

23. This demographic will populate all categories in Figure 8.3, but will make up a greater proportion of innovators and early adopters.

24. This ability may relate to self-efficacy (see *4.5 The Theory of Planned Behavior*) or to limitations imposed by their economic, political, or social condition (Galjart 1971).

25. For a good introduction to the expansive field of social network theory, see Kadushin (2012).

26. Burt (1999, p. 37).

27. E.g., Valente and Davis (1999).

28. E.g., Locock et al. (2001).

29. E.g., Kincaid (2000).

30. See Burt (1992) for a more extensive treatment of the role of structural holes in social networks.

31. Stern (2010).

32. "Wicked" problems are those in which complexity is increased due to disagreements about the definition of the problem itself, in addition to incomplete or contradictory knowledge and opinions, interconnectedness to other complex problems, and continuous change (Balint et al. 2011).

Chapter 9

1. Lewin (1951: p. 169).
2. https://www.npca.org/articles/1462-house-moves-to-encourage-drilling-in-national-par ks#sm.001n4zec218yad2us9p1g8e4w9ar7 Accessed, February 1, 2017.
3. http://fox6now.com/2017/02/03/the-rep-who-introduced-national-parks-drilling-bill-got-250k-from-big-energy-tmwsp/ Accessed February 4, 2017.
4. See Predmore, Stern, and Mortimer (2011).
5. See Hoover and Stern (2014) and Predmore, Stern, and Mortimer (2011).
6. The Federal Advisory Committee Act places some restrictions on these processes. In short, the Forest Service cannot officially convene meetings or treat recommendations from a collaborative group differently than other comments without forming a Federal Advisory Committee. However, they can be directly engaged with the group throughout the process and communicate on a regular basis to build trust and better understand the concerns of stakeholders. Unless they decide to make the group a federal advisory committee, they will have to partner with external groups, who can officially convene the process, to make this work. This has been done successfully in the Forest Service's Collaborative Forest Landscape Restoration Program multiple times (see Butler 2013).
7. She plans to rely on some of the persuasive communications theories in this book if she runs into any trouble in convincing them to participate. However, she is pretty confident they will want to be involved if they can see the Forest Service putting in an honest effort to better hear their concerns.
8. For more detail, see Matsuura and Schenk (2016).
9. Specific techniques include World Café (Fouché and Light 2011), structured decision-making (Gregory et al. 2012), community visioning (Walzer and Hamm 2012), and scenario planning (Peterson, Cumming, and Carpenter 2003; Scearce and Fulton 2004), among others.
10. See Coleman and Stern (2017) for more on this.
11. In most newly constructed office buildings this wouldn't be the case, but many older buildings commonly have multiple thermostats, especially those converted from other uses.
12. Another idea would be to use the money to fund special projects meaningful to the staff.

Chapter 10

1. Valid arguments could be made for additional theories in each of Figure 10.1's boxes. I've selected only those I feel are most directly related in each case.
2. See Norton (2015).

Literature Cited

Abrahamse, W., L. Steg, C. Vlek, and T. Rothengatter 2005. A review of intervention studies aimed at household energy conservation. *Journal of Environmental Psychology* 25: 273–91.

Agrawal, A., and C.C. Gibson 1999. Enchantment and disenchantment: The role of community in natural resource conservation. *World Development* 27(4): 629–49.

Ajzen, I. 1988. *Attitudes, personality, and behavior.* Stony Stratford, UK: Open University Press.

Ajzen, I. 1991. The theory of planned behavior. *Organizational Behavior and Human Decision Processes* 50: 179–91.

Armitage, C.J., and M. Conner 2001. Efficacy of the theory of planned behaviour: A meta-analytic review. *British Journal of Social Psychology* 40: 471–99.

Baard, P.P., E.L. Deci, and R.M. Ryan 2004. Intrinsic need satisfaction: A motivational basis of performance and well-being in two work settings. *Journal of Applied Psychology* 34(10): 2045–68.

Baldwin, M., and J. Lammers. 2016. Past-focused environmental comparisons promote proenvironmental outcomes for conservatives. *Proceedings of the National Academy of Sciences* 13(52): 14953–7.

Balint, P.J., R.E. Stewart, A. Desai, and L.C. Walters 2011. *Wicked environmental problems: Managing uncertainty and conflict.* Washington, DC: Island Press.

Ban, N.C., M. Mills, J. Tam, C.C. Hicks, S. Klain, N. Stoeckl, M.C. Bottrill, J. Levine, R.L. Pressey, T. Satterfield, and K.M.A. Chan 2013. A social-ecological approach to conservation planning: Embedding social considerations. *Frontiers in Ecology and the Environment* 11(4): 194–202.

Baral, N., and M.J. Stern 2011. Capital stocks and organizational resilience of conservation area management committees in Annapurna Conservation Area, Nepal. *Society and Natural Resources* 24(10): 1011–26.

Baral, N., M.J. Stern, and J.T. Heinen 2007. Integrated conservation and development project life cycles in the Annapurna Conservation Area, Nepal: Is development overpowering conservation? *Biodiversity and Conservation* 16: 2903–17.

Barata, R., P. Castor, and M.A. Martins-Loucao 2017. How to promote conservation behaviours: the combined role of environmental education and commitment. *Environmental Education Research* 23(9): 1322–34.

Barczak, G., F. Lask, and J. Mulki 2010. Antecedents of team creativity: An examination of team emotional intelligence, team trust, and collaborative culture. *Creativity and Innovation Management* 19(4): 332–45.

Bass, B.M., and R.E. Riggio 2006. *Transformational leadership.* Second edition. London: Laurence Erlbaum Associates.

Benford, R.D., and D.A. Snow 2000. Framing processes and social movements: An overview and assessment. *Annual Review of Sociology* 26: 211–39.

Bennis, W. 1984. The 4 competencies of leadership. *Training and Development Journal* 38(8): 14–19.

Berkes, F., J. Colding, and C. Folke (eds) 2008. *Navigating social-ecological systems: Building resilience for complexity and change.* Cambridge, UK: Cambridge University Press.

Bissing-Olson, M.J., K.S. Fielding, and A. Iyer 2016. Experiences of pride, not guilt, predict pro-environmental behavior when pro-environmental descriptive norms are more positive. *Journal of Environmental Psychology* 45: 145–53.

Blake, R.R., and J.S. Mouton 1982. *The versatile manger: A grid profile.* Homewood, IL: Irwin.

Brandon, K., and M. Wells 1992. Planning for people and parks. *World Development* 20: 357–70.

Breaux, A., J. Eickhoff, S. Neill, K. Sheppard, M. Smith, A. Taveras, H. Truong, and J. Valente 2015. *Bali, Indonesia: Opportunities for future engagement.* Arlington, VA: Center for Leadership in Global Sustainability.

Brønn, P.S., and C. Brønn 2003. A reflective stakeholder approach: Co-orientation as a basis for communication and learning. *Journal of Communication Management* 7(4): 291–303.

Brosius, J.P., and D. Russell 2004. Conservation from above: An anthropological perspective on transboundary protected areas. In U.M. Goodale, M.J. Stern, C. Margoluis, A.G. Lanfer, and M. Fladeland (eds.), *Transboundary protected areas: The viability of regional conservation strategies.* New York: Haworth Press.

Brown, M.L. 2000. *The wild east: A biography of the Great Smoky Mountains.* Gainesville, FL: University Press of Florida.

Brugha. R., and Z. Varvasovsky 2000. Stakeholder analysis: A review. *Health Policy and Planning* 15(3): 239–46.

Bryan, C.J., G.M. Walton, T. Rogers, and C.S. Dweck 2011. Motivating voter turnout by invoking the self. *Proceedings of the National Academy of Sciences* 108: 12653–56.

Bovens, M., R.E. Goodin, and T. Shillemans (eds.) 2014. *The Oxford handbook of public accountability.* Oxford, UK: Oxford University Press.

Burch, W.R., Jr., G.E. Machlis, and J.E. Force 2017. *The structure and function of human ecosystems.* New Haven: Yale University Press.

Burt, R.S. 1999. The social capital of opinion leaders. *The Annals of the American Academy of Political and Social Science* 566: 37–54.

Burt, R.S. 1992. *Structural holes: The social structure of competition.* Cambridge, MA: Harvard University Press.

Butler, R.W. 1980. The concept of a tourist area cycle of evolution: Implications for management of resources. *The Canadian Geographer/Le Géographe Canadien* 24(1): 5–12.

Butler, W.H. 2013. Collaboration at arm's length: navigating agency engagement in landscape scale ecological restoration collaboratives. *Journal of Forestry* 111(6): 395–403.

Candler, G., and G. Dumont 2010. A non-profit accountability framework. *Canadian Public Administration* 53(2): 259–79.

Chaffin, B.C., H. Gosnell, and B.A. Cosens 2014. A decade of adaptive governance scholarship: synthesis and future directions. *Ecology and Society* 19(3): 56. http://dx.doi.org/10.5751/ES-06824-190356

Christensen, R.A., and A. Ebrahim 2006. How does accountability affect mission? The case of a nonprofit serving immigrants and refugees. *Nonprofit Management and Leadership* 17(2): 195–209.

Cialdini, R.B. 2006. *Influence: The psychology of persuasion.* Revised edition. New York: Harper Business.

Cialdini, R.B., L.J. Demaine, B.J. Sagarin, D. Barrett, K. Rhoads, and P.L. Winter 2006. Managing social norms for persuasive impact. *Social Influence* 1(1): 3–15.

Cialdini, R.B., N. Eisenberg, B.L. Green, K. Rhoads, and R. Bator 1998. Undermining the undermining effect of reward on sustained interest: When unnecessary conditions are sufficient. *Journal of Applied Social Psychology* 28: 249–63.

Cialdini, R.B., C.A. Kallgren, and R.R. Reno 1991. A focus theory of normative conduct. *Advances in Experimental Psychology* 24: 201–34.

Cohen, G.L., J. Aronson, and C.M. Steele 2000. When beliefs yield to evidence: Reducing biased evaluation by affirming the self. *Personality and Social Psychology Bulletin* 26(9): 1151–62.

Cohen, G.L., and D.K. Sherman 2014. The psychology of change: Self-affirmation and social psychological intervention. *The Annual Review of Psychology* 65: 333–71.

Cohen, G.L., D.K. Sherman, A. Bastardi, L. Hsu, M. McGoey, and L. Ross 2007. Bridging the partisan divide: Self-affirmation reduces ideological close-mindedness and inflexibility in negotiation. *Journal of Personality and Social Psychology* 93(3): 415–30.

Coleman, K., and M.J. Stern 2017. Boundary spanners as trust ambassadors in collaborative natural resource management. *Journal of Environmental Planning and Management* 61(2): 291–308.

Coleman, K., M.J. Stern, and J. Widmer 2017. Facilitation, coordination, and trust in landscape-level forest restoration. *Journal of Forestry*. DOI: https://doi.org/10.5849/jof.2016-061.

Collins, S.L., S.R. Carpenter, S.M. Swinton, D.E. Orenstein, D.L. Childers, T.L. Gragson, N.B. Grimm, J.M. Grove, S.L. Harlan, J.P. Kaye, and A.K. Knapp 2011. An integrated conceptual framework for long-term social–ecological research. *Frontiers in Ecology and the Environment* 9(6): 351–7.

Covey, S.R. 2004. *The seven habits of highly effective people: Powerful lessons in personal change.* New York: Free Press.

Covey, S.R. 1992. *Principle centered leadership.* New York: Simon and Schuster.

Creighton, J.L. 2005. *The public participation handbook.* San Francisco, CA: Jossey-Bass.

Daniels, D., and V. Price 2009. *Essential enneagram: the definitive personality test and self-discovery guide.* New York, NY: HarperOne.

Daniels, S.E., and G.B. Walker 2001. *Working through environmental conflict: The collaborative learning approach.* Westport, CT: Praeger Publishers.

Daspit, J., C.J. Tillman, N.G. Boyd, and V. Mckee 2013. Cross-functional team effectiveness: An examination of internal team environment, shared leadership, and cohesion influences. *Team Performance Management* 19(1/2): 34–56.

Deci, E.L., R. Koestner, and R.M. Ryan. 1999. A meta-analytic review of experiments examining the effects of extrinsic rewards on intrinsic motivation. *Psychological Bulletin* 125(3): 627–68.

Drath, W.H., C.D. McCauley, C.J. Palus, E.V. Velsor, P.M.G. O'Connor, and J.B. McGuire 2008. Direction, alignment, and commitment: Toward a more integrative ontology of leadership. *The Leadership Quarterly* 19: 635–53.

Emery, M., and C. Flora 2006. Spiraling-up: Mapping community transformation with community capitals framework. *Journal of the Community Development Society* 37(1): 19–35.

Eisenhardt, K.M. 1989. Agency theory: An assessment and review. *The Academy of Management Review* 14(1): 57–74.

Fan, M., N. Lin, and C. Sheu 2008. Choosing a project risk-handling strategy: An analytical model. *International Journal of Production Economics* 112: 700–13.

Feinberg, M., and R. Willer 2013. The moral roots of environmental attitudes. *Psychological Science* 24(1): 56–62.

Feinberg, M., and R. Willer 2015. From gulf to bridge: When do moral arguments facilitate political influence? *Personality and Social Psychology Bulletin* 41(12): 1665–81.

Ferguson, R. 2014. *Finally! Performance assessment that works: Big five performance management.* North Charleston, SC: Create Space Independent Publishing Platform.

Fernandez-Gimenez, M.E., H.L. Ballard, and V.E. Sturtevant 2008. Adaptive management and social learning in collaborative and community-based monitoring: A study of five community-based forestry organizations in the western USA. *Ecology and Society* 13(2): 4. [online] URL: http://www.ecologyandsociety.org/vol13/iss2/art4/

Festinger, L. 1957. *A theory of cognitive dissonance.* Vol. 2. Stanford, CA: Stanford University Press.

Fey, S., C. Bregendahl, and C. Flora 2006. The measurement of community capitals through research, *Online Journal of Rural Research and Policy* 1(1): 1–28. https://doi.org/10.4148/ojrrp.v1i1.29

Fiedler, F.E., and M.M. Chemers 1984. *Improving leadership effectiveness: The leader match concept.* New York, NY: Wiley.

Firey, W. 1960. *Man, mind, and land: A theory of resource use.* Glencoe, IL: Free Press.

Fishbein, M. and I. Ajzen 2011. *Predicting and changing behavior: The reasoned action approach.* New York, NY: Psychology Press.

Fisher, R., and D. Shapiro 2005. *Beyond reason. Using emotions as you negotiate.* New York: Penguin Books.

Fisher, R., W. Ury, and B. Patton 1991. *Getting to yes: Negotiating agreement without giving in.* Second edition. New York: Penguin Books.

Fliegel, F.C., and P.F. Korsching 2000. *Diffusion Research in Rural Sociology: The record and prospects for the future.* Middleton, Wisconsin: Social Ecology Press.

Flora, C.B., J.L. Flora, and S.R. Gasteyer 2016. *Rural communities: Legacy and change.* Fifth edition. Boulder, CO: Westview Press.

Fouché, C., and G. Light 2011. An invitation to dialogue: "The World Café" in social work research. *Qualitative Social Work* 10(1): 28–48.

Folke, C., T. Hahn, P. Olsson, and J. Norberg 2005. Adaptive governance of social-ecological systems. *Annual Review of Environmental and Resources* 30: 441–73.

French, J., and B. Raven 1959. The Bases of Social Power. In D. Cartwright (ed.), *Studies in Social Power*, pp. 150–67. Ann Arbor, MI: Institute for Social Research.

Frey, B.S., and R. Jegen 2001. Motivation crowding theory. *Journal of Economic Surveys* 15(5): 589–611.

Galjart, B. 1971. Rural development and sociological concepts - a critique. *Rural Sociology* 36(1): 31–40.

Gifford, R., and L.A. Comeau 2011. Message framing influences perceived climate change competence, engagement, and behavioral intentions. *Global Environmental Change* 21: 1301–7.

Gillespie, N., and G. Dietz 2009. Trust repair after an organization-level failure. *Academy of Management Review* 34(1): 127–45.

Gilovich, T. 1991. *How we know what isn't so: The fallibility of human reason in everyday life.* New York, NY: Free Press.

Goffman, E. 1956. Embarrassment and social organization. *American Journal of Sociology* 62(3): 264–71.

Goldstein, N.J., S.J. Martin, and R.B. Cialdini 2008. *Yes! 50 scientifically proven ways to be persuasive.* New York, NY: Free Press.

Graham, J., B.A. Nosek, J. Haidt, R. Iyer, S. Koleva, and P.H. Ditto 2011. Mapping the moral domain. *Journal of Personality and Social Psychology* 101(2): 366–85.

Gregory, R., L. Failing, M. Harstone, G. Long, and T. McDaniels 2012. *Structured decision making: A practical guide to environmental management choices.* Hoboken, NJ: John Wiley & Sons.

Groves, C.R., D.B. Jensen, L.L. Valutis, K.H. Redford, M.L. Shaffer, J.M. Scott, J.V. Baumgartner, J.V. Higgins, M.W. Beck, and M.G. Anderson 2002. Planning for biodiversity conservation: Putting conservation science into practice: A seven-step framework for developing regional plans to conserve biological diversity, based upon principles of conservation biology and ecology, is being used extensively by The Nature Conservancy to identify priority areas for conservation. *BioScience* 52(6): 499–512.

Haidt, J. 2001. The emotional dog and its rational tail: A social intuitionist approach to moral judgment. *Psychological Review* 108(4): 814–34.

Haidt, J. 2012. *The righteous mind: Why good people are divided by politics and religion.* New York, NY: Vintage Books.

Hanleybrown, F., J. Kania, and M. Kramer 2012. Channeling change: Making collective impact work. *Stanford Social Innovation Review* January 26, 2012. https://ssir.org/articles/entry/channeling_change_making_collective_impact_work

Hardin, G. 1968. The tragedy of the commons. *Science* 162(3859): 1243–8.

Hastorf, A.H., and H.J. Cantril 1954. They saw a game: A case study. *The Journal of Abnormal Psychology* 49(1): 129–34.

Heberlein, T.A. 2012. *Navigating environmental attitudes.* New York: Oxford University Press.

Hersey, P., K.H. Blanchard, and D.E. Johnson 2008. *Management of organizational behavior: Leading human resources.* Ninth edition. Upper Saddle River, NJ: Pearson Education, Inc.

Hersey, P., and M. Goldsmith 1980. The changing role of performance management. *Training and Development Journal* 34: 18–32.

Herzberg, F. 1968. One more time: How do you motivate employees? *Harvard Business Review* 46: 53–62.

Hine, W., and R. Gifford 1996. Individual restraint and group efficiency in commons dilemmas: The effects of two types of environmental uncertainty. *Journal of Applied Psychology* 26: 993–1009.

Hines, G.H. 1973. Cross-cultural differences in two-factor motivation theory. *Journal of Applied Psychology* 58(3): 375–7.

Hoegl, M. 2005. Smaller teams – better teamwork: How to keep project teams small. *Business Horizons* 48: 209–14.

Hoegl, M., and H.G. Gemuenden 2001. Teamwork quality and the success of innovative projects: A theoretical concept and empirical evidence. *Organizational Science* 12(4): 435–49.

Hofstede, G. 1984. *Culture's consequences: International differences in work related values.* London: Sage Publications.

Hofstede, G., G.J. Hofstede, and M. Minkov 2010. *Cultures and organizations: Software of the mind.* Third edition. New York, NY: McGraw-Hill Education.

Hoover, K.N., and M.J. Stern 2014. Constraints to public influence in U.S. Forest Service NEPA processes. *Journal of Environmental Planning and Management* 57(2): 157–72.

House, R.J., P.J. Hanges, M. Javidan, P.W. Dorfman, and V. Gupta 2004. *Culture, leadership, and organizations: The GLOBE study of 62 societies.* Thousand Oaks, CA: Sage Publications, Inc.

House, R.J. 1996. Path-goal theory of leadership: Lessons, legacy, and a reformulated theory. *The Leadership Quarterly* 7(3): 323–52.

Hull, R.B. 2006. *Infinite Nature.* Chicago, IL: University of Chicago Press.

Hulsheger, U.R., N. Anderson, and J.F. Salgado 2009. Team-level predictors of innovation at work: A comprehensive meta-analysis spanning three decades of research. *Journal of Applied Psychology* 94(5): 1128–45.

Isaacs, W.N. 1993. Taking flight: Dialogue, collective thinking and organizational learning. *Organizational Dynamics* 22(2): 24–39.

Judge, T.A., J.E. Bono, R. Ilies, and M.W. Gerhardt 2002. Personality and leadership: A qualitative and quantitative review. *Journal of Applied Psychology* 87(4): 765–80.

Kahan, D. 2010. Fixing the communications failure. *Nature* 463: 296–7.

Kahan, D.M. 2012. Cultural cognition as a conception of the cultural theory of risk. In S. Roeser, R. Hillerbrand, P. Sandin, and M. Peterson (eds). *Handbook of Risk Theory: Epistemology, Decision Theory, Ethics, and Social Implications of Risk,* pp. 725–9. Netherlands: Springer.

Kahan, D.M., H. Jenkins-Smith, and D. Braman. 2011. Cultural cognition of scientific consensus. *Journal of Risk Research* 14(2); 147–74.

Kahan, D.M., E. Peters, M. Wittlin, P. Slovic, L.L. Ouellette, D. Braman, and G. Mandel 2012. The polarizing impact of science literacy and numeracy on perceived climate change risks. *Nature Climate Change* 2: 732–5.

Kahneman, D. 2011. *Thinking, fast and slow.* New York, NY: Farrar, Strauss, and Giroux.

Kahneman, D., and A. Tversky 1979. Prospect theory: An analysis of decision under risk. *Econometrica* 47(2): 263–71.

Kania, J., and M. Kramer 2011. Collective impact. *Stanford Social Innovation Review* 9(1): 36–41.

Kania, J., and M. Kramer 2013.Embracing emergence: How collective impact addresses complexity. *Stanford Social Innovation Review.* Blog Report, January 21, 2013. https://ssir.org/articles/entry/embracing_emergence_how_collective_impact_addresses_complexity

Kaplan, S. 2001. Meditation, restoration, and the management of mental fatigue. *Environment and Behavior* 33(4): 480–506.

Kaplan, S., and R. Kaplan 2009. Creating a larger role for environmental psychology: The Reasonable Person Model as an integrative framework. *Journal of Environmental Psychology* 29: 329–39.

Keen, M., V.A. Brown, and R. Dyball 2005. *Social Learning in Environmental Management: Towards a Sustainable Future.* New York, NY and London: Earthscan.

Kellert, S.R. 2014. *Birthright: People and nature in the modern world.* New Haven, CT: Yale University Press.

Kellert, S.R. 1996. *The value of life: Biological diversity and human society.* Washington, DC: Island Press.

Kincaid, D.L. 2000. Social networks, ideation, and contraceptive behavior in Bangladesh: a longitudinal analysis. *Social Science and Medicine* 50: 215–31.

Kirkpatrick, S.A., and E.A. Locke 1991. Leadership: Do traits matter? *The Executive* 5(2): 48–60.

Knowlton, L.W., and C.C. Phillips 2013. *The logic model guidebook: Better strategies for great results*, Volume two. Los Angeles, CA: Sage Publications.

Kolb, D.A. 1984. *Experiential learning: Experience as the source of learning and development.* Englewood Cliffs, NJ: Prentice Hall.

Kozlowski, S.W.J., and D.R. Ilgen 2006. Enhancing the effectiveness of work groups and teams. *Psychological Science in the Public Interest* 7(3): 77–124.

Kroeger, O., J.M. Thuesen, and H. Rutledge 2002. *Type talk at work: How the 16 personality types determine your success on the job.* New York, NY: Delta.

Kutsch, E., and M. Hall 2010. Deliberate ignorance in project risk management. *International Journal of Project Management* 28(3): 245–55.

Lansing, J.S. 2006. *Perfect order: Recognizing complexity in Bali.* Princeton, NJ: Princeton University Press.

Lerner, J.S., and P.E. Tetlock 2003. Bridging individual, interpersonal, and institutional approaches to judgment and decision making: The impact of accountability on cognitive bias. In S.L. Schneider and J. Shanteau (eds), *Emerging Perspectives on Judgment and Decision Research*, pp. 431–457. Cambridge, UK: Cambridge University Press.

Levin, I.P., and G.J. Gaeth 1988. Framing of attribute information before and after consuming the product. *Journal of Consumer Research* 15: 374–8.

Levin, I.P, S.L. Schneider, and G.J. Gaeth 1998. All frames are not created equal: A typology and critical analysis of framing effects. *Organizational Behavior and Human Decision Processes* 76(2): 149–88.

Lewicki, R.J., B. Gray, and M. Elliott (eds) 2003. *Making sense of intractable environmental conflicts.* Washington, DC: Island Press.

Lewin, K. (1951) *Field theory in social science; selected theoretical papers.* D. Cartwright (ed.). New York: Harper & Row.

Likert, R. 1967. *The human organization.* New York: McGraw-Hill.

Lipsky, M. 1980. *Street-level bureaucracy: Dilemmas of the individual in public services.* New York, NY: Russell Sage Foundation.

Locock, L., S. Dopson, D. Chambers, and J. Gabbay 2001. Understanding the role of opinion leaders in improving clinical effectiveness. *Social Science and Medicine* 53: 745–57.

Louv, R. 2006. *Last child in the woods: Saving our children from nature-deficit disorder.* Chapel Hill, NC: Algonquin Books of Chapel Hill.

Lynam, T., and K. Brown (eds) 2012. Mental models in human–environment interactions: Theory, policy implications, and methodological explorations (Special feature). *Ecology and Society* 17(3).

Magis, K. 2010. Community resilience: An indicator of social sustainability. *Society and Natural Resources* 23(5): 401–16.

Maloney, E.K., M.K. Lapinski, and K. Witte 2011. Fear appeals and persuasion: A review and update of the extended parallel process model. *Social and Personality Compass* 5(4): 206–19.

Margoluis, R., C. Stem, V. Swaminathan, M. Brown, A. Johnson, G. Placci, N. Salafsky, and I. Tilders 2013. Results chains: A tool for conservation action design, management, and evaluation. *Ecology and Society* 18(3): 22. http://dx.doi.org/10.5751/ES-05610-180322

Marks, M.A., J.E. Mathieu, and S.J. Zaccaro 2001. A temporally based framework and taxonomy of team processes. *Academy of Management Review* 26(3): 356–76.

Maslow, A. 1943. A theory of human motivation. *Psychological Review* 50(4): 370–96.

Maslow, A. 1954. *Motivation and personality.* New York: Harper.

Mathieu, J., M.T. Maynard, T. Rapp, and L. Gilson 2008. Team effectiveness 1997–2007: A review of recent advancements and a glimpse into the future. *Journal of Management* 34(3): 410–76.

Mathieu, J.E., S.I. Tannenbaum, J.S. Donsbach, and G.M. Alliger 2014. A review and integration of team composition models: Moving toward a dynamic and temporal framework. *Journal of Management* 40(1): 130–60.

Matsuura, M., and T. Schenk 2016. *Joint fact-finding in urban planning and environmental disputes.* New York, NY: Routledge.

Maxwell, R. and R. Dickman 2009. *The elements of persuasion: Use storytelling to pitch better, sell faster, and win more business.* New York: Harper Collins.

Mayer, R.C., J.H. Davis, and F.D. Schoorman 1995. An integrative model of organizational trust. *Academy of Management Review* 20(3): 709–34.

Maynard, M.T., J.E. Mathieu, T.L. Rapp, and L.L. Gilson 2012. Something(s) old and something(s) new: Modeling drivers of global virtual team effectiveness. *Journal of Organizational Behavior* 33: 342–65.

McCright, A.M., M. Charters, K. Dentzman, and T. Dietz 2016. Examining the effectiveness of climate change frames in the face of a climate change denial counter-frame. *Topics in Cognitive Science* 8: 76–97.

McGregor, D. 1960. *The human side of enterprise.* New York, NY: McGraw-Hill.

McLeod, J.M., and S.H. Chaffee 1973. Interpersonal approaches to communication research. *American Behavioral Scientist* 16: 469–99.

McQueen, A., and W.M.P. Klein 2006. Experimental manipulations of self-affirmation: A systematic review. *Self and Identity* 5(4): 289–354.

McShane, T.O., and M.P. Wells (eds) 2004. *Getting biodiversity projects to work: Towards more effective conservation and development.* New York: Columbia University Press.

Merton, R.K. 1968. *Social theory and social structure.* New York: The Free Press.

Meyer, E. 2014. *The culture map: Breaking through the invisible boundaries of global business.* New York: Public Affairs.

Meyerowitz, B.E., and S. Chaiken 1987. The effect of message framing on breast self-examination attitudes, intentions and behavior. *Journal of Personality and Social Psychology* 52: 500–10.

Mintzberg, H. 1983. *Structure in fives: Designing effective organizations.* Englewood Cliffs, NJ: Prentice Hall.

Morgeson, F.P., D.S. DeRue, and E.P. Karam 2010. Leadership in teams: A functional approach to understanding leadership structures and processes. *Journal of Management* 36(1): 5–39.

Morton, T.A., A. Rabinovich, D. Marshall, and P. Bretschneider 2011. The future that may (or may not) come: How framing changes responses to uncertainty in climate change communications. *Global Environmental Change* 21: 103–9.

Murray-Johnson, L., Witte, K., Liu, W., and A.P. Hubbel 2001. Addressing cultural orientations in fear appeals: Promoting AIDS-protective behaviors among Mexican immigrant and African American adolescents and American and Taiwanese college students. *Journal of Health Communication* 6: 335.

Nonaka, I. 1994. A dynamic theory of organizational knowledge creation. *Organization Science* 5(1): 14–37.

Nonaka, I., R. Toyama, and N. Konno 2000. SECI, *ba*, and leadership: A unified model of dynamic knowledge creation. *Long range Planning* 33: 5–34.

Nonaka, I., G. von Krogh, and S. Voelpel 2006. Organizational knowledge creation theory: Evolutionary paths and future advances. *Organization Studies* 27(8): 1179–208.

Norton, B.G. 2015. *Sustainable values, sustainable change: A guide to environmental decision making*. Chicago, IL: The University of Chicago Press.

Onwezen, M.C., G. Antonides, and J. Bartels 2013. The norm activation model: An exploration of the functions of anticipated pride and guilt in pro-environmental behavior. *Journal of Economic Psychology* 39: 141–53.

Ostrom, E. 1990. *Governing the commons: The evolution of institutions for collective action*. New York: Cambridge University Press.

Ostrom, E. 2005. *Understanding institutional diversity*. Princeton, NJ: Princeton University Press.

Ostrom, E., J. Burger, C.B. Field, R.B. Norgaard, and D. Policansky 1999. Revisiting the commons: Local lessons, global challenges. *Science* 284(5412): 278–82.

Pahl-Wostl, C. 2009. A conceptual framework for analyzing adaptive capacity and multi-level learning processes in resource governance regimes. *Global Environmental Change* 19: 354–65.

Parkins, J.R., and B.L. McFarlane 2015. Trust and skepticism in dynamic tension: Concepts and empirical refinements on the mountain pine beetle outbreak in Alberta, Canada. *Human Ecology Review* 21(1): 133–53.

Peterson, G.D., G.S. Cumming, and S.R. Carpenter 2003. Scenario planning: A tool for conservation in an uncertain world. *Conservation Biology* 17(2): 358–66.

Petty, R.E., and J.T. Cacioppo 1986. The elaboration likelihood model of persuasion. *Advances in Experimental Psychology* 19: 123–205.

Pinker, S. 2014. *The sense of style: The thinking person's guide to writing in the 21st century*. New York, NY: Penguin Books.

Predmore, S.A., M.J. Stern, and M.J. Mortimer 2011. Constructing the public: the 'substantive sieve' and personal norms in US Forest Service Planning. *Journal of Environmental Planning and Management* 54(3): 403–19.

Pretty, J. 2003. Social capital and the collective management of resources. *Science* 302(5652): 1912–14.

Pretty, J., and D. Smith 2004. Social capital in biodiversity conservation and management. *Conservation Biology* 18(3): 631–8.

Pretty, J., and H. Ward 2001. Social capital and the environment. *World Development* 29(2): 209–27.

Project Management Institute 2013. *A guide to the project management body of knowledge*. Fifth edition. Upper Darby, UK: Project Management Institute.

Raven, B.H. 1965. Social influence and power. In I.D. Steiner and M. Fishbein (eds), *Current studies in social psychology*, pp. 371–82. New York: Holt, Rinehart, Winston.

Reed, M.S., A. Graves, N. Dandy, H. Posthumus, K. Hubacek, J. Morris, C. Prell, C.H. Quinn, and L.C. Stringer 2009. Who's in and why? A typology of stakeholder analysis methods for natural resource management. *Journal of Environmental Management* 90: 1933–49.

Riso, D.R., and R. Hudson 2003. *Discovering your personality type: The essential introduction to the enneagram.* New York, NY: Mariner Books.

Robbins, S.P., and T.A. Judge 2011. *Organizational Behavior.* Fourteenth edition. Upper Saddle River, NJ: Prentice Hall.

Robinson, J.A., and R. Torvik 2005. White elephants. *Journal of Public Economics* 89(2–3): 197–210.

Rogers, E. 2003. *Diffusion of Innovations.* Fifth edition. New York, NY: Free Press.

Romzek, B., K. LeRoux, J. Johnston, R.J. Kempf, and J.S. Piatak 2013. Informal accountability in multisector service delivery collaborations. *Journal of Public Administration Research and Theory* 24(4): 813–42.

Rosenthal, R. and L. Jacobson 1966. Teachers' expectancies: Determinants of pupils' IQ gains. *Psychological Reports* 19: 115–18.

Rousseau, V., C. Aube, and A. Savoie 2006. Teamwork behaviors: A review and an integration of frameworks. *Small Group Research* 37(5): 540–70.

Ryan, R.M., and E.L. Deci 2000a. Self-determination theory and the facilitation of intrinsic motivation, social development and well-being. *American Psychologist* 55(1): 68–78.

Ryan, R.M., and E.L. Deci 2000b. Intrinsic and extrinsic motivations: Classic definitions and new directions. *Contemporary Educational Psychology* 25: 54–67.

Scanell, L., and R. Gifford 2013. Personally relevant climate change: The role of place attachment and local versus global message framing in engagement. *Environment and Behavior* 45(1):60–85.

Scearce, D., and K. Fulton 2004. *What if? The art of scenario thinking for nonprofits.* San Francisco, CA: Global Business Network.

Schein, E.H. 2010. *Organizational culture and leadership.* Fourth edition. San Francisco, CA: Jossey-Bass.

Schultz, P.W., J.M. Nolan, R.B. Cialdini, N.J. Goldstein, and V. Griskevicius 2007. The constructive, destructive, and reconstructive power of social norms. *Psychological Science* 18: 429–34.

Schwartz, S.H. 1997. Normative influences on altruism. In L. Berkowitz. (ed.), *Advances in experimental social psychology,*. New York: Academic Press.

Sedikides, C. 2012. Chapter 16. Self-protection. In Leary, M.R., and J.P. Tangney (eds), *Handbook of self and identity,* pp. 327–53. New York: The Guilford Press.

Simon, H.A. 1997. *Models of bounded rationality: Empirically grounded economic reason.* Vol. 3. Cambridge: MIT Press.

Simons, T.L., and R.S. Peterson 2000. Task conflict and relationship conflict in top management teams: The pivotal role of intragroup trust. *Journal of Applied Psychology* 85(1): 102–11.

Sivasubramaniam, N., S.J. Liebowitz, and C.L. Lackman 2012. Determinants of new product development team performance: A meta-analytic review. *Journal of Product Innovation Management* 29(5): 803–20.

Smith, J.W., J.E. Leahy, D.H. Anderson, and M.A. Davenport 2013. Community/agency trust and public involvement in resource planning. *Society and Natural Resources* 26(4): 452–71.

Spence, A., and N. Pidgeon 2010. Framing and communicating climate change: The effects of distance and outcome frame manipulations. *Global Environmental Change* 20: 656–67.

Stern, M.J. 2006. *Understanding local reactions to national parks: The nature and consequences of local interpretations of park policies, management, and outreach.* Ph.D. dissertation. New Haven: Yale University.

Stern, M.J. 2008a. Coercion, voluntary compliance, and protest: the role of trust and legitimacy in combating local opposition to protected areas. *Environmental Conservation* 35(3): 200–10.

Stern, M.J. 2008b. The power of trust: Toward a theory of local opposition to neighboring protected areas. *Society and Natural Resources* 21(10): 859–65.

Stern, M.J. 2010. Payoffs vs. process: Expanding the paradigm for park/people studies beyond economic rationality. *Journal of Sustainable Forestry* 29(2–4): 174–201.

Stern, M.J., and T.D. Baird 2015. Trust ecology and the resilience of natural resource management institutions. *Ecology & Society* 20(2): 14.

Stern, M.J., and K.J. Coleman 2015. The multi-dimensionality of trust: Applications in collaborative natural resource management. *Society and Natural Resources* 28(2): 117–32.

Stern, M.J., C.A. Martin, S.A. Predmore, and W.C. Morse 2014. Risk tradeoffs in adaptive ecosystem management: The case of the United States Forest Service. *Environmental Management* 53(6): 1095–108.

Stern, M.J. and R.B. Powell 2013. What leads to better visitor outcomes in live interpretation? *Journal of Interpretation Research* 18(2): 9–44.

Stern, M.J., R.B. Powell, and D. Hill 2014. Environmental education program evaluation in the new millennium: what do we measure and what have we learned? *Environmental Education Research* 20(5): 581–611.

Stern, M.J., S.A. Predmore, M.J. Mortimer, and D. Seesholtz 2010. From the office to the field: Areas of consensus and tension in the implementation of the National Environmental Policy Act within the U.S. Forest Service. *Journal of Environmental Management* 91(6): 1350–6.

Stern, M.J., and S.A. Predmore 2011. Decision making, procedural compliance, and outcomes definition in U.S. Forest Service planning processes. *Environmental Impact Assessment Review* 31(3): 271–8.

Stern, M.J., and S.A. Predmore 2012. The importance of team functioning to natural resource planning outcomes. *Journal of Environmental Management* 106: 30–39.

Stern, P.C. 2000. Toward a coherent theory of environmentally significant behavior. *Journal of Social Issues* 56(3): 407–24.

Stets, J.E., and P.J. Burke 2005. New directions in identity control theory. *Advances in Group Processes* 22: 43–64.

Stets, J.E., and R.T. Serpe 2013. Chapter 2. Identity theory. In J. DeLamater and A. Ward (eds), *Handbook of social psychology*, pp. 31–60. Netherlands: Springer.

Stevens, S.F. 1993. *Claiming the high ground: Sherpas, subsistence, and environmental change in the highest Himalaya.* Berkeley, CA: University of California Press.

Stewart, G.L. 2006. A meta-analytic review of relationships between team design features and team performance. *Journal of Management* 32(1): 29–54.

Stogdill, R.M., and A.E. Coons (eds) 1957. *Leader behavior: Its description and measurement.* Columbus, OH: Bureau of Business Research, Ohio State University.

Susskind, L., and P. Field 1996. *Dealing with an angry public: The mutual gains approach to resolving disputes.* New York: The Free Press.

Susskind, L.E., S. McKearnen, and J. Thomas-Lamar (eds) 1999. *The consensus-building handbook: A comprehensive guide to reaching agreement.* Thousand Oaks, CA: Sage publications.

Tannenbaum, R., and W.H. Schmidt 1973. How to choose a leadership pattern. *Harvard Business Review* May–June: 3–12.

Tenbensel, T., J. Dwyer, and J. Lavoie 2013. How not to kill the golden goose: Reconceptualizing accountability environments of third-sector organizations. *Public Management Review* 16(7): 925–44.

Thaler, R.H., and C.R. Sunstein 2008. *Nudge: Improving decisions about health, wealth, and happiness.* New Haven, CT: Yale University Press.

Thøgersen, J. 2006. Norms for environmentally responsible behavior: An extended taxonomy. *Journal of Environmental Psychology* 26: 247–61.

Thompson, C. 2007. "Clive Thompson thinks: Desktop orb could reform energy hogs." Wired. https://www.wired.com/2007/07/st-thompson-5/. Accessed, February 19, 2017.

Turner, S., K. Merchant, J. Kania, and E. Martin 2012. Understanding the value of backbone organizations in collective impact. *Stanford Social Innovation Review*, July 17, 2012. https://ssir.org/articles/entry/understanding_the_value_of_backbone_organizations_in_collective_impact_1

Tybout, A.M., and R.F. Yalch 1980. The effect of experience: A matter of salience? *Journal of Consumer Research* 6: 406–13.

Vaisey, S. 2009. Motivation and justification: A dual-process model of culture in action. *American Journal of Sociology* 114(6): 1675–1715.

Valente, T.W., and R. L. Davis 1999. Accelerating the diffusion of innovations using opinion leaders. *The Annals of the American Academy of Political and Social Science* 566: 55–67.

Van Boven, L., G. Loewenstein, E. Welch, and D. Dunning. 2012. The illusion of courage in self-predictions: Mispredicting one's own behavior in embarrassing situations. *Journal of Behavioral Decision Making* 25: 1–12.

van der Linden, S., E. Maibach, and A. Leiserowitz 2015. Improving public engagement with climate change: Five "best practice" insights from psychological science. *Perspectives on Psychological Science* 10(6):758–63.

Vroom, V.H., and P.W. Yetton 1973. *Leadership and decision making.* Pittsburgh, PA: University of Pittsburgh Press.

Walker, B., and D. Salt 2012. *Resilience thinking: Sustaining ecosystems and people in a changing world.* Washington, DC: Island Press.

Walzer, N., and G.F. Hamm (eds) 2012. *Community visioning programs: Processes and outcomes.* New York, NY: Routledge.

White, D.D., A. Wutich, K.L. Larson, P. Gober, T. Lant, and C. Senneville 2010. Credibility, salience, and legitimacy of boundary objects: water managers' assessment of a simulation model in an immersive decision theater. *Science and Public Policy* 37(3):219–32.

Widiger, T.A. (ed.) 2017. *The Oxford handbook of the five factor model.* Oxford, UK: Oxford University Press.

Wilson, J.Q. 1989. *Bureaucracy: What government agencies do and why they do it.* New York, NY: Basic Books, Inc.

Witte, K., and K. Morrison 1995. Using scare tactics to promote safer sex among juvenile detention and high school youth. *Journal of Applied Communication Research* 23: 128–42.

Wondolleck, J.M., and S.L. Yaffee 2000. *Making collaboration work: Lessons from innovation in natural resource management.* Washington, DC: Island Press.

Index